DIETRICH BONHOEFFER WORKS, VOLUME 3

Creation and Fall

This series is a translation of
DIETRICH BONHOEFFER WERKE
Edited by
Eberhard Bethge, Ernst Feil,
Christian Gremmels, Wolfgang Huber,
Hans Pfeifer, Albrecht Schönherr,
Heinz Eduard Tödt†, Ilse Tödt

This volume has been made possible through a generous gift from Dr. John and Cleo Young of Eau Claire, Wisconsin, a grant from the University of Cape Town, as well as the ongoing support of the Lilly Endowment, Inc., the Aid Association for Lutherans, the Bowen H. and Janice Arthur McCoy Charitable Foundation, and the Lusk-Damen Charitable Gift Fund.

DIETRICH BONHOEFFER WORKS

General Editor
Wayne Whitson Floyd, Jr.

DIETRICH BONHOEFFER

Creation and Fall

A Theological Exposition of Genesis 1–3

Translated from the German Edition
Edited by
MARTIN RÜTER AND ILSE TÖDT

English Edition
Edited by
JOHN W. DE GRUCHY

Translated by
DOUGLAS STEPHEN BAX

FORTRESS PRESS   MINNEAPOLIS

DIETRICH BONHOEFFER WORKS, Volume 3

Originally published in German as *Dietrich Bonhoeffer Werke, Band 3*, by Chr. Kaiser Verlag in 1988. First English-language edition of *Dietrich Bonhoeffer Works, Volume 3*, published by Fortress Press in 1997.

Schöpfung und Fall first published in German by Chr. Kaiser Verlag in 1937. Original English-language edition of *Creation and Fall* published in 1959 by SCM Press, Ltd., and in 1965 by Macmillan Publishing Company. New English-language translation of *Creation and Fall* with new supplementary material first published in 1997 by Fortress Press as part of *Dietrich Bonhoeffer Works*.

Translation of this work was generously supported by the Inter Nationes agency, Bonn.
Jacket design: Cheryl Watson
Cover photo: Dietrich Bonhoeffer. Used by permission of Chr. Kaiser/Gütersloher Verlagshaus, Gütersloh, Germany.
Internal design: The HK Scriptorium, Inc.

Library of Congresss Cataloging-in-Publication Data

Bonhoeffer, Dietrich, 1906–1945.
    [Schöpfung und Fall. English]
    Creation and fall : a theological exposition of Genesis 1–3 /
Dietrich Bonhoeffer ; translated from the German edition edited by
Martin Rüter and Ilse Tödt ; English edition edited by John W. de
Gruchy ; translated by Douglas Stephen Bax.
        p.   cm. – (Dietrich Bonhoeffer works ; v. 3)
    Includes bibliographical references (p.   ) and indexes.
    ISBN 0-8006-8303-X (alk. paper)
    1. Bible. O.T. Genesis I–III—Commentaries.   2. Creation.
3. Fall.   I. De Gruchy, John W.   II. Bax, Douglas S.   III. Title.
IV. Series: Bonhoeffer, Dietrich, 1906–1945. Works. English. 1996; v. 3.
BR45.B6513   1996 vol. 3
[BS1235.B653]
230'.044—dc21
[222'.1106]   97-36937
                                                              CIP

The paper used in this publication meets the minimum requirements of American National Standard for Information Sciences—Permanence of Paper for Printed Library Materials, ANSI Z329.48-1984.

Manufactured in the U.S.A.

CONTENTS

General Editor's Foreword
to Dietrich Bonhoeffer Works

Since the time that the writings of Dietrich Bonhoeffer (1906–1945) first began to be available in English after World War II, they have been eagerly read both by scholars and by a wide general audience. The story of his life is compelling, set in the midst of historic events that shaped a century.

Bonhoeffer's leadership in the anti-Nazi Confessing Church and his participation in the *Abwehr* resistance circle make his works a unique source for understanding the interaction of religion, politics, and culture among those few Christians who actively opposed National Socialism. His writings provide not only an example of intellectual preparation for the reconstruction of German culture after the war but also a rare insight into the vanishing world of the old social and academic elites. Because of his participation in the resistance against the Nazi regime, Dietrich Bonhoeffer was hanged in the concentration camp at Flossenbürg on April 9, 1945.

Yet Bonhoeffer's enduring contribution is not just his moral example but his theology. As a student in Tübingen, Berlin, and at Union Theological Seminary in New York — where he also was associated for a time with the Abyssinian Baptist Church in Harlem — and as a participant in the European ecumenical movement, Bonhoeffer became known as one of the few figures of the 1930s with a comprehensive and nuanced grasp of both German- and English-language theology. His thought resonates with a prescience, subtlety, and maturity that continually belies the youth of the thinker.

In 1986 the Chr. Kaiser Verlag, now part of Gütersloher Verlagshaus, marked the eightieth anniversary of Bonhoeffer's birth by issuing the first of the sixteen volumes of the definitive German edition of his writings, the *Dietrich Bonhoeffer Werke*. Preliminary discussions about an English translation began even as the German series was beginning to emerge. As a consequence, the International Bonhoeffer Society, English Language Section, formed an editorial board, initially chaired by Robin Lovin, assisted by Mark Brocker, to undertake this project. Since 1993 the *Dietrich Bonhoeffer Works* translation project has been located in the Krauth Memorial Library of the Lutheran Theological Seminary at Philadelphia, under the leadership of its general editor — Wayne Whitson Floyd, Jr., the director of the seminary's Dietrich Bonhoeffer Center — and its executive director — Clifford J. Green of Hartford Seminary.

Dietrich Bonhoeffer Works provides the English-speaking world with an entirely new, complete, and unabridged translation of the written legacy of one of the twentieth century's most notable theologians; it includes a large amount of material appearing in English for the first time. Key terms are translated consistently throughout the corpus, with special attention being paid to accepted English equivalents of technical theological and philosophical concepts.

The *Dietrich Bonhoeffer Works* strives, above all, to be true to the language, style, and — most importantly — the theology of Bonhoeffer's writings. Translators have sought, nonetheless, to present Bonhoeffer's words in a manner that is sensitive to issues of language and gender. Consequently, accurate translation has removed sexist formulations that had been introduced inadvertently or unnecessarily into earlier English versions of his works. In addition, translators and editors generally have employed gender-inclusive language, so far as this was possible without distorting Bonhoeffer's meaning or dissociating him from his own time.

At times Bonhoeffer's theology sounds fresh and modern, not because the translators have made it so, but because his language still speaks with a hardy contemporaneity even after more than half a century. In other instances, Bonhoeffer sounds more remote, a product of another era, not due to any lack of facility by the translators and editors, but because his concerns and his rhetoric are, in certain ways, bound to a time that is past.

Volumes include introductions written by the editors of the English edition, footnotes provided by Bonhoeffer, editorial notes added by the

German and English editors, and afterwords composed by the editors of the German edition. In addition, volumes provide tables of abbreviations used in the editorial apparatus, as well as bibliographies which list sources used by Bonhoeffer, literature consulted by the editors, and other works related to each particular volume. Finally, volumes contain pertinent chronologies, charts, and indexes of scriptural references, names, and subjects.

The layout of the English edition has retained Bonhoeffer's original paragraphing (indicating by a ¶ any paragraph breaks added by the English Edition editors), as well as his manner of dividing works into chapters and sections. The pagination of the German critical edition, the *Dietrich Bonhoeffer Werke,* is indicated in the outer margins of the pages of the translated text. At times, for the sake of precision and clarity of translation, a word or phrase that has been translated is provided in its original language, in normal type, set within square brackets at the appropriate point in the text. All biblical citations come from the New Revised Standard Version, unless otherwise noted. Where versification of the Bible used by Bonhoeffer differs from the NRSV, the verse number in the latter is noted in the text in square brackets.

Bonhoeffer's own footnotes — which are indicated by plain, superscripted numbers — are reproduced as they appear in the German critical edition, complete with his idiosyncrasies of documentation. In these, as in the accompanying editorial notes, existing English translations of books and articles have been substituted for their counterparts in other languages whenever available. When non–English titles are not listed individually in the bibliographies (along with an English translation of those titles), a translation of those titles has been provided within the footnote or editorial note in which they are cited.

The editorial notes — which are indicated by superscripted numbers in square brackets, except in volume five where they are indicated by plain, superscripted numbers — provide information on the intellectual, ecclesiastical, social, and political context of Bonhoeffer's pursuits during the first half of the twentieth century. These are based on the scholarship of the German critical edition; they have been supplemented by the contributions of the editors of the English edition. Where the editors or translators of the English edition have substantially added to or revised a German editor's note, the initials of the person making the change(s) appear at the note's conclusion. When any previously translated material is quoted within an editorial note in an altered form, such changes should be assumed to be the responsibility of the translators.

Bibliographies at the end of each volume provide the complete information for each source that Bonhoeffer or the various editors have mentioned in their work. References to the archives, collections, and personal library of materials that had belonged to Bonhoeffer and that survived the war — as cataloged in the *Nachlaß Dietrich Bonhoeffer* — are indicated within the *Dietrich Bonhoeffer Works* by the initials NL followed by the appropriate reference code within that published index.

The production of any individual volume of the *Dietrich Bonhoeffer Works* requires the assistance of numerous individuals and organizations, whose support is duly noted on the verso of the half-title page. A special note of gratitude, however, is owed to all those prior translators, editors, and publishers of various portions of Bonhoeffer's literary legacy who heretofore have made available to the English-speaking world the writings of this remarkable theologian.

This English edition depends especially upon the careful scholarship of all those who labored to produce the critical German edition from which these translations have been made. Their work has been overseen by a board of general editors — responsible for both the concept and the content of the German edition — composed of Eberhard Bethge, Ernst Feil, Christian Gremmels, Wolfgang Huber, Hans Pfeifer, Albrecht Schönherr, Heinz Eduard Tödt†, and Ilse Tödt.

The present English edition would have been impossible without the creative and untiring dedication of the members of the editorial board of the *Dietrich Bonhoeffer Works:* Mark Brocker, James H. Burtness, Keith W. Clements, Clifford J. Green, Barbara Green, John W. de Gruchy, Barry A. Harvey, James Patrick Kelley, Geffrey B. Kelly, Reinhard Krauss, Robin W. Lovin, Michael Lukens, Nancy Lukens, Paul Matheny, Mary Nebelsick, and H. Martin Rumscheidt.

The deepest thanks for their support of this undertaking is owed, as well, to all the various members, friends, and benefactors of the International Bonhoeffer Society; to the National Endowment for the Humanities, which supported this project during its inception; to the Lutheran Theological Seminary at Philadelphia and its Auxiliary who established and help support the Dietrich Bonhoeffer Center on its campus specifically for the purpose of facilitating these publications; and to our publisher, Fortress Press, as represented with uncommon patience and *Gemütlichkeit* by Michael West, Rachel Riensche, Pam McClanahan, and Debbie Finch. Such a collaboration as this is fitting testimony to the spirit of Dietrich Bonhoeffer, who was himself always so attentive to the creative mystery of community and that ever-deepening collegiality that is engendered by our social nature as human beings.

Wayne Whitson Floyd, Jr. , General Editor
January 27, 1995
The Fiftieth Anniversary of the Liberation of Auschwitz
Revised on October 1, 1997

ABBREVIATIONS

AB (*DBW* 2)	*Act and Being* (*DBW*, German Edition)
AB (*DBWE* 2)	*Act and Being* (*DBWE*, English Edition)
CC	*Christ the Center* (U.K. title *Christology*)
CD	*The Cost of Discipleship*
CS	*The Communion of Saints* (U.K. title *Sanctorum Communio*)
DB-E	Eberhard Bethge, *Dietrich Bonhoeffer* (English Edition)
DB-G	Eberhard Bethge, *Dietrich Bonhoeffer* (German Edition)
DBW	*Dietrich Bonhoeffer Werke,* German edition
DBWE	*Dietrich Bonhoeffer Works,* English edition
E	*Ethics*
EK	Erich Klapproth's notes on Bonhoeffer's 1932–33 lectures
FL	Ferenc Lehel's notes on Bonhoeffer's 1932–33 lectures
GS	*Gesammelte Schriften* (Collected works)
HP	Hilde Pfeiffer's notes on Bonhoeffer's 1932-33 lectures
LB	*Die Bibel,* Martin Luther translation in German
LPP	*Letters and Papers from Prison,* 4th Edition
LT (*DBW* 5)	*Life Together* (DBW, German Edition)
LT (*DBWE* 5)	*Life Together* (DBWE, English Edition)
LW	[Martin] *Luther's Works,* American edition
NL	*Nachlaß Dietrich Bonhoeffer*
NL-A	Manuscript of *Creation and Fall* prepared by Bonhoeffer himself
NL-B	Students' notes from Bonhoeffer's lectures, or transcripts

NRS	*No Rusty Swords*
SC (DBW 1)	*Sanctorum Communio* (*DBW*, German Edition)
UK	Udo Köhler's notes on Bonhoeffer's 1932–33 lectures
WA	*Weimar Ausgabe* (Weimar edition), Martin Luther
WA-BR	Martin Luther's Letters (*Briefe*), Weimar edition
WA-TR	Martin Luther's Table Talk (*Tischreden*), Weimar edition

JOHN W. DE GRUCHY

EDITOR'S INTRODUCTION TO THE ENGLISH EDITION[1]

Listening to the Word of God in a Winter of Discontent

READING *CREATION AND FALL* makes one part of the audience of students to whom Dietrich Bonhoeffer lectured at the University of Berlin in the winter semester of 1932–33. Bonhoeffer, a *Privatdozent*[2] at the university, announced his course under the title *Schöpfung und Sünde. Theologische Auslegung von Genesis 1–3* (Creation and sin. A theological exposition of Genesis 1–3). The course proved to be an immediate success among the students who crowded into his lecture room. It was a winter of profound discontent in Germany; it was also a time of confusion, anxiety, and, for many, false hope, as social and political upheavals led to the demise of the Weimar Republic and the birth of the Third Reich. In the midst of these events Bonhoeffer called his students to focus their attention on the word of God as the word of truth in a time of turmoil.

The students who attended the course responded by pressing Bonhoeffer to publish the lectures. He sent a typed copy of the manuscript he had written for the lectures to the well-known publishing house Chr. Kaiser Verlag. For publication, however, he had to change the original

---

[1.] This Introduction incorporates most of the Editors' Foreword to the 1989 German edition (7–16), including most of the notes. The section entitled "A Turning Point in Bonhoeffer's Theological Development" is new to this English edition. Notes from the German edition that have been altered, or new notes for this edition, have not been indicated in this Introduction.

[2.] A university lecturer who was not yet part of the university's regular, salaried academic staff.

1

title to *Creation and Fall*. This was because in 1931 a book by Emanuel Hirsch had appeared with the title *Schöpfung und Sünde* (Creation and sin). On July 4, 1933, the proprietor, Albert Lempp, informed his theological advisor, pastor Georg Merz, that the manuscript had arrived. He wondered whether it was necessary for Merz to read it, and commented that Karl Barth had a good impression of Bonhoeffer.[3] The contract was signed on July 11, 1933, and the slim volume appeared later that same year.[4] Thus began the history of "Bonhoeffer and the Chr. Kaiser Publishing House."[5]

The students' urging that this particular course of university lectures be published resulted in its being the only one to have been preserved in its entirety in Bonhoeffer's own words. Apart from scanty notes, all records of his other lecture courses at Berlin have been lost. What made his students respond to Bonhoeffer and these lectures with such enthusiasm? Was it the way Bonhoeffer accomplished what he announced would be a "theological exposition," a way of dealing with biblical texts not previously experienced in the academic context of the faculty at Berlin? Was it the "essential topical relevance" of the lectures that became so evident in the face of the revolutionary changes then brewing in the political, ecclesiastical, and social spheres, even though the lec-

---

[3.] Georg Merz was also editor of the journal *Zwischen den Zeiten*, to which Karl Barth was a regular contributor. The letter from Lempp to Merz was found by Ulrich Kabitz.

[4.] On January 12, 1936, Bonhoeffer agreed to a second edition, which came out in 1937. For the third, paperback edition in 1955 the text was reset in Latin script instead of Gothic. The fourth edition came out in 1958. The first English edition, translated by John C. Fletcher, was published by SCM in London and Macmillan in New York in 1959. These publishers brought out a new edition in 1966 that included Bonhoeffer's biblical study *Temptation*. This combination was followed by Chr. Kaiser Verlag in 1968, when *Creation and Fall* was reset and bound together with *Temptation*. *Creation and Fall* has also been published in Japanese (1962), Spanish (1972), and Italian (1977).

[5.] This was the title of what Ernst Wolf contributed to Wolf-Dieter Zimmermann's book *Begegnungen mit Dietrich Bonhoeffer* as "an epilogue" (his subtitle) (220–25). Wolf supervised the republication of Bonhoeffer's doctoral dissertation and of his *Habilitationsschrift*, or postdoctoral dissertation required to qualify as a university lecturer, by Chr. Kaiser Verlag in 1954 and 1956 respectively. Wolf's article was not retained in the English edition of Zimmermann's book, *I Knew Dietrich Bonhoeffer*.

tures kept a steady focus on the text of Genesis?[6] Was it the particular content of the lectures, the close reflection on the image of God, on community, on sexuality, and on how the fall changed what "life" means? Evidently all these things together played a role.

Hans Hinrich Flöter, who attended the lectures as a student of the history of religion rather than as a theology student, provides a personal answer. In a letter[7] he recalls:

> It was Dietrich Bonhoeffer! Already in his first lecture he struck me — and thereafter the impression was reinforced — as a man who dug deeply . . . , who from "a point of view outside history" — so it seemed to me — found in the text new things of basic importance for life and understanding. . . . The whole lecture pressed toward, and strove for, semantic correctness and clarity. The style of speaking was of the *genus subtile*[8] — without, I was sure, any conscious use of rhetorical technique. It proceeded in all seriousness and without compromise. . . . It was thus no usual lecture course in dogmatics. Systematics and exegesis were naturally there in the background, but the speaker was — Bonhoeffer! . . . In these lectures this extraordinary man, Bonhoeffer, exploded everything I had taken for granted as custom or tradition in theology/the church, the state/politics, academic scholarship [*Wissenschaft*]/research and so on.

Flöter testifies that the announcement of the course struck him as at once provocative and fascinating.

Albrecht Schönherr, who also attended these lectures as a student, confirms Flöter's impressions. By contrast, Hilde Enterlein, who later married Schönherr, could not go along with Bonhoeffer's "fairy tales"; she regarded the lectures as unphilosophical. Ferenc Lehel, who attended Bonhoeffer's lectures, reports:

> He was an extremely infectious personality and wholly engrossed in the problems of his subject. Hence he did not resort to any emotional display or rhetorical artifice. A Kierkegaardian profundity, a talent for analysis like

---

[6.] Cf. *DB-G* 263: ". . . one cannot sidestep the depth of the statements; one also cannot deny that those in the battle line are here being well equipped to recognize the deception of the day and to resist it." Bethge used the expression "substantial topical relevance" to characterize the lecture course on "Contemporary Theology" that Bonhoeffer gave during the same semester (ibid.). [trans. DBS]

[7.] Written by H. H. Flöter to Reinhart Staats on May 27, 1987.

[8.] Latin term that in classical rhetoric meant "plain" or "unadorned."

that of [Adolf von] Harnack, a deep familiarity with the context such as [Ernst] Troeltsch had, a knowledge of the material like [Karl] Holl had, and a gift for formulating issues as sharply as [Karl] Barth did drew more and more students to this young lecturer's course. We listened to his sentences with such intensity that one could hear the flies buzzing. Often when we laid our pens down, we were literally bathed in sweat.[9]

On the basis of the notes made by Lehel and especially by Hilde Pfeiffer, who recorded the date of every lecture, we know that the course began on Tuesday, November 8, 1932, and ended on Tuesday, February 21, 1933.

In addition to the course on "Schöpfung und Sünde" ("Creation and sin"), Bonhoeffer that term gave another course of one-hour lectures on "Jüngste Theologie" ("Contemporary theology") as well as a course of "Dogmatische Übungen" ("Dogmatic exercises") on the theological analysis of the human person [über theologische Psychologie].[10] This was a heavy curriculum of work in the midst of the unrest and tensions that were manifesting themselves in the political situation. At the beginning of the second half of the semester Bonhoeffer wrote to his brother, Karl Friedrich:

> The semester is under way again, and preparations for my lecture course and seminar claim the major part of my time. I often have the feeling housewives must have when they have gone to great trouble to cook something special and then see how one eats it up together with other food. But I just cannot give a poorly prepared course; I would get hopelessly stuck.[11]

This letter betrays incidentally a further reason for the fascination that Bonhoeffer's lectures aroused: the freshness of the preparation behind them. Bonhoeffer was not reading from a seasoned manuscript; instead the students witnessed at first hand how his insights gained in depth as he struggled to put them into words.

The exposition of Genesis 1–3 was in fact unusual among the acade-

---

[9.] Ferenc Lehel in Wolf-Dieter Zimmermann and Ronald Gregor Smith, *I Knew Dietrich Bonhoeffer*, 68 [trans. DSB from the original German text]. In a letter to the editors dated January 4, 1988, Lehel confirms that it was not the topic in Old Testament exegesis but Bonhoeffer's personality that made Lehel register for the course on Genesis 1–3.

[10.] Cf. the parallel term *theologische Anthropologie*, "theological anthropology."

[11.] Letter to Karl Friedrich Bonhoeffer dated January 12, 1933, *GS* 3:23–24. On Bonhoeffer's uneasiness with "lectures that were monologues," see *DB-E* 161.

mic courses Bonhoeffer taught. Both of his previous lecture courses, each of which lasted for two hours per week, dealt with systematic theology and ecclesiology.[12] In this particular winter semester of 1932–33 he divided his lecture time, giving one hour a week to the discussion of new developments in systematic theology and the other weekly lecture period to listening to what the Bible had to say.

Looking back on this time a few years later, Bonhoeffer wrote: "I came to the Bible for the first time."[13] Hearing the word of God demands practice, *exercitium*, he said on November 8, 1932, in his introduction to the course on Genesis 1–3.[14] To this exercise Bonhoeffer now found himself drawn with great intensity. "It was a great liberation."[15] The profoundest reason for the students' fascination with the lectures on "Creation and Sin" was surely that they saw how personally captivated Bonhoeffer was by the word.

Delivered with passion in kerygmatic style rather than in the language of academic discourse, *Creation and Fall* retains the sense of immediacy, relevance, and power that first spoke to Bonhoeffer's students. It was not his intention to enter into debate on matters of science and religion or evolution and creation or even the kind of philosophical issues he had addressed at length in *Act and Being*. His concern was to hear the word of God that had spoken in the beginning — and that was seeking even then to speak to Germany and the nations of the world. It is a word that still addresses us in our own situations out of the silence of the universe in the redemptive power of the Crucified.

A Turning Point in Bonhoeffer's Theological Development

Despite the impact Bonhoeffer's lectures had on his students, systematic theologians at the time ignored their publication, and most biblical scholars scorned Bonhoeffer's Barthian method of "theological exege-

[12.] "The History of Systematic Theology in the Twentieth Century" (winter semester 1931–32), "The Essence of the Church" (summer semester 1932). Cf. the student notes from the lecture courses for 1931–32 and 1932–33 in *DBW* 11:139–213, 239–303 (*GS* 5:181–358).

[13.] Letter from Finkenwalde dated January 27, 1936, *DBW* 14:113 (*GS* 6:367).

[14.] Transcript by Erich Klapproth, *NL-B* 5,2(1).

[15.] Letter dated January 27, 1936, *DBW* 14:113 (*GS* 6:368). Meanwhile Bonhoeffer had worked on "exercises" on the Sermon on the Mount; see the letter to his friend Erwin Sutz dated April 28, 1934, *DBW* 13:129 (*GS* 1:41).

sis."[16] Notwithstanding this indifferent and critical reception, *Creation and Fall* provided "a first small literary success for Bonhoeffer."[17] One of the book's readers was Karl Barth; indeed it was the only work by Bonhoeffer on which Barth was to express an opinion during the author's lifetime.[18] Barth's influence on Bonhoeffer is clear in *Creation and Fall*, and Barth found it congenial and helpful for his own work.

Creation and Fall is not as well known as Bonhoeffer's other books; it has also been studied less.[19] Nevertheless it retains much of its relevance for Christian theology and witness. It is also important for the study of Bonhoeffer, providing a link between his earlier, seminal writings (*Sanctorum Communio* and *Act and Being*) and those that were later to make such an impact on the theology and life of the ecumenical church in the twentieth century (*[The Cost of] Discipleship*, *Ethics*, and *Letters and Papers from Prison*). In it he reworks ideas from his earlier writings in ways that anticipate their development and expression in his later writings. Indeed *Creation and Fall* represents a turning point in Bonhoeffer's theological development and as such is of particular significance for our understanding of it.

To begin with, these lectures were Bonhoeffer's first attempt to do theology in direct dialogue with the Bible. Traditional Christianity had accepted Genesis 1–3 as an accurate account of the beginning of the world and of the history of humankind. The development of modern historical and critical scholarship together with sciences such as astronomy, geology, biology, zoology, and paleontology, however, had rendered this worldview more and more untenable. By the 1930s when Bonhoeffer was lecturing, many biblical scholars and other people, espe-

---

[16.] A similar reaction met the publication of Barth's commentary on Romans, *Der Römerbrief*, when it was first published in 1918, and for the same reasons. This edition was never published in English, but Barth explains his "theological exegesis" in the Prefaces published in the English translation of the sixth edition, *The Epistle to the Romans*. Both Bonhoeffer's *Creation and Fall* and Barth's commentary on Romans were written at times of historical crisis in Europe; they demonstrate their authors' concern as preachers of the word of God to listen for that word in scripture in relation to their contexts. On Bonhoeffer's "theological exegesis" see John Godsey, *The Theology of Dietrich Bonhoeffer*, 119–43; John A. Phillips, *The Form of Christ in the World*, 84–88.

[17.] *DBE* 163.

[18.] Karl Barth, *Church Dogmatics*, 3/1, 194–206.

[19.] See the bibliography for details of the few major studies on *Creation and Fall* that have been published in German and English.

cially in Germany, regarded the first chapters of Genesis as primitive tales of little relevance for modern people. This resulted in confusion in the church over how to regard these chapters (and the Bible in general) and how to think about God in relation to the origin of the world and of humankind. More broadly it resulted in a crisis that disoriented European culture regarding the place of humankind in time and history.

As the German editors point out in the Afterword,[20] in his lectures on creation and sin Bonhoeffer was broadly following Karl Barth's example of how to expound scripture. Barth had published three commentaries on books of the Bible;[21] the most famous was his commentary on *The Epistle to the Romans*.

Biblical scholars at that time wished above all to be *wissenschaftlich*, that is, 'scientific' in the sense of applying one's scholarship in an objective, unbiased way so as to produce work that was acceptable to the academic world. As a result, like most modern commentators today still, they tended to limit their commentaries to such scholarly questions as the reconstruction of the text, the exact meaning of the words in which the text was written, the historical background, relevant information from archaeology, and parallels from other religions. More generally, they limited themselves to making the text intelligible in terms of the historical and religious context of its author or authors. They made little or no attempt to wrestle with the text in order to understand and interpret its message *theologically*, so as to enable that message to address *contemporary* people in their *contemporary* cultural, philosophical, social, and political situation. This, however, amounted to treating the text as though it were a mere religious relic, of only historical interest. It was to ignore what Barth regarded as the essential task: seeking to hear and expound "the Word . . . in the words."[22]

Barth, by contrast, in a way that was very controversial at the time, sought to develop a 'post-critical' method of expounding scripture. That is, he in principle accepted the findings of historical and literary criticism but sought to move *beyond* them to grapple with the question, What is the word of God as it addresses itself to us today in this scripture? Bon-

---

[20.] See below, 151–53.

[21.] *The Epistle to the Romans* (1st ed. 1918, 2d ed. 1922, English trans. 1933); *The Resurrection of the Dead* (1924, English trans. 1933); *The Epistle to the Philippians* (1928, English trans. 1962).

[22.] Karl Barth, *The Epistle to the Romans*, 8.

hoeffer likewise sought to grapple with the same question and to produce a "theological exposition" of the biblical text. There were differences, however. Whereas Barth had published commentaries only on books in the New Testament, Bonhoeffer chose to expound the first book in the Old Testament. He also did not use the particular 'dialectical' language that Barth had used in his commentary on Romans. He brought his own particular questions to scripture and developed his own particular way of expounding it on the basis of his own theological and philosophical training.

Thus in choosing to lecture on the first chapters of Genesis at a university in the contemporary academic context, Bonhoeffer faced two challenges. One was to provide an exposition that showed itself to be genuinely scholarly. The other challenge was much more profound. Throughout the course he was above all intensely concerned with the question: How can these words live? How can they once more be heard not as just the expression of an ancient cosmology and worldview but as God's word to humankind in the twentieth century, in all its sin and confusion?

In facing this challenge, Bonhoeffer followed Barth in discerning "the living word" for today in the witness of scripture.[23] The God whom Genesis 1 portrayed as creating the world by the word of God was speaking that same word of creation and redemption as a word of judgment and salvation to Nazi Germany — and by inference is doing the same to our situation today. Indeed, as will be seen in the text, several of the key themes in Bonhoeffer's exposition of Genesis 1–3 recur in his addresses and lectures of this period in the church struggle against Nazism and in his passionate advocacy of international peace through the ecumenical movement.

Thus we see with these lectures a turning point in Bonhoeffer's development from an abstruse academic theologian whose context was solely the university to a theologian for preachers.[24] As his later writings and his work for the church show, he was now to be more and more concerned with the witness of the church to the word of God in the world.

[23.] On Bonhoeffer's use of the Bible see his essay "The Interpretation of the New Testament," *NRS* 308–25, and *LT* (*DBW* 5), 58–65. For an overview of the development of Bonhoeffer's use of the Bible see James Woelfel, *Bonhoeffer's Theology: Classical and Revolutionary*, 208–38.

[24.] Bonhoeffer's use of the Bible in preaching exemplifies this existential concern. See *Worldly Preaching*.

More concretely we see Bonhoeffer's own ability and willingness to listen to and trust that word and obey its command. It was this evangelical[25] obedience that was to find such masterful expression four years later in *[The Cost of] Discipleship*. Still later, in taking part in the conspiracy against Hitler at the risk of his own life, Bonhoeffer was seeking in a different way to be obedient to God.

A second way in which *Creation and Fall* was a pivotal point in Bonhoeffer's theological development follows from what has just been said. For Bonhoeffer, the Old Testament was certainly the Hebrew Bible, but it was also part of the Christian canon.[26] Therefore it had to be read in the light of God's self-disclosure in Jesus Christ. In the Introduction to *Creation and Fall*, which Bonhoeffer actually wrote after the lectures for their published version, he explained that the subtitle, *A Theological Exposition of Genesis 1–3*, meant that the Old Testament as well as the New was to be regarded as the book of the church and therefore to be read in light of its fulfillment in Christ. Later, as one can see from his letters from prison, he preferred to read the New Testament from the perspective of the Hebrew Bible rather than the other way around. For Christian hermeneutics both approaches are appropriate, and they complement each other. For it remains fundamental to the proper understanding of Christianity to affirm the Old Testament as an integral part of Christian scripture. The reasons for this were argued by the anti-Marcionite theologians of the second and early third centuries; they remained essentially the same for Bonhoeffer in the Third Reich.

The denial or downplaying of the Old Testament as scripture by Christians has contributed to a dualistic separation of creation and redemption and of the public and the private spheres of life. This separation has plagued Christianity ever since it first was confronted by Gnosticism and infiltrated by Neoplatonism. The practical consequences have been far-reaching and destructive. In Bonhoeffer's own situation such an attitude to the Old Testament led inevitably to the reinforcement of German anti-Semitism. More universally this dualism has bred a perverse attitude to human sexuality, a piety that denies the

---

[25.] The word "evangelical" has several meanings. In this context it refers to the theology of the Protestant Reformation that is described in German as *"evangelisch."*

[26.] For Bonhoeffer's understanding of the Old Testament as Christian scripture see Martin Kuske, *The Old Testament as the Book of Christ*, 7–17.

social and political responsibilities of Christians, and an attitude toward the environment that has allowed its destruction. Bonhoeffer's own growing love for the Old Testament contributed a great deal to his quite different approach. This love, which is already so apparent in *Creation and Fall*, was expressed in the prison writings especially in his appreciation of the "earthiness" of the Hebrew Bible.[27] His later biblical insight into the "worldliness" of Christianity in "a world come of age" is also rooted in his understanding that the New Testament must be read in the light of the Old.[28] For Bonhoeffer the God of Israel and of Jesus Christ is always in the midst of the world and can only be encountered there.[29] Thus what he wrote in his letters from prison is already foreshadowed in *Creation and Fall*.[30]

A third way in which *Creation and Fall* is a turning point has to do directly with the christocentric character of his interpretation of the creation narrative. In Bonhoeffer's previous theology Christology was at the service of ecclesiology, which was primary. As he argued in *Sanctorum Communio* and *Act and Being*, "Christ exists as community." But now he sees, and emphasizes, that Christ is the cosmic word of God that speaks from the center of world history. Within a year he was to develop this Christology more systematically in his programmatic lectures on the subject in the summer of 1933.[31]

Creation and Fall, however, is written at a transitional stage; its focus is still on questions of human identity and sociality. Indeed in many respects *Creation and Fall* is an exposition of Bonhoeffer's earlier "theology of sociality" (*Sanctorum Communio*) in a more accessible form.[32] For

---

[27.] Letters to Bethge, April 30, 1944, May 20, 1944, June 27, 1944, *LPP* 278–81, 302–3, 335–37.

[28.] Letter to Bethge, June 27, 1944, *LPP* 335–37. For the influence of the Old Testament on Bonhoeffer's understanding of "the world come of age" see Kuske, 132–58.

[29.] See André Dumas, *Dietrich Bonhoeffer: Theologian of Reality*, 142–45.

[30.] On the continuity between Bonhoeffer's theology in *Creation and Fall* and his later theology, see Eberhard Bethge, "The Challenge of Dietrich Bonhoeffer's Life and Theology," in Ronald Gregor Smith, ed., *World Come of Age*, 76.

[31.] Lectures on christology, *DBW* 12.

[32.] For a detailed discussion of Bonhoeffer's "theology of sociality" with special reference to these lectures see Clifford J. Green, *The Sociality of Christ and Humanity*, 235–48.

instance, in discussing the *imago dei* (Gen. 1:26-27) Bonhoeffer points to human sociality as its central meaning.

Fundamental to this interpretation is Bonhoeffer's discussion of what he refers to as the *analogia relationis*, a concept that is already anticipated in *Act and Being*.[33] Despite some criticism of Bonhoeffer's exposition, Barth appropriated the concept of *analogia relationis*; he did so in developing his *analogia fidei* in opposition to the *analogia entis* of traditional Roman Catholic natural theology and in his christocentric interpretation of the *imago dei*. But he recast the *imago dei* in terms of gender relations in a way that went beyond Bonhoeffer's own approach.[34]

A fourth way in which *Creation and Fall* is a turning point for Bonhoeffer has to do with his emphasis on human freedom in relation to the freedom of God. Human beings have been given the freedom to rule over the created order but must do so responsibly. Genuine human freedom is freedom "for others," just as God's freedom expresses itself in covenantal love for the world. This anticipates much of what Bonhoeffer was to write later in the manuscripts for his *Ethics*.[35] Especially it anticipates his "ethic of free responsibility," which provided the theological basis for his participation in the Resistance. Bonhoeffer's Christ-centered anthropology is in fact the central theme of *Creation and Fall* and prepares the way for his prison theology. In Eberhard Bethge's words,

> The change of direction from the metaphysical elements of Christology to its place at the "center of life," and also the reference to Christ as the one who refuses to be relegated to the psychological or moral boundaries of life but is at the center and the "strongest places" of man, all this we have read before in *Creation and Fall*.[36]

A fifth way in which *Creation and Fall* represents a turning point for Bonhoeffer and for our understanding of his thought has to do with the way in which he dealt with natural theology. Following Barth, he adopted a christological interpretation of the Bible to oppose the misuse

---

[33.] See Bonhoeffer's critique of the "Thomistic" doctrine of the *analogia entis* in *AB* (*DBWE* 5), 73–75, 138. On "analogia relationis" in Bonhoeffer's theology, see Benjamin A. Reist, *The Promise of Bonhoeffer* (Philadelphia: J. B. Lippincott, 1969), 48–52.

[34.] Green, *The Sociality of Christ and Humanity*, 286, n. 19.

[35.] *E* 224–54.

[36.] Bethge, *DB-E* 793, trans. altered.

by some German theologians of the Lutheran doctrine of the "orders of creation" to support the Nazi ideology of "blood and soil."[37]

Creation does not provide a basis for autonomous orders — state, family, culture — that function independently of God's revelation and redemption in Christ; instead the orders must be understood from the perspective of that very revelation and redemption.[38] Thus Bonhoeffer in *Creation and Fall* chooses the term "orders of preservation." In other words, the orders are not given with creation and cast in concrete forever afterward; they are the means by which God preserves the world from plunging into chaos in anticipation of its redemption. Later Bonhoeffer was to move away from this formulation as well, speaking in his *Ethics* rather of "divine mandates."[39] As in the *Ethics*, however, he was following Barth in rejecting natural theology. He also was anticipating the first article of the Barmen Theological Declaration of 1934 with its firm rejection of Nazi ideology as a form of divine revelation supplementary to the gospel of Jesus Christ.

Reconstructing the German Text

What was published in *Creation and Fall* corresponds largely with the original lecture material, both in content and in order. Only in the exposition of Gen. 2:18-25, "The Power of the Other," did Bonhoeffer choose to rearrange his material, so that its order in the book is different from its order in the lectures.

Bonhoeffer, however, seems to have no longer concerned himself with texts he had written once he had handed them over to others. Eberhard Bethge was later to witness how he treated another of his "products," *[The Cost of] Discipleship*, in such a "stepmotherly" way, when Bonhoeffer rejected a request that he revise it, saying instead with a smile, "What I

[37.] For example, the distinguished Lutheran theologian Paul Althaus published a pamphlet entitled *Theologie der Ordnungen* (Theology of the orders) in which the German race and nation, or *Volk*, were understood as part of God's created order and law. See Robert P. Eriksen, *Theologians under Hitler*, 98–104.

[38.] The National Socialist abuse of the Lutheran doctrine of the "orders of creation" was paralleled in South Africa, where the doctrine of the "sovereignty of spheres" developed by the Dutch theologian Abraham Kuyper was used to give theological legitimation to apartheid. See Douglas S. Bax, *A Different Gospel*, 29–45; John W. de Gruchy, *Bonhoeffer and South Africa*, 108–12.

[39.] *E* 286–92.

have written, I have written."[40] In the case of *Creation and Fall* this attitude resulted in errors that had crept into the text already in the first edition of 1933. For this reason the German text was reconstructed for the 1989 edition, on the basis of which the translation for the present English edition has been made. The reconstructed text of the 1989 edition was based on three sources:

1. *NL-A* 31.3: A photocopy of the manuscript of the Introduction and Preface that Dietrich Bonhoeffer wrote for the publication of the lectures in the winter semester of 1932–33, on six octavo size pages; this was in the possession of Bertha Schulze.
2. *Schöpfung und Fall. Theologische Auslegung von Genesis 1–3* (Munich: Christian Kaiser Verlag, 1933), 87 pages.
3. The notes of four students who attended the lecture course. These are used sparingly to correct the text of the 1933 edition, although they are quoted frequently in the notes of the 1989 edition and in the editorial notes of the present translation.

The first of these sources comes from photographs made by Jørgen Glenthøj, who on a tour of the archives authorized in 1959 photographed three sheets covered with Bonhoeffer's handwriting that comprised Bonhoeffer's draft of the Introduction and Preface for the printed version of *Creation and Fall*. These sheets were in the possession of Bertha Schulze (1896–1987), a doctoral student of Adolf von Harnack who became an acquaintance of Bonhoeffer during his student days. Especially from 1931 until 1934 she transcribed many of Bonhoeffer's manuscripts into typed copy.[41] In all probability Bertha Schulze typed the Introduction and the Preface in a copy for publication that is now lost. Presumably she also typed the remainder of the text; but both the manuscript and the typed copy are lost.

Bonhoeffer's handwriting in the German script is very difficult to read, so we have to reckon with the possibility of errors already in Bertha Schulze's draft as a result of misreading the original manuscript. The German editors based the 1989 edition on the photocopied manuscript

---

[40.] *DB-G* 167; cf. Pilate in John 19:22! In a letter to Erwin Sutz dated February 28, 1932, Bonhoeffer called his postdoctoral dissertation a "product" with which he no longer felt much empathy (*DBW* 11:63) [*GS* 1:26]; cf. *AB* (*DBW* 2):12.

[41.] Cf. *DB-G* 96, *DB-E* 101 (*DB-G* 174); Jørgen Glenthøj, *Dokumente*, 26.

NL-A 31.3. The footnotes indicate a selection of the words crossed out in the manuscript.

The second source of the 1989 German edition, apart from the Introduction and the Preface, is the first edition of 1933. The editors of the 1989 edition, however, compared the text with the editions that had come out between the end of the war and 1968. They restored paragraph divisions that were not clear or omitted in later editions, and they corrected the incorrect printing of three sets of chapter-and-verse numbers as headings. The table of contents was also correctly restored. In all these matters the present English edition follows the 1989 German edition.

The third source for the reconstruction of Bonhoeffer's text is the archives of Bonhoeffer's literary remains, which includes the notes of four students who attended the lecture course:

- The lecture notes of *Hilde Pfeiffer*, which are written on 70 International Paper Size (IPS) A5 pages (original: *NL* appendix B2).
- The lecture notes of *Udo Köhler*, on 46 pages of an IPS A5 notepad (photocopy: *NL-B* 5,1).
- The more abbreviated notes of the Hungarian student *Ferenc Lehel*, comprising 76 pages and written to begin with on small IPS A6 sheets of paper and then in a small IPS A6 notebook (transcription: *NL* Suppl. 9). His notes contain much that none of the others copied down. In such cases the German editors' notes indicate: "(only) FL."
- A transcribed draft in standard German shorthand of notes ending with the sixth lecture and two other pages of still untranscribed notes of the seventh lecture, the last in 1932, by *Erich Klapproth* (photocopy: *NL-B* 5,2).[42]

The students' notes show clearly that even the printed text of the 1933 edition was based in several places on reading errors. In reconstructing the text for the critical edition of 1989, wherever the 1933 edition seemed clearly based on a reading error that had resulted from words that are similar in their handwritten form and where the students' wording fitted the context more precisely, the German editors drew on the above four sets of students' notes. Such cases are indicated in the editors'

[42.] The number following each abbreviation in the editors' comments in round brackets gives the page number of the manuscript or archival form of the document in Bonhoeffer's literary remains.

notes and in the text itself by material enclosed in square brackets, indicating that the editors have substituted material from the students' notes for the text as published in the 1933 edition.

Because the students' notes showed that the 1933 edition contained mistakes, the German edition of 1989 also replaced words in the 1933 edition that seemed to be intrusions (because they failed to fit the sense) with words that were similar in written form and made more sense — even where the students' notes did not support the substitution. In the present English edition, the editors' notes provide the necessary information in every case.

Bonhoeffer apparently wanted to allow as little erudition as possible to spill over into his manuscript;[43] for instance, he referred the students in his audience to literature without including references to this literature in the printed edition. Information about these references is to be found in the editorial notes.

As already indicated, Bonhoeffer's original lecture notes are lost, and the version of *Creation and Fall* that he submitted to the publisher contained no footnotes. The German editors of the *Dietrich Bonhoeffer Werke* edition of *Schöpfung und Fall* have addressed this situation in a way that may not be evident to the reader, especially in English translation, without explanation. In lieu of any footnotes by Bonhoeffer himself, they have in their editorial notes cited pertinent works in the portion of Bonhoeffer's personal library that survived the war and that they have strong reason to think he consulted in preparing the lectures published as *Creation and Fall*. These notes in the German edition have been retained among the editorial notes of the present English edition. All the sources cited on this basis are among those cataloged in the *Nachlaß Dietrich Bonhoeffer*. They have been listed in the Bibliography under "Literature Used by Bonhoeffer," which therefore in this volume alone of the *Dietrich Bonhoeffer Works* must be understood as an editorial reconstruction.

The first section of the Bibliography provides details about these books; the second section lists other publications to which the editors refer. As is appropriate for this translation, we have included the titles and publishing details of those books that have been published in an English translation. Also listed are those books on Bonhoeffer's theology that are relevant to *Creation and Fall* and have been published in

---

[43.] Expressions he uses in languages other than German are translated in the notes in the English translation.

English. When publications are cited in the editorial notes, usually the name of the author is given with an abbreviated title; in the case of very frequently cited titles, however, only the name is given (e.g., Hans Schmidt, Kautzsch). The indexes at the end include Bible passages, persons, and subjects (including places).

A Note on the Translation

This English edition is a wholly new translation of Bonhoeffer's text according to the critical German edition of 1989. It also translates much of the German editors' Foreword (incorporated into the Editor's Introduction to the English edition), practically all their footnotes, and the whole of their Afterword.[44]

Bonhoeffer began each section of his book with the biblical passage from Genesis which that section expounded, and he sometimes went on to quote from the passage in the exposition. These biblical passages for the most part followed either the contemporary (1911) revision of Martin Luther's translation or the fourth edition (1922) of Emil Kautzsch's translation; in some places, however, Bonhoeffer chose to make his own rendering. All these biblical passages have been translated to accord as closely as possible with Bonhoeffer's version (as well as with the Hebrew text). Accepted modern English versions, particularly the New Revised Standard Version, have been consulted in the process. This means that the English version of each of these passages in this edition fits Bonhoeffer's exposition of it, which was not always the case in the earlier translation of *Creation and Fall*, rather than merely quoting the New Revised Standard Version.

The German term *der Mensch* occurs often in *Schöpfung und Fall*. In order both to be gender inclusive by avoiding the term "man" and to convey the solidarity and unity of human beings "in Adam" that *der Mensch* normally intends, this word generally has been translated as "humankind" (or occasionally "the human being") and used with the singular pronoun "it."

[44.] This translation has been checked word for word with the earlier English translation by John Fletcher published in 1959. Fletcher's wording has been adopted when that seemed the best way to render the German, even though this translation differs from his in detail and *in extenso* in the endeavor to make as correct, clear, and idiomatic a rendering of the German as possible. [DSB]

All footnotes added by the translator, and all the translator's interpolations in the editors' footnotes, are marked by the initials DSB, set within square brackets.

Acknowledgments

The translator wishes to thank all those whom he consulted on difficult points of translation, particularly Robert Steiner. Most especially, however, he thanks Dr. Ilse Tödt, one of the editors of the German critical edition of 1989, who checked through his translation meticulously, saving it from many mistakes and making it much more exact. She also located all the references to Bonhoeffer's works that appear in the volumes so far published in the *Dietrich Bonhoeffer Werke*. The translator, however, takes responsibility for the final wording chosen.

The *Dietrich Bonhoeffer Works*, as indicated in the General Editor's Foreword, are intended for the English-speaking world as a whole. It is therefore appropriate that those involved in the translating and editing of the volumes have been drawn from several English-speaking countries. This particular volume has been translated and edited by South Africans. In drawing attention to this fact, I wish to express a word of gratitude to Douglas Bax for his conscientious work as translator (and his many editorial suggestions) amidst his responsibilities as the minister of the Rondebosch United Church (Congregational/Presbyterian) in Cape Town. Bax's linguistic skills, his eye for detail, and his theological acumen are widely respected and have been demonstrated once again.

Together we would like to express our thanks to the editorial board of the *Dietrich Bonhoeffer Works* for inviting us to share in this project, and to the general editor, Wayne Whitson Floyd, Jr., for all his work on the translation, the notes, and the bibliography — and particularly his patience and guidance in enabling us to bring our task to completion. Of course, what we have produced was possible only because of the scholarly thorough and dedicated labors of the editors of the German edition, Martin Rüter and Ilse Tödt.

We wish to join in thanking the numerous individual members and friends of the International Bonhoeffer Society who, in addition to the sources listed at the front of the volume, provided financial support for our undertaking.

PREFACE

THIS COURSE OF LECTURES was delivered at the University of Berlin in the winter semester 1932–33. It is being published at the request of students who heard them. The translation of the biblical text conforms as closely to Luther's version as the original seemed to allow; where it diverges from this, it essentially follows the version by Kautzsch.[1]

[1.] The 1933 edition reads, "where it diverges from this, it seeks to follow Kautzsch." Bonhoeffer's handwriting gave rise to this wording, but it is actually a faulty deciphering of what he wrote.

INTRODUCTION

THE CHURCH OF CHRIST witnesses to the end of all things. It lives from the end, it thinks from the end, it acts from the end, it proclaims its message from the end. "Do not remember the former things or consider the things of old. I am about to do a new thing"[1] (Isa. 43:18-19). The new is the real end of the old; the new, however, is Christ. Christ is the end of the old. Not the continuation, not the goal, the completion in line with the old, but the end and therefore the new. The church speaks within the old world about the new world. And because it is surer of the new world than of anything else, it sees the old world only in the light of the new world.

¶The church cannot please the old world because the church speaks of the end of the world as though this has already happened, as though the world has already been judged. The old world is not happy to let itself be declared dead. The church has never been surprised at this. It also is not surprised that again and again there appear within it people who think as the old world does. Who after all does not still at times think like this? What must certainly arouse the church to real indignation,[2] however, is that these children of the world that has passed away

---

[1.] *NL-A* 31.3 (Bonhoeffer's own manuscript) has only the words, "Remember not what happened before"; above the dots Bonhoeffer added the word, "create." From this it appears that he had in mind Isa. 43:19a ("I wish to create something new"). For the 1933 edition the quotation was completed in the words of the *LB*.

[2.] Instead of the word for "indignation," the 1933 edition printed another German word meaning "uproar, agitation, turmoil, revolt." "Indignation" occurs also before this in a deletion from *NL-A* 31.3.

wish to claim the church, the new, as belonging to them. They want the new, and they know only the old. And in that way they deny Christ, the Lord.

¶Only the church, which knows of the end, knows also of the beginning. It alone knows that between the beginning and now there lies the same breach as between now and the end, that the beginning and now are related in the same way as life is to death, as the new is to the old. The church therefore sees the beginning only in dying, from the viewpoint of the end.[3] It views the creation from Christ; or better, in the fallen, old world it believes in the world of the new creation, the new world of the beginning and the end, because it believes in Christ and in nothing else.

22

The church does all this because it is founded upon the witness of Holy Scripture.[4] The church of Holy Scripture — and there is no other 'church' — lives from the end. Therefore it reads the whole of Holy Scripture as the book of the end, of the new [vom Neuen], of Christ.[5] Where Holy Scripture, upon which the church of Christ stands, speaks of creation, of the beginning, what else can it say other than that it is only from Christ that we can know what the beginning is? The Bible is after all nothing other than the book of the church. It *is* this in its very essence, or it is nothing. It therefore needs to be read and proclaimed wholly from the viewpoint of the end. In the church, therefore, the story of creation must be read in a way that begins with Christ and only then moves on toward him as its goal; indeed one can read it as a book that moves toward Christ only when one knows that Christ is the beginning, the new, the end of our whole world.

Theological exposition takes the Bible as the book of the church and interprets it as such. This is its presupposition and this presupposition constitutes its method; its method is a continual returning from the text (as determined by all the methods of philological and historical research)[6] to this presupposition. That is the objectivity [Sachlichkeit] in

---

[3.] In *NL-A* 31.3 the words follow, crossed out: "The world, which does not wish to know about the end, because it does not wish to die, sees." The 1933 edition reads "the end" in place of "dying."

[4.] In *NL-A* 31.3 this replaces: "because Holy Scripture is its only authority."

[5.] In *NL-A* 31.3 the words follow, crossed out: "Christ is the center of Scripture."

[6.] The parenthesis is a late addition in *NL-A* 31.3.

the method of theological exposition. And on this objectivity alone does it base its claim to have the nature of a science [Wissenschaftlichkeit].[7]

¶When Genesis says "Yahweh," it 'means', from a historical or psychological point of view, nothing but Yahweh; theologically, i.e., from the viewpoint of[8] the church, however, it is speaking of God.[9] For in the whole of Holy Scripture God is the one and only God [der Eine Gott][10]; with this belief the church and theological science [Wissenschaft] stand or fall.[11]

[7.] See above, 7.

[8.] In *NL-A* 31.3 the words follow, crossed out: "God's revelation in."

[9.] Cf. Hans Schmidt, *Die Erzählung von Paradies und Sündenfall*, 29: "The god whom this ancient story [of the tree of knowledge] knows is not the God in whom we believe; nor is this god Yahweh, the God of the great Israelite prophets, or the God of Moses" but the Canaanite god Baal.

[10.] In *NL-A* 31.3 Bonhoeffer replaced "God is God" with this wording.

[11.] Bonhoeffer wrote the Introduction and the Preface, in this order (see *NL-A* 31.3), for the 1933 edition, after the lecture course. Erich Klapproth gives an impression of how the lecture course itself started on November 8, 1932: "The word of God [is] neither fiction nor fairy tale nor myth; on the contrary one must read it word for word [*buchstabieren*] like a child and learn to rethink *completely* what the historical critical commentaries teach us. One can never hear it, if one does not at the same time live it — and this involves especially *exercitium* ['practice']. For *us* the word of God always lies hidden like a treasure in a field [Matt. 13:44], for we always have to come to the knowledge of God via the cross of Christ. In its catechumenate the ancient church allowed the story of creation to be discussed only at the *end* of the course of instruction [for baptism]; in the same way we come to it not just with a speculative approach but from the center of the Bible. We must place ourselves under the same Lord under whom the Bible stands. That is the only 'methodological presupposition'" (*EK* [1]). The comment about the catechumenate of the ancient church appears also in *FL* (1). In Hilde Pfeiffer's notes taken down during the lecture the concluding sentences of the introduction read: "In these three chapters the very God speaks to us as those who are under judgment, as those who have been put to death in and with Christ, as children and heirs of Adam who was driven out [of Paradise], as those who know about the church. We take the Bible into our hands here as the church of Christ" (*HP* [1]).

THE BEGINNING

In the beginning God created heaven and earth, and the earth was formless   25
and empty [wüst und leer];[1] *and it was dark upon the deep. And the spirit*
of God hovered over the water.

THE PLACE WHERE THE BIBLE begins is one where our own most impas-
sioned waves of thinking break, are thrown back upon themselves, and
lose their strength in spray and foam. The first word of the Bible has
hardly for a moment surfaced before us, before the waves frantically
rush in upon it again and cover it with wreaths of foam. That the Bible
should speak of the beginning provokes the world, provokes us. For we
cannot speak of the beginning. Where the beginning begins, there our
thinking stops; there it comes to an end.[2] Yet the desire to ask after the
beginning is the innermost passion of our thinking; it is what in the end
imparts reality to every genuine question we ask. We know that we continually have to ask about the beginning — and yet that we can never ask
about it. Why not? Because [the beginning is the infinite, and because

---

[1.] The adjective *wüst* can mean either "deserted, waste" or "chaotic, formless." The Hebrew noun *tohu* that it translates can also mean either "desert" or
"chaos." As we shall see in what follows, however, Bonhoeffer understands the
word here in the latter sense. For, like Luther, whose translation he here follows,
and Augustine before him, he interprets the text to mean that a formless chaos
was the first step of creation itself — not something that preexisted creation and
supplied the necessary matter out of which the world was created. [DSB]

[2.] Cf. Friedrich Gogarten, *Ich glaube*, "Belief in God the Creator": "This 'In
the beginning' is something absolutely inconceivable. Thought tumbles into
infinity, because before every beginning it must posit another beginning" (47).

we can conceive of the infinite only as what is endless] and so as what has
no beginning.[3] Because the beginning is freedom, and we can never
conceive of freedom except in terms of necessity[4] and thus as one thing
among others but never as the one thing that utterly precedes all other
things [das Eine schlecthin vor allem anderen].[5]

¶We may ask why it is that we always think from the beginning and
with reference to it and yet can never conceive it, never indeed ask after
26 the beginning to find out about it. The question why, however, only gives
expression to a series of questions that could be pushed back endlessly,
yet would not reach the beginning. Thinking can never answer its own
last question why, because an answer to this would produce yet another
why? The question 'why' is really only an expression, an expression κατ'
ἐξοχήν,[6] of thinking that lacks a beginning. Our thinking, that is, the
thinking of those who have to turn to Christ to know about God, the
thinking of fallen humankind, lacks a beginning because it is a circle. We
think in a circle. But we also feel and will in a circle. We exist in a circle.[7]
It is possible to say that in that case the beginning is everywhere. But
against that stands the equally valid statement that for that very reason
there is no beginning at all. The decisive point, however, is that thinking

---

[3.] In the 1933 edition this sentence began: "Because we can conceive of the
beginning only as something finite. . . ." *EK* (1), in agreement with *FL* (2) and
UK (1), attests the wording that stands in the square brackets.

[4.] Friedrich Brunstäd in his *Idee der Religion* expounds the Hegelian idea of
the unity of freedom and necessity; e.g., "True freedom is necessity that has
been comprehended and appropriated" (113). Bonhoeffer had discussed Brunstäd's book in his *Habilitationsschrift* or postdoctoral dissertation (*AB* [*DBWE*
2]:40–41) and in many other places.

[5.] *EK* reads, ". . . goes *beyond* every other thing" (1). *HP* also reads "beyond"
(2).

[6.] Gk. for *par excellence*. The literal meaning of ἐξοχή is "prominence, emi-
nence." Cf. Acts 25:23. [DSB]

[7.] For the image of the circle see Bonhoeffer's "Dogmatische Übungen
[Theologische Psychologie]" (Dogmatic exercises [on the theological analysis of
the human person]) in the winter semester of 1932–33: "Kant: The I can never
conceive of itself. Hegel: dialectics. The I comes back to itself. Circle"(*GS* 5:342).
[trans. DSB] Also see Friedrich Nietzsche, *Zarathustra*, "Concerning the Virtu-
ous": "The circle's thirst is within you; every circle curves and turns in order to
catch itself up again" (206). [trans. altered DSB] Cf. also Emil Brunner, *God and
Man: Four Essays on the Nature of Personality*, "The Philosophers' Idea of God and
the Creator God of Faith": "The ring of 'mine' encloses all" (58).

takes this circle to be the infinite, the beginning itself, and is thereby caught in a *circulus vitiosus*.[8] For where thinking looks to itself as the beginning, it posits itself as an object, as an entity over against itself, and so again and again withdraws behind this object — or rather, finds itself in every instance before the object it is positing. It is therefore impossible for thinking to make this final pronouncement about the beginning. Thinking pounds itself to pieces on the beginning. Because thinking wants to reach back to the beginning and yet never can want it, all thinking pounds itself to pieces, shatters against itself, breaks up into fragments, dissolves, in view of the beginning that it wants and cannot want.

¶The Hegelian question how we are to make a beginning in philosophy can therefore be answered only by the bold and violent action of enthroning reason in the place of God.[9] That is why critical philosophy is but a systematic despair of its own beginning, indeed of any beginning.[10] Critical philosophy may proudly renounce what it lacks the

27

[8.] Latin, meaning a faulty or erroneous circle, i.e., a circular argument. [DSB]

[9.] Georg Wilhelm Friedrich Hegel (1770–1831) begins the main body of the 1827 version of his *Lectures on the Philosophy of Religion* saying: "The question with which we have to begin is this: How are we to secure a beginning?" (1:365). In Bonhoeffer's copy of the Georg Lasson edition of the *Vorlesungen über die Philosophie der Religion*, this passage is marked with exclamation marks in indelible pencil in the margin (Lasson, 79). Also marked with a lead pencil is the passage which reads: The "true relation of the finite and the infinite is one in which their opposition finds its resolution in *reason*" (*Philosophy of Religion*, Pt. 1, *The Concept of Religion*, 1:301 [Lasson, 141]). See *Internationales Bonhoeffer Forum* 8:61, 78. While one may be surprised to find Hegel figuring so prominently in a commentary on Genesis, we need to remember both that Bonhoeffer's first two books up to this point — *Sanctorum Communio* and *Act and Being* — had engaged in a significant dialogue with Hegel and that in fact the final lecture series that Bonhoeffer was to give at the University of Berlin the following summer of 1933 was on the philosophy of Hegel.

[10.] Hegel in the *Philosophy of Religion* compares Kant to a person from Gascony — by reputation a blustering person who, when it comes down to it, turns out to be irrationally cautious — "who does not want to go into the water until he can swim" (1:169, n. 51). This passage is marked in Bonhoeffer's copy of the Lasson edition with a double exclamation mark in pencil in the margin (57). It is particularly against Immanuel Kant that Hegel directs his diagnosis that "despair about knowledge" is the "plague of our time in view of what reason or knowledge is" (Lasson, 55). He scornfully reproaches Kant with even being

power to attain, or else lapse into a resignation that leads to its complete destruction; either alternative stems from the same human hatred of the unknown beginning.

¶Humankind no longer lives in the beginning; instead it has lost the beginning. Now it finds itself in the middle, knowing neither the end nor the beginning, and yet knowing that it is in the middle. It knows therefore that it comes from the beginning and must move on toward the end. It sees its life as determined by these two factors, concerning which it knows only that it does not know them. The animals know nothing about the beginning and the end; they therefore know no hatred and no pride. Humankind knows itself to be totally deprived of its own self-determination, because it comes from the beginning and is moving toward the end without knowing what that means. This makes it hate the beginning and rise up in pride against it.

There can therefore be nothing more disturbing or agitating for human beings than to hear someone speak of the beginning as though it were not the totally ineffable, inexpressibly dark beyond of our own blind existence. People will fall upon such a person; they will call such a person the chief of liars, or else indeed the savior, and they will kill that person when they hear what he says.

¶Who can speak of the beginning? There are two possibilities. The speaker may be the one who has been a liar from the beginning,[11] the evil one, for whom the beginning is the lie and the lie is the beginning, whom human beings believe because the evil one deceives them with lies. And as one who lies, the evil one will say: I am the beginning, and you, O humankind, are the beginning. You were with me from the beginning. I have made you what you are, and with me your end is done away [aufgehoben].[12] I am the Beginning and the End, the A[lpha] and the

28

---

proud that he has renounced the knowledge of God (see, e.g., Lasson, 5f.). These passages are marked by Bonhoeffer. See *Internationales Bonhoeffer Forum*, 8:57 and 28–29. See also *AB* (DBWE 2) where, speaking of 'Being in Adam' as opposed to 'Being in Christ,' Bonhoeffer wrote: "The thinking and philosophizing of human beings in sin is self-glorifying, even when it seeks to be self-critical or to become 'critical philosophy'" (138).

[11.] See John 8:44: The devil "was a murderer from the beginning. . . . When he lies, he speaks according to his own nature." Augustine cites part of this text in his exposition of the creation story in the *Confessions*, 12/25:290.

[12.] *Aufheben* is a key term in Hegel. The Hegelian meaning of this term is a dialectical one: it means "negating" or "overcoming," and yet at the same time

O[mega];[13] worship me. I am the truth out of which comes the lie; for I am the lie that first gives birth to the truth. You are the beginning and you are the end, for you are in me. Believe me, the liar from the beginning: lie, and you will be in the beginning and will be lord of the truth. Discover your beginning yourself. So speaks the evil one, as the liar from the beginning. It is either *the evil one* who speaks or that other who speaks, the one who has been the truth from the beginning, and the way and the life,[14] the one who was in the beginning, the very God, Christ, the Holy Spirit. No one can speak of the beginning but the one who was in the beginning.[15]

¶Thus the Bible begins with the free confirmation, attestation, or revelation of God by God: In the beginning God created. . . .[16] But this rock hardly surfaces for a moment in the sea, before the sea, roused to a furious storm by the sight of the one who is immovable, covers it again. What does it mean that in the beginning God is? Which God? Your God, whom you make for yourself out of your own need because you need an idol, because you do not wish to live without the beginning, without the end, because being in the middle causes you anxiety? In the beginning, God — that is just your lie, which is not better but even more cowardly than the lie of the evil one. How do you, an unknown stranger, you, the writer of this sentence, know about the beginning? Have you seen it, were you there in the beginning? Does your God not say to you, "Where were you when I laid the foundations of the earth? Tell me, if you are so clever!" (Job 38:4).[17]

¶So what sort of statement are these first words of Scripture? An illusion produced by the fainthearted imagination of a person who is unable to live in the middle with pride or with resignation? And are we

---

"preserving" or "sustaining" in a higher unity (cf. *AB* [*DBWE* 2]: 31, editorial note 20). Thus the German sentence could also be interpreted to mean "and your end has been raised up to [be with] me." [DSB]

[13.] Revelation 1:8. Alpha and Omega are the first and last letters of the Greek alphabet.

[14.] John 14:6.

[15.] John 1:1-2.

[16.] Here *EK* adds: "Whoever asks after the beginning asks after God; when you do not know the beginning, then you know you are not with God" (2). Similarly, *UK* (3).

[17.] The NRSV reads, "Where were you when I laid the foundation of the earth? Tell me, if you have understanding." [DSB]

not all that person — we who out of the faintheartedness of our own lives,
with their lack of a beginning and an end, cry out to a god who is but our
own ego?[18] How can we meet this reproach? It is after all true that one
who speaks of the beginning speaks of one's own anxiety within life's circle. This is true even of the person who wrote the Bible. Or rather it is
not that person who speaks; it is God, the absolute beginning or primal
reality, who had being before our life and thinking, with all its anxiety.
God alone tells us that God is in the beginning; God testifies of God by
no other means than through this word, which as the word of a book, the
word of a pious human being, is wholly a word that comes from the middle and not from the beginning. In the beginning God created. . . . This
word, spoken and heard as a human word, is the form of a servant in
which from the beginning God encounters us and in which alone God
wills to be found. It is neither something profound nor something frivo-
lous but God's truth, to the extent that *God* speaks it.

In the beginning — God. That is true if by this word God comes alive
for us here in the middle, not as a distant, eternal being in repose but as
the Creator. We can *know* about the beginning in the true sense only by
hearing[19] of the beginning while we ourselves are in the middle,
between the beginning and the end; otherwise it would not be the beginning in the absolute sense which is also our *beginning*. Here in the middle, between the beginning we have lost and the end we have lost, we
know of God as the beginning only — as God the Creator.

In the beginning God *created* heaven and earth. Not that first God was
and then God created, but that in the beginning God created. This
beginning is the beginning in the anxiety-causing middle and at the
same time beyond the anxiety-causing middle in which we have our
being. We do not know of this beginning by stepping out of the middle

---

[18.] Cf. Hegel, *Lectures on the Philosophy of Religion*: "God is in the same way
also the finite, and I am in the same way the infinite" (308, n. 97). In Bonhoeffer's copy of the Lasson edition this passage is marked with wavy lines in
pencil, indicating disapproval (148). See *Internationales Bonhoeffer Forum*, 8:81.
Cf. the comment Bonhoeffer wrote in 1926: "'heavenly double' [*Doppelgänger*] of
my earthly ego!" (*DBW* 9:377).

[19.] The word "*hearing*" is underlined in *FL* (5), just as in its repetition at the
beginning of the second lecture (which *HP* [5] dates November 11, [1932]). *FL*
reads, "In the middle one can *hear* of the beginning; otherwise it is speculation"
(6). Similarly, see *EK* 2. Bonhoeffer stressed the hearing of the word in opposition to Hegel with his talk of a (speculative) human knowledge of God.

and becoming a beginning ourselves. Because we could accomplish that only by means of a lie, we would then certainly not be in the beginning but only in the middle that is disguised by a lie. This needs to be kept clearly in mind in everything that follows. It is only in the middle that we come to learn about the beginning. 30

The twofold question arises: Is this beginning God's own beginning, or is it God's beginning with the world? But the very fact that this question is asked shows that we no longer know what the beginning means. When the beginning can be spoken about only by those who are in the middle and worry about the beginning and the end, those who tug at their own chains, those who — to anticipate for a moment something that comes later — know only in their sin about having been created by God,[20] then it can no longer be asked whether this beginning is God's own beginning or God's beginning with the world. This is because for us God as the beginning is no other than the one who in the beginning created the world and created us, and because we can know nothing at all of *this* God except as the Creator of our world. Luther was once asked what God was doing before the creation of the world. His answer was that God was cutting sticks to cane people who ask such idle questions.[21] In this way Luther was not just cutting the questioner short; he was also saying that where we do not recognize God as the merciful Creator, we can know God only as the wrathful judge — that is, only standing in relation to the middle, between the beginning and the end. There is no possible question that could go back behind this God who created in the beginning. Thus it is also impossible to ask why the world was created, what God's plan for the world was, or whether the creation was necessary. These questions are exposed as godless questions and finally disposed of by the statement: In the beginning God created heaven and earth. The statement declares not that in the beginning God had this or that idea about the purpose of the world, ideas that we must now try to discover, but that in the beginning God *created*. No question can go back

---

[20.] See the exposition of Gen. 2:8-17 below, e.g., pages 90–92.

[21.] *EK* reads, "God sat behind a hazelbush, cutting canes for such useless questions" (2). Bonhoeffer is referring to the passage in Luther's *Table Talk* where Luther is recalling Augustine, who wrote in his *Confessions* that God "was preparing hell for those who pry too deep" (11/12:253). Luther's actual words were: ". . . Once, when he was asked, [Augustine] said, 'God was making hell for those who are inquisitive'" (*LW* 54:377 [*WA-TR* 4:611, no. 5010]).

behind the creating God, because one cannot go back behind the beginning.

31   From this it follows that the beginning is not to be thought of in temporal terms. We can always go back behind a temporal beginning. But the beginning is distinguished by something utterly unique — unique not in the sense of a number that one can count back to, but in a qualitative sense, that is, in the sense that it simply cannot be repeated, that it is completely free. One could conceive of a continual repetition of free acts;[22] such a concept would be basically mistaken only because freedom does not allow itself to be repeated. Otherwise freedom would have freedom as its own precondition, that is, freedom would be unfree, and no longer the beginning κατ᾽ ἐξοχήν.[23]

This quite unrepeatable, unique, free event in the beginning, which must in no way be confused with the number 4800[24] or any such date, is the creation. In the beginning God created heaven and earth. In other words the Creator — in freedom! — creates the creature. The connection between them is conditioned by nothing except freedom, which means that it is unconditioned. This rules out every application of causal categories for an understanding of the creation. The relation between Creator and creature can never be interpreted in terms of cause and effect, because between the Creator and the creature there stands no law of thought or law of effect or anything else. Between Creator and creature there is simply *nothing* [das Nichts].[25] For freedom is exercised in,

---

[22.] Cf. below, pages 46–47, concerning *creatio continua*.

[23.] See above, editorial note 6. [DSB]

[24.] This is a calculation based on the figures given in the Bible, e.g., in Genesis 5 (the genealogy from Adam to Noah). Bonhoeffer noted in pencil next to this chapter in his copy of *LB*: "1656 yr. fr[om]. Adam to the Flood." [In the English-speaking world the equivalent traditional date of creation was 4004 B.C.E. This date was calculated by the seventeenth-century Irish Archbishop James Ussher, and was then printed above Genesis 1 in many editions of the KJV.] [DSB]

[25.] "*das Nichts*": the italics are Bonhoeffer's. Here and later, John Fletcher's previous translation of *Creation and Fall* used the term "the void" to translate *das Nichts*. While this term does convey something of the force of *das Nichts* as a noun, the problem is that many English translations render the Hebrew word *bohu* in Gen. 1:2 as "void" (= empty). Thus to translate *das Nichts* as "the void" here would convey the impression to the unwary English reader that Bonhoeffer's comments about *das Nichts* have to do with this word, *bohu*, in Gen. 1:2. In fact, however, Bonhoeffer is still expounding v. 1 ("In the beginning God created heaven and earth"), not yet v. 2. [DSB]

and on the basis of, this nothing [in und aus dem Nichts]. No kind of necessity that could, or indeed had to, ensue in creation can therefore be demonstrated to exist in God.[26] There is simply nothing that provides the ground for creation. Creation comes out of this nothing.

Now human beings could certainly once again attempt to move away from the middle that causes them anxiety and become a beginning themselves. They could endeavor to think of this nothing as something that in turn gives birth to creation. But where one speaks of *creation* — that is, theologically — there nothingness has a wholly different meaning from where it appears as the endless end in thinking that lacks a beginning. Nothingness, nonbeing,[27] arises in our philosophical thinking at the point where the beginning cannot be conceived. Thus it is in the end never anything but the ground for being. Nothingness as the ground for being is understood as a creative nothingness. One then has to ask what lies back beyond this nothingness, yet without coming up against the beginning. Nothingness, as humankind in the middle conceives it without knowing about the beginning, is the ultimate attempt at explanation. It is the point through which that which is has passed in coming to be. We call it a filled, charged, self-glorifying nothingness.[28]

¶The nothingness that lies between the freedom of God and creation

---

[26.] According to Hegel, God — even in terms of the traditional idea of God as the One who created the world out of nothing — as the infinite *had* to choose to be determined as the finite, because outside of God nothing existed that could determine itself. See Hegel's *Lectures on the Philosophy of Religion* (Lasson, 146–48). Bonhoeffer's copy of the Lasson edition has this passage heavily marked in colored pencil; see also *Internationales Bonhoeffer Forum*, 8:81–82.

[27.] Here I have used two terms to translate *das Nichts*: "nothingness" and "nonbeing." But "nonbeing" corresponds more exactly to the German term *Nichtsein*, which Bonhoeffer uses elsewhere and which in other places in the English edition of Bonhoeffer has been translated "nonbeing" (e.g., *AB* [*DBWE 2*]: 99). [DSB]

[28.] *HP* (7), with reference to "the speculative creative primeval ground of what has being," notes: "(cf. Idealism Heidegger's philosophy)." *UK* (5) reads, "(Heidegger: Metaphysics of nonbeing.)" *FL* (7) says, "What is Metaphysics." The last of these is the title of Martin Heidegger's inaugural lecture, which considered the theme of nothingness. Heidegger's lecture was delivered three and a half years earlier at the University of Freiburg in Breisgau on July 24, 1929. (Only) *FL* mentions the name Hegel (7). Cf. Hegel, *Lectures on the Philosophy of Religion* with reference to "God created the world out of nothing. . ." (Lasson, 147); and see *Internationales Bonhoeffer Forum*, 8:13 and 81.

32

is by contrast not an attempted explanation for the creation of that which has being. It is thus not a substance out of which, paradoxically, the world then arose, the point through which what has being had to pass. It is not a something at all, not even a negative something. It is the particular word that alone is able to define and express the relation between God's freedom and God's creation.

¶This nothingness is therefore not a primal possibility or a ground of God; it 'is' absolutely 'nothing'. It happens instead in God's action itself, and it happens always as what has already been negated, as the nothing that is no longer happening but has always already happened. We call it the obedient nothing, the nothing that waits on God, the nothing whose glory and whose existence [Bestand] are neither in itself nor in its nothingness but only in God's action. Thus God needed no link between God and the creation; even the nothing constitutes no such 'between'. On the contrary God affirms the nothing only to the extent that God has already overcome it. This is what people of a bygone time[29] tried to express with their somewhat clumsy description of the nothing as the nihil negativum (as distinct from the nihil privativum,[30] which was understood as primal being). The nothing poses no reason for anxiety to the first creation. Instead, it is itself an eternal song of praise to the Creator who created the world out of nothing.

¶The world exists in the midst of nothing, which means in the beginning. This means nothing else than that it exists wholly by God's freedom. What has been created belongs to the [free] Creator.[31] It means also, however, that the God of creation, of the utter beginning, is the God of the resurrection. The world exists from the beginning in the sign

---

[29.] *EK* reads, ". . . the older dogmatic theologians" (3). Probably this referred above all to Johannes Andreas Quenstedt, a Lutheran theologian in the time of the old seventeenth-century Protestant orthodoxy. See Heinrich Schmid, *Dogmatik*, 113. Bonhoeffer liked to use Schmid's *Dogmatik*, along with von Hase's *Hutterus redivivus*, as is evident already in 1926 (see *DBW* 9:430, 438–39).

[30.] From the Latin *privatio*, meaning "(a state of) privation or deprivation." *EK* reads *nihil negativum* "over against the philosophical '*nihil privativum*'" (3). *UK* also has the characterization "philosophical" (5). The German 'school philosophy' employed this idea of the '*nihil*'. This is evident already in Alexander Gottlieb Baumgarten (1714–1762). Immanuel Kant (1724–1804) provided it with its definitive categorization in his *Critique of Pure Reason*, 295–96 (B 348).

[31.] *HP* provides the evidence for the word in square brackets (8). The 1933 edition lacks it.

of the resurrection of Christ from the dead.[32] Indeed it is because we know of the resurrection that we know of God's creation in the beginning, of God's creating out of nothing. The dead Jesus Christ of Good Friday and the resurrected κύριος[33] of Easter Sunday — that is creation out of nothing, creation from the beginning. The fact that Christ was dead did not provide the possibility of his resurrection but its impossibility; it was nothing itself, it was the nihil negativum. There is absolutely no transition, no continuum between the dead Christ and the resurrected Christ, but the freedom of God that in the beginning created God's work out of nothing. Were it possible to intensify the nihil negativum even more, we would have to say here, in connection with the resurrection, that with the death of Christ on the Cross the nihil negativum broke its way into[34] God's own being. — O great desolation! God, yes God, is dead.[35] — Yet the one who is the beginning lives, destroys the nothing, and in his resurrection creates the new creation. By his resurrection we know about the creation. For had he not risen again,[36] the

34

[32.] Cf. Wilhelm Vischer's 1927 article, "Das Alte Testament als Gottes Wort": "As absurd as it may seem to base the exposition of the first book of Moses on the Easter faith, so much does it make sense and so pertinent and essential is it to do so. For the Easter message is the verification of the message of the creation story, and the message of the creation story is the presupposition of the Easter message" (388).

[33.] "Lord."

[34.] *FL* (8) and *EK* (3) provide the evidence for this wording; the 1933 edition reads "was taken into."

[35.] [In his *Lectures on the Philosophy of Religion* Hegel discusses the idea of the death of God as meaning that there is suffering, pain, and negation in God. He quotes the words of the Lutheran hymn, "God, yes God, is dead" (*Gott selbst ist tod*).] [JDEG] Georg Lasson, the editor of the edition of Hegel's *Philosophie der Religion* used by Bonhoeffer, comments as follows: "'O great desolation! God, yes God, is dead' is the second verse of the hymn, 'O Traurigkeit, O Herzeleid' of Johannes Rist (1607–1667)" (14:157–58). In Bonhoeffer's copy of Lasson's edition these lines are marked with a pencil. See *Internationales Bonhoeffer Forum*, 8:99–100. By 1932–33 the 'patripassian' wording, "God, yes God, is dead," had disappeared from German hymnbooks; see the *Evangelisches Gesangbuch für Brandenburg und Pommern* (1931), hymn 43, verse 2, and the *Evangelisches Gesangbuch erarbeitet im Auftrag der Evangelischen Kirche in Deutschland* (1992), hymn 80, verse 2: "O great desolation! The Son of God lies dead." [Bonhoeffer quoted the German text of the hymn as: "oh grosse Not, Gott selbst ist tot."] [DSB]

[36.] Cf. the *Evangelisches Gesangbuch für Brandenburg und Pommern*, hymn 56, verse 2, and the *Evangelisches Gesangbuch* (1992): "Had he not risen, the world were undone."

Creator would be dead and would not be attested. On the other hand we know from the act of creation about God's power to rise up again, because God remains Lord [over nonbeing].[37]

In the beginning — that is, out of freedom, out of nothing — God created heaven and earth. That is the comfort with which the Bible addresses us who are in the middle and who feel anxiety before the spurious nothingness, before the beginning without a beginning and the end without an end. It is the gospel, it is Christ, it is the resurrected one, who is being spoken of here. That God is in the beginning and will be in the end, that God exists in freedom over the world and that God makes this known to us — that is compassion, grace, forgiveness, and comfort.

"And the earth was formless and empty; and it was dark upon the deep; and the spirit of God hovered over the waters."[38]

The beginning has been made. But attention still remains fixed on that event, on the free God. That it is true, that it has been done, that heaven and earth are there, that the miracle has come to pass, deserves all wonder. Not the created work, no, but the Creator wills to be glorified. The earth is formless and empty; but the Creator is the Lord, the one who brings about the wholly new, the strange, inconceivable work of God's dominion and love. "The earth was formless and empty." It was nevertheless our earth which came forth from God's hand and now lies ready for God, subject to God in devout worship. God is praised first by the earth that was formless and empty. God does not need us human beings to be glorified, but brings about divine worship out of the world which is without speech, which, mute and formless, rests, slumbering, in God's will.

¶"And it was dark upon the deep, and the spirit of God hovered over the waters. . . ." What can be said about the work considering the act, and what can be said about the creature considering the Creator, except that it is dark and that it is in the deep? That the creature is God's work, that is its honor; and that it lies dark before God, that is the glory of God's majesty as Creator. It lies in the abyss beneath God. Just as we look down, dizzy, from a high mountain into the depths, and the darkness of

35

[37.] *UK* provides evidence for the words in square brackets (5), which are lacking in the 1933 edition.

[38.] The wording of the text here follows the Kautzsch translation (10) in differing from the *LB*, which is quoted at the beginning of the section ("upon the water").

the depths lies beneath us, so the earth is at God's feet — distant, strange, dark, deep, but God's work.[39]

The dark deep — that is the first sound of the power of darkness, of the passion of Jesus Christ. The darkness, the tehōm, the tihāmat, the Babylonian "primeval sea [Urmeer],"[40] contains within itself — precisely in its depth — power and force. This power and force still serve to honor the Creator now, but once torn away from the origin, from the beginning, they become tumult and rebellion. In the night, in the abyss, there exists only what is formless. Thus the formless [wüste], empty, dark deep, which is not able to take on form by itself, the agglomeration of formlessness [die Zusammenballung des Gestaltlosen], the torpid unconscious, the unformed, is both the expression of utter subjection and the unsuspected force of the formless, as it waits impatiently to be bound into form.

It is a moment [Augenblick] in God in which the unformed mass and its Creator exist over against each other. It is a moment of which it is said

---

[39.] Bonhoeffer takes v. 1 (in *LB*: "In the beginning God created heaven and earth. And . . .") to be not a heading or superscription for the acts of creation depicted from v. 3 on ("And God spoke: . . . ") but the start of creation itself. Hermann Gunkel by contrast regards it as "an impossible interpretation" that God first created the world in a chaotic condition, only then to refashion it as an organism (*Urgeschichte*, 102). Bonhoeffer's interpretation corresponds to the reflections of Augustine in the twelfth and thirteenth books of his *Confessions* (see 12/29:294–95 and 13/33:330) about the *informitas* (formlessness) of what was created out of nothing *primo* (at first), the *materia* (matter, material, stuff) that waited to be given form.

[40.] In both the Luther and Kautzsch translations of the Bible the Hebrew word *tehom* is translated with *Tiefe* ("deep, depth, abyss" [DSB]). Hans Schmidt proposes the translation "primeval sea" (*Paradies und Sündenfall*, 36). According to Kautzsch, 10, note d, *tehom* corresponds to the "Babylonian *tiâmat.*" Cf. Kautzsch, 9 (in the Introduction), where he says that *tiamat* means the sea which is hostile to the gods on high but which "Marduk, the god of the spring sun," finally conquered. Hans Schmidt mentions the Babylonian story of creation, the *Enuma elish* (7, note 1). [In the *Enuma elish*, Tiamat represents salt water or the sea and so primeval chaos. Out of the original chaos which is constituted by her mingling with her mate Apsu (fresh or sweet water) is born the next generation of gods. Marduk, the god of Babylon, eventually kills Tiamat, bringing order to chaos, and thereby also justifying redemptive violence. He then divides her body, leaving half as the sea and using the other half to make the sky. The text of the myth can be found in Barbara Sproul, *Primal Myths: Creating the World.*] [JDEG]

that the spirit of God hovered over the waters; it is a moment in which God is thinking, planning, and bringing forth form. It cannot be said that the relation of Creator and creature is in any way affected, that God here espouses what God has created in order to make it fruitful,[41] or that God becomes one with it. The cosmogonic idea of the world-egg over which the divine being broods[42] is at any rate not intended here. God remains utterly Creator *over* the deep, *above* the waters.[43]

¶But this God who is the Creator now begins again. The creation of that which is formless, empty, and dark is distinguished from the creation of form by a moment in God that is described here as the hovering of the spirit over the waters. God reflects upon the divine work. The unbinding or release of formless force and the simultaneous binding of it into form, so that what merely exists [Dasein] begins to exist in a particular way [Sosein],[44] is a moment of hesitation in God. The divine praise that God prepares out of the rude darkness of the unformed is to

37

[41.] Hans Schmidt (37) refers in a footnote to Albrecht Dietrich's 1905 book, *Mutter Erde*: "The cosmogonic myths of many primitive peoples know of a primary couple from whom everything originates: the female is the earth, the male is often 'heaven' or alternatively the sun god. The fructifying element is naturally a sunbeam or rain" (15, note 2). In Gen. 2:6 and even in Gen. 1:2 Schmidt finds a corresponding idea: the "divine storm" passes over the "Mother of All Things, here the *tehom*" (38).

[42.] Hermann Gunkel, for instance, finds this idea here (*Urgeschichte*, 102). Kautzsch very tentatively leaves open the possibility that it stands in the background (10, note e). Stiasny quotes Luther as saying that ". . . just as a hen sits on the eggs," so the Holy Spirit settles upon the work that had been created out of nothing (Stiasny ed., 4).

[43.] Cf. Augustine's *Confessions* (13/4:301), according to which the Holy Spirit hovered "'super aquas,' non ferebatur ab eis" ("'over the face of the waters,' . . . not borne up by them"). *FL* (alone) records at this point the comment that the creation may not be played off against revelation: "There is a unique problem: *creation and revelation*. (This is the question about God today.) It concerns at bottom the *theologia naturalis* ['natural theology'] (*gnosis* in the second century)" (10). At this point the second lecture period ended. The third period is dated by *HP* (11) and *FL* (11) as November 22, 1932. At the beginning of the third period *FL* reads, "(Must hold together the uniqueness of the revelation in creation and the revelation in Christ — therein lies the difficulty in the world today)" (11). Cf. *UK*: "Revelation happens only once: creation and the resurrection of Jesus are one" (6).

[44.] Cf. Bonhoeffer's discussion of "Definition of 'Being' in Adam" in *AB* (*DBWE* 2):136–50.

be completed through its being given form. The creation still rests entirely in God's hand, in God's power; it has no being of its own. Yet the praise of the Creator is completed only when the creature receives its own being from God and praises God's being by its own being. In the creation of form the Creator denies [the Creator's own self],[45] in that this grants form to what is created and grants to it its own being or existence before the Creator; in that the existence of what is created serves the Creator, however, the Creator chooses to be glorified. Thereby the Creator enormously increases the power of the creation, by giving to creation its own being as that which has form. In this form creation exists over against God in a new way, and in existing over against God it wholly belongs to God.[46]

[45.] *HP* (11) and *EK* (4) record that in the lecture Bonhoeffer used the words "the Creator denies the Creator's own self"; the 1933 edition lacks the reflexive.

[46.] In the recapitulation at the beginning of the third lecture period *EK* adds "That today we can no longer think of form and material as separated is an indication of our origin and our end: we *wholly* come from God and *wholly* go to God. On the other hand it is an indication of the Fall; by our existing in a particular way [*So-Sein*] we have also snatched our being away from God" (4). *HP* (11) and *FL* (11) also have the last sentence, almost word for word.

THE WORD

And God said: Let there be light,[1] *and there was light.*

THERE ARE MYTHS OF CREATION in which the deity imparts its own nature, so that the world springs from the natural fecundity of the deity. In these myths, then, creation is understood as the self-unfolding of the deity or the deity's giving form to itself or giving birth; the creation itself is a portion of what belongs to God's very nature, and the pangs of nature, in its birth and in its decay, are pangs that the deity itself suffers.[2]

¶In opposition to all such myths, however, the God of the Bible remains wholly God, wholly the Creator, wholly the Lord, and what God has created remains wholly subject and obedient, praising and worshiping God as Lord. God is never the creation but always the Creator. God is not the substance [Substanz] of nature. There is no continuum that ties God to, or unites God with, God's work — except God's *word*. God said. . . . The only continuity between God and God's work is the word. That is, 'inherently' ['an sich'][3] there is no continuum; were the word not there, the world would drop into a bottomless abyss.[4] This word of

---

[1.] The *LB* and Kautzsch's version (10) both read: "Let there be light!"

[2.] August Dillmann, *Genesis*, 4–9, and Hermann Gunkel, *Urgeschichte*, 113–15, provide lists of such cosmogonies.

[3.] The phrase *an sich,* "in itself" or "as such," is an allusion to the term *das Ding an sich,* "the thing in itself, the thing as such," which Kant used to distinguish the reality of something from what it appears to be, i.e., from the way we experience it. [DSB]

[4.] Cf. Emil Kautzsch, who said that biblical cosmogony is quite different

God is neither the nature [Natur] nor the essence [Wesen] of God; it is the commandment of God. It is the very God who thinks and creates in this word, but as One who chooses to encounter the creature as its Creator. God's creatorship is not the essence, the substance, but the will or commandment of God; in it God gives us God's very self as God wills. That God creates by the word means that creation is God's order or command, and that this command is free.

¶God *says*, God *speaks*.[5] This means that God creates in complete freedom. Even in creating, God remains wholly free over against what is created. God is not bound to what is created; instead God binds it to God. God does not enter into what is created as its substance [substantiell]; instead what relates God to what is created is God's command. That is, God is never in the world in any other way than as one who is utterly beyond [jenseits] it. God is, as the word, *in* the world, because God is the one who is utterly beyond, and God is utterly beyond the world, because God is in the world *in the word*. Only in the word of creation do we know the Creator; only in the word addressed to us in the middle do we have the beginning. It is not 'from' God's works, then, that we recognize the Creator[6] — as though the substance, the nature, or the essence of the work were after all ultimately somehow identical with God's essence or as if there were some kind of continuum between them, such as that of cause and effect. On the contrary we believe that God is the Creator only because by this word God acknowledges these works as God's own, and we *believe* this word about these works. There is no via eminentiae, negationis, causalitatis![7]

39

---

from the Babylonian cosmogony in that the Bible sees God as standing "over against the world, which is fundamentally distinct and different from God. . . . God called it into being through a mere word and from the beginning provided it with the laws of its preservation" (9). *EK* reads, "Were the word not there, the world would be without God — more correctly, would not be. This word [is] thought and deed in one, *the* beginning" (4). *HP* (12) and *FL* (12) read similarly.

[5.] The German has just "Gott *spricht*." The two English verbs bring out the two nuances here of the single German verb; for it both refers back to "And God said" in Gen. 1:3 and means that "God speaks," as Bonhoeffer discusses here. [DSB]

[6.] Cf. Emil Brunner, *God and Man*, 60–61: "The God who is known from the world is precisely not the creator. . . . As the creator he is only to be known by the fact that he is not to be known in continuity with the world, but from his Word alone."

[7.] According to Bernhard Bartmann, *Dogmatik*, scholastic theology identi-

First of all we need to understand in exactly what sense one can say that God speaks. The term *word* means a spoken word, not a symbol, a meaning, or an idea, but just what it designates.[8] That God creates by speaking means that in God the thought, the name, and the work are in their created reality one. What we must understand, therefore, is that the word does not have 'effects'; instead, God's word *is* already the

40   work.[9] What in us breaks hopelessly asunder — the word of command and what takes place — is for God indissolubly one. With God the imperative is the indicative. The indicative does not result from the imperative; it is not the effect of the imperative. Instead it *is* the imperative.

¶One cannot call God's act of creating an 'effecting' either, because this term does not include within its meaning the character of creation as a command,[10] the absolute freedom of the act of creation, and the freedom from the creation of the one who creates, all of which expresses itself in the word. The 'word' thus encompasses a specific reality. The 'word' expresses the fact that the act of creation is done out of freedom, just as the taking place of creation expresses the fact that it is done out of

---

fied "a threefold procedure on the one way to the knowledge of God: that of affirmation (*via affirmationis* or *causalitas*), that of negation (*via negationis*) and that of perfection (*via eminentiae*). It wished thereby to say that we are able to discern from created things that God exists as their cause, but is not identical with them; on the contrary God is essentially distinct from them and without any of their imperfections and can be thought of only in terms of the infinite heightening of creaturely perfections" (94). See *FL*: "*The only way that God proceeds* [=] *by speaking*" (13). *HP* reads, "Not the miracle of law or of beauty" (13) as a way ("via"). According to *EK*: "The miracles of causality and nature could also be works of the devil; they are not that only because God *calls* them God's work" (4).

[8.] Kautzsch states concerning Gen. 2:20 that "the name, according to the ancient Hebrew way of looking at things, is completely identical with the object that it signifies" (13, note c; cf. Kautzsch, 10, note g, on Gen. 1:5). Brunner comments: "The thing indicated is at all times detachable from the symbol" (*God and Man*, 55).

[9.] *HP* reads, "*The word itself is the deed*" (13). *UK* (7) and *EK* (4) have the same, word for word; *FL* has the same except that it omits "itself" (13).

[10.] (Only) *FL* has a note, in pencil: "Titius" (13). For Arthur Titius, the obvious way in which to differentiate the idea of creation from the idea of the world being formed as an emanation from a primeval being is by the analogy of an act of will. He sees this understanding of creation in terms of a command as most consistently developed in Israelite prophecy. He also refers to Ps. 33:9, which says (as translated in *LB*) "as he commands, so it stands forth" (see Arthur Titius, *Natur und Gott*, 111–12).

omnipotence. Our complete inability to hold the indicative and the imperative together in our minds shows that we no longer live in the unity of the active word of God but are fallen. We can never conceive of any connection between imperative and indicative except as something mediated by a continuum, usually in the framework of a pattern of causality, of cause and effect. This then justifies the inference from the 'effect' to the 'cause'.[11] That, however, is just what does not apply to the creation. Creation is not an 'effect' of the Creator from which one could read off a necessary connection with the cause (the Creator); instead it is a work created in freedom in the word.

God speaks and by speaking creates. Strangely enough the Bible first says this when it comes to the creation of form, the wresting of form out of the formless. Form corresponds to the word. The word brings into relief; it outlines and limits the individual, the real, the whole. The word summons that which comes to be out of nonbeing, so that it may be.[12] It is a completely dark, wholly inaccessible background that discloses itself here behind the word of creation. For us it remains simply impossible to comprehend that first, wordless act of creation — because the Creator is One, and we as creatures are created by the Creator's word.[13] These two moments [Augenblicke] in God are one act; we can express it no other way.

41

"Let there be light, and there was light." Because it was dark upon the formless deep, the light must create form. As the formless night takes form in the light of morning, as the light unveils and creates form, so that primeval light had to order the chaos and unveil and create form. If the preceding word about the darkness upon the deep was the first thing that pointed to the passion of Jesus Christ, so now the light that

---

[11.] Cf. the form of oath prescribed by Pope Pius X against modernism (1910): "I profess that *God* . . . can be *known with certainty,* and that his existence can also be proved . . . from the visible works of creation, as the Cause from its effect" (Neuner and Dupuis, eds., *The Christian Faith in the Doctrinal Documents of the Catholic Church,* 49). Cf. Brunner, *God and Man,* 61–62: "He *creates* it out of nothing — that is the stumbling block for all idealism. . . . He creates the world *through his Word* — that is the stumbling block for realism, which tries to conceive of the creation by means of the category of causality. . . ."

[12.] See Rom. 4:17.

[13.] According to *HP,* "As creatures we are dependent on his word" (12–13). *FL* (alone), emphasized with a line down the margin: "The word is the key to *understanding election*" (14).

frees the subjected, formless deep so that it comes to have its own being points to the light that shines in the darkness.[14] The light awakens the darkness to its own being and to free praise of the Creator. Without the light we would not exist, because without the light things do not exist over against each other — for then no form exists. But without existing over against one another there is no freely offered worship of God. The deep that was made subject worshiped God in a subject, torpid state that was unfree, a state in which nothing stood over against anything else. In the light, however, form becomes aware of existing over against something else and so becomes aware of its own existence; and it gives all thanks for this to the Creator. The light dispenses to the created form the limpid, clear, and carefree nature of its own being in existing over against the other created form and over against the Creator. That is the work of the first word of the Creator. In the created light the creation sees the Creator's light.[15]

[14.] See John 1:7.
[15.] See Ps. 36:9.

V. 4 A

GOD'S LOOK

And God saw that the light was good.

THIS IS THE THIRD MOMENT [Augenblick][1] in God, when God looks at God's created work. It is a moment we can no more think of as separate from the first two moments than we can think of them as separate from each other. God looks at God's work and is pleased with it, because it is good. This means that God loves God's work and therefore wills to uphold and preserve[2] it. Creation and preservation are two sides of the same activity of God. It could after all not be otherwise than that God's work is good and that God does not reject or destroy it but loves and upholds it. As God looks at it, that work comes to rest and becomes aware of God's pleasure in it. God's looking keeps the world from falling back into nothingness [Nichts], from complete destruction [Vernichtung].

¶God's look sees the world as good, as created — even where it is a fallen world. And because of God's look, with which God embraces God's work and does not let it go, we live. That God's work is good in no way means that the world is the best of all conceivable worlds[3]; what it means is that the world lives wholly before God, that it lives from God

---

[1.] Bonhoeffer engages in a wordplay on *Augenblick*, which literally means "blink of an eye," but here is meant in the everyday sense of a "moment," thus alluding to the instant in which God looks at what has been created. [DSB]

[2.] The German verb *erhalten* is translated "uphold" in what follows. The noun *Erhaltung* is translated as "upholding" where this fits and "preservation" where it does not. This first instance of *erhalten* is therefore translated "uphold and preserve." [DSB]

[3.] Cf. Gottfried Wilhelm von Leibniz, *Theodicy: Essays on the Goodness of God, the Freedom of Man and the Origin of Evil* (originally published in 1710): "In conclusion, there is an infinitude of possible worlds, among which God must have chosen the best" (128).

and toward God and that God is its Lord. What is meant here is a good-ness that has not yet been distinguished as such over against evil,[4] a goodness that consists in being under the dominion of God. It is thus the work itself that is good; the creation is God's good work, a work that God does for God's self. That the work and not only the will is good, and is intended to be good, is a biblical as opposed to a Kantian insight.[5] The whole Bible is concerned to teach that the work that has been done, the state of things, the embodiment of the will, the world, is good, that God's kingdom is on earth, that God's will is done on earth.[6] Because the world is God's world, it is good. God, the Creator and Lord of the world, wills a good world, a good work. The flight from the created work to bodiless spirit, or to the internal spiritual disposition [*die Gesinnung*], is prohibited.[7] God wills to look upon God's work, to love it, call it good, and uphold it.

There is an essential difference between creatio continua and uphold-ing creation.[8] In the concept of creatio continua the world is continually

---

[4.] Cf. the students' notes at the beginning of the ninth lecture period: see below, 93, editorial note 37.

[5.] Immanuel Kant's *Groundwork of the Metaphysic of Morals*, after its Pro-logue, begins: "The only thing that is good without qualification or restriction is a good will. That is to say, a good will alone is good *in all circumstances* and in that sense is an absolute or unconditioned good" (17). Cf. Bonhoeffer's discussion of Kant in his lecture, "A Theological Basis for the World Alliance?" in Cierno-horské Kúpele on July 26, 1932 (*DBW* 11:342 [*GS* 1:156]): "It is not correct that only the will can be good. A state of things can also be good: God's creation was as such 'very good.' Even in the fallen world a state of things can be good — never in and through itself but always only with God's own act, the new creation, in view." [trans. DSB] [The World Alliance to which the title of the lecture refers was the World Alliance for Promoting International Friendship through the Churches, one of the ecumenical movements that was a forerunner of the World Council of Churches. Another version of this text can be found in *NRS* 157–73.] [JDEG]

[6.] Cf. Matt. 6:10, the third petition of the Lord's Prayer.

[7.] *FL* (alone) adds to the words "flight to spirit, internal spiritual disposi-tion etc.": "(Protestant idea!)" (16).

[8.] In what follows Bonhoeffer takes issue with ideas to which Bernhard Bartmann had referred in his *Dogmatik*, 256: "*Preservation and Creation.* In God both are one single, eternal act. Therefore it has been maintained in line with Augustine that preservation is a continuing creation: *conservatio continua creatio est.*" Bartmann criticizes this idea on the ground that "through creation being was first brought forth out of nonbeing, but in its preservation no new being is produced; instead what already exists is preserved and protected in its continu-ity." Erich Przywara in his *Religionsphilosophie* regards the "*analogia entis as an*

wrested anew out of nothingness. But this idea, with its concept of a discontinuous continuity, deprives God's creatorship of its utter freedom and uniqueness. It fails to respect our very inability to anticipate God's action.[9] The concept of a creatio continua also ignores the reality of the fallen world, which is *the creation upheld*, not created ever anew. To say that God upholds the created world is a judgment that accepts the present moment in its reality as from God. It means that the world, which was 'once'[10] wrested from nothingness, is upheld in its being. That which was created out of nothing and called forth into being through God's word is kept in place through God's look. It does not, in the moment of becoming, sink back again; instead God looks at it and sees that it is good, and God's look, resting upon God's work, upholds that work in being. Thus the world is upheld only by the one who is its Creator and only for the one who is the Creator. It is upheld not for its own sake but because of God's look. But the work that is upheld is still God's good work.[11]

Creation means wresting out of nonbeing [Nichtsein]; *upholding* means affirming being. *Creation* is a real *beginning*, always 'before' my knowledge[12] and *before* the *upholding* of what has been created. Creation and upholding are at this point still one; they are related to the same object, God's original good work. Upholding is always *with reference to* creation, whereas creation is in itself. But upholding the original creation and upholding the fallen creation are different things.[13]

44

---

expression in philosophical terms of the *creatio ex nihilo*, and indeed of the *creatio continua*; every possible 'is' that applies to a creature [derives] from the unchanging 'Is' who is God" (24). On *analogia entis* see below, 64–66.

[9.] *Creatio continua*, continuous creation. *EK* adds the comment that the idea of the *creatio continua* "anticipates the moment that is still to come" (5). *FL* reads, "The moment has come — Enough! Say no more" (16).

[10.] Cf. the ἐφάπαξ ("once for all") in Rom. 6:10 or, e.g., in Heb. 10:10.

[11.] According to *HP*, what follows is the beginning of the fourth lecture period, dated Nov. 29, 1932 (15).

[12.] *EK* reads, "Creation is not 'before' so many years but always 'before' the moment in which I reflect on it, that is before my existence" (5). *FL* reads very much the same (17).

[13.] *EK* adds that "The world is upheld not as inherently valuable but as something that has been given direction and receives its value only from being directed in this way. As a φιλοσοφούμενον [i.e., philosophical expression] the idea of the *creatio continua* is unjustified and mistaken; as a θεολογούμενον [i.e., theological expression], however, it is justified, so long as it does not affect the once-for-all nature [of creation]" (5; cf. above, editorial note 10).

THE DAY

45   *And God separated the light from the darkness and called the light day and the darkness night. So with evening and morning the first day came to be.*[1]

THE FIRST FINISHED WORK of God is the day. God creates the day in the beginning. The day bears along everything else; the world exists in the process of one day's turning into another [im Wechsel des Tages]. The day has its own being, its own form, its own power. It is not to be understood in physical terms as the rotation of the earth around the sun or as the change of darkness and light that can be calculated as a period of time; it is something beyond all that, something that determines the essence of the world and of our existence. It is, one might almost say if the term did not suit the context here so badly, what we call a mythological entity. To be sure, the gods of the day and of the night who in pagan belief animate and fill the world are here wholly dethroned; the day nevertheless remains God's first creature, something wondrous and mighty in God's hand.

¶The day in its creatureliness and wonder is wholly lost to us. We have withdrawn from its power. We no longer allow ourselves to be determined by it. We count up the days and tick them off. We do not accept the day as a gift; we do not live it. Today we do so less than ever, for technology wars against the day. The Bible itself already speaks of days in the way we speak of them, namely, as periods of time that can be counted. But the Bible still knows that days cannot simply be counted up as

---

[1.] The text is close to that of *LB*; cf. Kautzsch, "And it became evening and became morning, a first day" (10).

48

periods of time determined by the earth's rotation but are instead the great rhythm, the natural dialectic[2] of creation. What the Bible means when it speaks of the creation of the day is that what is formless becomes form in the morning and sinks back into formlessness in the evening, that the clear and distinct existence of things over against one another in the light dissolves into oneness in the dark, that the noise of life dies away in the silence of the night, that expectant wakening in the light is followed by sleep, and that there are times (reaching far beyond the physical day) of wakening and of slumbering in nature, in history, and in the nations [in den Völkern]. The Bible means all of that when it speaks of the creation of the day, of the day without humankind, a day that sustains everything, including the fate of humankind.[3] The rhythm that is both rest and movement, that gives and takes and gives again and takes again and so points forever to God's giving and taking, to God's freedom beyond rest and movement — that is what the day is.

¶When the Bible speaks of six days of creation, the term "day" may well have been meant in the sense of a day of morning and evening. Even so, however, it did not mean such days as periods of time that one could just count up; instead what is being thought of is the power of the day, which alone makes the physical day what it is: the natural dialectic of creation. Where the Bible speaks of the "day," it is not at all the physical problem that it is discussing. Whether the creation occurred in rhythms of millions of years or in single days, this does no damage to biblical thinking. We have no reason to assert the latter or to doubt the former; the question as such does not concern us. That the biblical author, to the extent that the author's word is a human word, was bound by the author's own time, knowledge, and limits is as little disputed as the fact that through this word God, and God alone, tells us about God's creation. God's daily works are the rhythms in which the creation rests.[4]

[2.] Cf. Friedrich Gogarten, *Ich glaube*, 55.

[3.] The German has an untranslatable wordplay, "von dem menschenlosen Tag, der alles, auch das Menschenlos, trägt," in which *los* as the suffix in *menschenlosen* means "without" and as a noun in *Menschenlos* means "fate, destiny." [DSB].

[4.] *EK* reads, "For the Bible the six days are nothing other than the rhythm which God put in his creation and to which God gave the power to bear along the world" (5).

THAT WHICH IS FIRMLY FIXED

---

47   *Vv. 6-10. And God said: Let there be a firmament in the midst of the waters and let it form a partition between the separate waters. And so it came to be.*[1] *And God made the firmament to be a partition between the waters under the firmament and the waters above the firmament. And God called the firmament heaven. So with evening and morning the second day came to be. And God said: Let the water under heaven gather together in one place,*[2] *so that the dry land may be seen. And so it came to be. And God called the dry land earth, but the gathering of the water God called sea. And God saw that it was good.*

HERE THE ANCIENT IMAGE of the world confronts us in all its scientific naïveté. To us today its ideas appear altogether absurd. In view of the rapid changes in our own knowledge of nature, a derisive attitude that is too sure of itself is not exactly advisable here; nevertheless in this passage the biblical author is exposed as one whose knowledge is bound by all the limitations of the author's own time. Heaven and the sea were in any event not formed in the way the author says, and there is no way we

---

[1.] The phrase, "And so it came to be" (rendered in *LB* as "and so it came to pass" and by Kautzsch as "And it came to pass in this way"), stands in the Hebrew (Masoretic) text, and so in *LB*, at the end of verse 7. Kautzsch comments on verse 6 that "according to v. 9, 11, 15 etc." the formula belongs "after the creation command" (10). Bonhoeffer accordingly placed it at the end of verse 6.

[2.] In *LB* this reads "in separate places." The singular is emphasized by Kautzsch's rendering, "in *one* place." Bonhoeffer follows Kautzsch's translation of vv. 6-10.

could escape having a very bad conscience if we let ourselves be tied to assertions of that kind. The theory of verbal inspiration will not do. The writer of the first chapter of Genesis sees things here in a very human way.[3] This state of affairs makes it seem then that there is very little to say about this passage. Yet on this next day of creation something completely new takes place. The world of what is fixed, or solid, the changeless, the inert, begins to exist. That is what is peculiar: that in the beginning just those works of creation are created which in their fixedness, their immutability, their repose, are to us the most distant, the most strange. Completely unaffected by human life, that which is fixed stands before God in undisturbed repose. An eternal law holds it fast.[4] This law is nothing other than the command of the word of God itself.

    48

To the firmament of heaven belongs also the world of the stars. Therefore we look here in advance at

> Vv. 14-19. *And God said, Let there be lights on the firmament of heaven that separate day and night and give signs, times, days, and years and let them be lights on the firmament of heaven to shine upon earth. And so it came to be. And God made two great lights: a great light that rules the day and a small light that rules the night. God also made the stars. And God placed them on the firmament of heaven to shine upon the earth, to rule over the day and the night, and to separate light and darkness. And God saw that it was good. And with evening and morning the fourth day came to be.*

[3.] The doctrine of "verbal inspiration" was developed above all in the old Protestant orthodoxy (on which see Bonhoeffer, *DBW* 9:309, written in 1925), but was evident already in antiquity. According to this doctrine, the Holy Spirit (as the *causa principalis*) inspired the prophets and apostles (as the *causa instrumentalis*) with what was to be written in terms of form and content, so that everything contained in Holy Scripture, throughout and in every detail, was true and free of any error. See Heinrich Schmid, *Dogmatik* (*Prolegomena*, chap. 4, sect. 6, "Notio scripturae sacrae et inspiratio"), 18. *EK* reads, "Luther himself, though he opposed verbal inspiration, took these words far more seriously" (5). *HP* reads, "According to Luther one may not simply dismiss it as unscientific. See Luther's Lectures on Genesis. We cannot do that without becoming untrue" (16–17). *FL* reads, "(Luther concerning the snake . . . in his Lectures on Genesis he develops quite abstruse ideas)" (19). See Luther, Stiasny ed., 53 and 67–69. [On "verbal inspiration" see also Frederic W. Farrar, *History of Interpretation,* and Francis Turretin, *The Doctrine of Scripture.*] [JDEG]

[4.] *EK* reads, " — 'Law' here for the first time!" (5); *UK* reads similarly (9).

As the firmament determines,[5] days, years, and epochs of time happen with complete regularity and without change. Here it is number that rules with its inflexible law. What does this have to do with our existence? Nothing — the stars go their way, whether or not human beings endure suffering, guilt, or bliss. And in being fixed they praise the Creator. The stars do not look down on human beings; they do not accuse, nor do they comfort. They are wholly themselves in unapproachable remoteness. They shine day and night, but they do so without any concern about us. The stars take no part in human existence. Human beings participate in the world of what is fixed, however. For they know *numbers* [*Zahl*].[6] Humankind in the middle retains a knowledge of numbers, of the unchanging, the fixed, of that which is apparently unaffected by humankind's fall. It is peculiar to human beings to realize that the higher they climb in the world of numbers,[7] the purer the air around them becomes; it also becomes thinner and more rarefied, however, so that they cannot live in this world. It is the great temptation of human beings who can count to want to seek comfort in the world of the unchanging, to flee to the world that is unaffected by their own existence,[8] without recognizing that this world existed before the

49

[5.] *HP* reads, "*The fixed pole of the created world is the firmament*" (17); *UK* (9), *FL* (19), and *EK* (5) read very similarly. Bonhoeffer follows *LB* in vv. 14-19.

[6.] [The German uses the singular, *Zahl*, "number," throughout; but the plural "numbers" is more idiomatic in English.] [DSB] Cf. the work by the philosopher of history Oswald Spengler, *The Decline of the West*, in the chapter "Concerning the Meaning of Numbers": "Pure numbers . . . were for the Greeks also the key to the meaning of that which had come to be, that which is *fixed* and *therefore transitory*" (1:95). "Number" is important in the definition of time that Plato puts in the mouth of a Pythagorean in Plato's dialogue *Timaeus*: an eternal image of eternity that advances (and is therefore movable) "by number" — κατ' ἀριθμόν — and to which we have given the name "time" — χρόνος (37d). In Plato's view, time came into existence with the heavenly bodies (*Timaeus*, 38b). Cf. Luther's statement that the movement of the "heavenly bodies above" is what enables us to count the days and years — that "is God's act of kindness and gracious order [*Ordnung*]." "Where number is lacking, however, there is also no time" (Stiasny ed., 14-15).

[7.] *HP* reads, ". . . climb in mathematics" (17).

[8.] *EK* reads, "Humanity cannot flee to the eternal law of the firmament (Kant), because that too is only God's creation. At this point theology's debate with exact natural science has to begin" (6). *HP* (18), *FL* (20), and *UK* (10) read similarly. Cf. Kant's "Conclusion" to his *Critique of Practical Reason*: "Two things fill the mind with ever new and increasing admiration and awe, the oftener and

world of humankind and takes no part in human life. Why do they not recognize this? Because human beings, to be sure, know about numbers and their laws[9] but no longer know that even numbers, which determine days, years, and periods of time, are not self-contained; human beings no longer know that numbers too are upheld by God's word and command alone. Numbers are not the truth of God itself.[10] On the contrary, like everything else, they are God's creatures and so receive their   50 truth wholly from the Creator. We have forgotten this connection; when we have numbers, we believe we have truth and eternity. What draws our attention to our loss of truth and eternity is the fact that in the end mathematics too does not rise above paradox.[11] A knowledge of numbers that is godless ends in paradox and contradiction.

¶So it is with us, who hear in the middle about the beginning of the world. We know about that which is fixed, about numbers, only in the middle, not otherwise, yet thereby the world of that which is fixed discloses itself to us anew in its essence. Because we no longer understand number at its inception, we no longer understand the language of the world of that which is fixed. What we grasp is the godless language we speak ourselves, the language of an eternal law of the world that rests in itself, language that is silent about the Creator and sounds forth about the glory of the creature. When we hear of the Creator who created the world in the beginning, however, we know about the lost connection and believe in God as the Creator — without grasping in what way God rules over the world of what is fixed, without seeing the world of what is fixed,

---

more steadily we reflect on them: the starry heavens above me and the moral law within me" (166).

[9.] *HP* reads, Humankind "knows the law of number" (18).

[10.] Cf. *EK*, who reads, "Number is not itself already the word of God and the truth (as Pythagoras held)" (6). This Greek mathematician (who died about 500 B.C.E.) is mentioned also in *FL* (19). Cf. Überweg's paraphrase of Aristotle's account of the doctrine of the Pythagoreans (*Metaphysics*, A 5, 985b 23ff.): "because numbers seemed to them to be the first principle in all of nature and everything else seemed by its nature to have been modeled on numbers, they also supposed that the elements of numbers were the elements of everything that existed and that the whole of heaven was harmony and number" (1:67).

[11.] Cf. *UK*, "the paradox of final numbers" (10). In opposition to the theory of sets advanced by the mathematician Georg Cantor (1845–1918), which was intended to make aggregates with "uncountably" numerous terms accessible to mathematical treatment, Bertrand Russell (1872–1970) showed that Cantor's set theory led to insoluble contradictions (the Russell Paradox or Antinomy).

the world of numbers, in its proper creatureliness. Thus we fail also to see the world of the fixed, the unchanging, in its original creatureliness — the law has become autonomous — but we do believe in God as its Creator.[12]

The development that the formless undergoes in the form of what is fixed breaks down its power and at the same time increases it. Being that has form limits the primeval power of the unformed. At the same time this being in a distinctive form means that the praise of the Creator grows ever more complete, ever more powerful. The Creator brings about worship out of the distinctive being of what is fixed. This, however, also admits of the idea that once the world is torn away from its origin, from the Creator, then the peculiar being of what is fixed, of law, of numbers, relies on itself and snatches its own power away from the Creator. To us in the middle who hear of this beginning of what is fixed, of law and numbers, is also given the different knowledge that now, in this age, that which is fixed boasts of its own being in opposition to God and snatches its power away from the Creator — by way of our guilt and our loss of the beginning. For this reason we no longer see the Creator in the world of what is fixed, but instead believe in the Creator. We see law, numbers, but in their godlessness, and we believe in God beyond this created world.[13]

There remains the old rationalistic question about the creation of light on the first day and of the sun on the fourth day. [Gottfried] Herder spoke beautifully of how the biblical author was thinking of a dawn in which the light breaks forth before the sun appears.[14] Perhaps he was right. But one must at least add to that the point that after all it is primarily the light that makes the sun what it is and not the sun the light. The physical explanation of the origin of light after all amounts to no more than an indication of the chain of phenomena whose end is 'light'. The factual reality of light, however, is not thereby explained. It is much

---

[12.] Cf. John 20:29.

[13.] *FL* reads, it is the "καύχημα ['glory, pride'] of our knowledge of nature that is judged here. *In spite of* the law we believe in God beyond the law" (20). *HP* reads, "Even knowledge of nature is right only when it does not wish to be God itself" (18).

[14.] *UK* reads, "Herder says: God already on the first day sees the light that makes the sunshine bright dawn" (11). See Johann Gottfried Herder, *Aelteste Urkunde des Menschengeschlechts* (1787), 1:70ff. Dillmann, *Genesis*, referred to this work (15).

truer to say that the light makes the sun what it is, that because there is meant to be light, the sun shines. The fact that we are not able to conceive of light as existing independently of any source in no way invalidates this relation between it and the sun. The light of creation that was unbound, the light that shone formlessly upon the formless darkness,[15] becomes bound to form, to law, to what is fixed, to numbers. It remains in God, however; it remains God's creation and never itself becomes a calculable number.

[15.] *UK* reads, "The light, as God's creation in the beginning, makes the sun (and, that is, the moon and the stars)" (11).

THAT WHICH LIVES[1]

52   *And God said: Let the earth put forth grass and plants that bear seed and*
trees that bear fruit, each bearing fruit on earth according to its kind and
with its own seed. And so it came to be. And the earth put forth grass
and plants that bore seed, each according to its kind, and trees that bore
fruit with their own seed, each according to its kind. And God saw that it
was good. And with evening and morning the third day came to be.

And God said: Let the water swarm with living creatures, and let birds
fly above the earth near the firmament of heaven. And God created the
great sea animals and all the living creatures that gambol about, with
which the waters swarm,[2] each according to its kind, and also every kind
of feathered bird, each according to its kind. And God saw that it was good.
And God blessed them and said: Be fruitful and multiply and fill the water
in the sea, and let the birds multiply on the earth. And with evening and
morning the fifth day came to be. And God said: Let the earth bring forth
living animals, each according to its kind.[3] And so it came to be. And God

---

[1.] At this point the fifth lecture period began, which *HP* (19) and *FL* (21) date Dec. 6, 1932.

[2.] The text on the third day (vv. 11-13) mostly follows *LB*, while that on the fifth and sixth days up to v. 25 mainly follows Kautzsch, 10–11; cf. *LB* (vv. 20-21): ". . . let the waters be agitated with creatures that live and move, and birds fly over the earth under the firmament of heaven. And God created great whales and all kinds of animals that live and move there, with which the waters were agitated. . . ."

[3.] Here in v. 24 the words are left out: "Cattle and reptiles and wild animals each according to its kind" (Kautzsch, 11).

made the wild animals, each according to its kind, and the cattle according
to their kind, and every kind of reptile on the earth according to its kind.
And God saw that it was good.

LIKE A WATERFALL that plunges from the heights down into a valley, creation moves from on high down to its final work. First there is formless,
then form in rhythm, and then a second form in law, in numbers. More   53
and more creation attains its own being, more and more sharply it
stands out in distinction from the form of the Creator, and more and
more jubilantly it proclaims the Creator's nearness.

¶The peculiar being of what has been created so far is dead, however.
It does not praise the Creator by carrying on the Creator's work but only
by its own existence. But now something totally new occurs, with no continuity with what has happened before. The Creator wills that the creation should itself, in obedience, endorse and carry on the Creator's
work — wills that creatures should live and should in turn[4] themselves
create life. That which is living differs from that which is dead in that it
can itself create life. God gives to God's work that which makes God
Lord, namely the ability to create. God calls it to life. And that God does
so, and that what lives belongs to God now as something that itself
creates and lives in an obedience of its own — that is the new way in
which the Creator is glorified by the Creator's work. God does not will to
be Lord of a dead, eternally unchangeable, subservient world; instead
God wills to be Lord of life with its infinite variety of forms.

¶Thus at God's word there breaks forth out of the dead stone, out of
the unfruitful earth, that which is alive and fruitful. It is no process of
evolution from death to life; instead it is God's command which creates
that which lives out of what is dead — it is God's being able to raise up
children to Abraham out of these stones,[5] and calling Christ to rise up
from the dead earth. The earth becomes the mother of the living; from
now on life will break forth out of her dead darkness, and the world of
plants, with their seed and their fruit, comes to be. This means that what
comes to be is life, the peculiar nature of which is to create life again —
plants with seed according to their kind, which means in all the manifold

---

[4.] Instead of the German word *wieder* (translated here as "in turn"), to
which *HP* (19), *FL* (21), and *EK* (6) bear evidence, the 1933 edition incorrectly
reads *weiter*, "further."
[5.] Cf. Luke 3:8b.

variety of things that live.[6] Not only the earth but also the sea, which is without life, and heaven, which is fixed, become animated with living creatures that move about. While the plants cling to the ground, the animals move about; they are in control of the ground, free to move over it, and are not bound to it. Fish and birds according to their kind and cattle and reptiles and wild animals according to their kind with their seed, in their fecundity.

¶It is not the Creator's own nature that the Creator here places within what lives and creates life. That which lives and is creative is not something divine; instead it is and remains a work that is creaturely, that has been created, that is separate from the Creator and under the Creator's free command. In the lively process of its coming to be, however, the Lord wills to look upon the Lord's own doing in what now stands over against the Lord; the Creator wills to see the Creator's own self in the process of creating, and the work is obliged to honor the one who made it.

¶One could suppose that God has now handed over to living creatures the work of upholding, so that the world or nature would provide for itself and so that the fixed nature of law and the fecundity of living things are the powers that together uphold the world. The clock is wound up and now runs on its own.[7] But what the Bible knows is just this, that in the created world nothing runs 'on its own'. Law and life that creates life are, as God's work, created out of nothing and exist only in the midst of nothingness, only in the freedom of God's word. If God withdraws the word from the work, it sinks back into nothingness. Thus

---

[6.] Cf. *UK*, which reads "in all the manifold variety of the individual" (11). *HP* also has "individual" (19, 20).

[7.] Christian Wolff (1679–1754) compared the world to a clock or a machine, so that no chance accident was conceivable for it. See Überweg 3:452. *FL* refers to the "Deists" (22). Deism was the way in which God was conceived in the English and French Enlightenment. It assumed that once the world was created, its author no longer intervened in the course of things. [The Enlightenment rebelled against a dogmatic Christianity that claimed to be based on scriptures that were inerrant and on a revelation that was 'proved' by prophecies and miracles and was not subject to rational evaluation. The Deists thus attempted to substitute for traditional Christianity a 'natural' or rational religion. In content this was a belief in a benevolent God, who had created the world so that it was governed by natural laws that precluded miracles, and in an unchanging moral law.] [JDEG]

neither the subjection of the course of the world to law nor the living nature of what has been created is to be identified with God's upholding activity; on the contrary, law and life are upheld only by the free word of God. Neither law nor life is worthy of adoration — they are creatures like everything else; only the Lord of the law and the Lord of the living is so worthy.

This section too closes with the words that the text repeats again and again: "and God saw that it was good." For us this has two meanings. On the one hand God's work in the unspoiled form in which God's will has shaped it is good. On the other hand it is "good" only in the way that the creaturely can be good, that is, by the Creator's looking upon it, acknowledging it as the Creator's own, and saying about it, "It is good." That God looks upon God's work is the only thing that makes the work good. This really means, however, that the work is good only because the Creator alone is good. The work never has its goodness in itself, but only in the Creator. The goodness of the work consists precisely in its pointing emphatically away from itself to the Creator and to the Creator's word alone as that which is good — that is, in its pointing out that "none is good but God alone."[8] It is in the sense of this word of Jesus that the first creation is "good." If none is good except God alone, then God alone will be given the glory. And the creature's being good — but now being genuinely good — consists in this: that it lets the Creator, as the only Lord, be good and receives its own being good from the Creator's word alone and knows this word alone to be good. One is saying the same thing in other words when one says that the peculiar being of the creature, that is, its creaturely being, is wholly suspended and sustained [aufgehoben][9] in God's being and is fully obedient to God. After all, the being of that which is without form — of that which in greater and greater intensification of its own being[10] is given form as rhythm, as what is fixed, and as what lives — always remains wholly created being, that is, obedient being. It never knows about its own being except by looking at the word of God, at the freedom with which God creates and upholds.

55

[8.] Mark 10:18b. *LB* translates, "No one is good, except the one God." *EK* reads, "Jesus is good in that he points to God as good" (6). *UK* adds: ". . . and does not make the claim for himself that he is good" (12). Cf. *FL* (22).

[9.] See page 28, editorial note 12.

[10.] The 1933 edition incorrectly reads *Tun*, "activity," instead of *Sein*, "being," both at this point and later in the sentence.

THE IMAGE OF GOD ON EARTH

56   *Then God said: Let us make humankind in our image, according to our*
likeness; and let it have dominion over the fish in the sea and over the birds
in[1] the sky and over the cattle and over all wild animals and over all rep-
tiles that creep about upon the earth. And God created human beings in
God's own image – God created them in the image of God, created them as
man and woman.[2]

GOD LOVES GOD'S WORK, loves it in that it has its own existence; for the
creature honors the Creator. God still does not recognize God's self in
the work, however; God beholds that work but not God's own self. To
behold oneself means, so to speak, to recognize one's own face in a mirror, to see oneself in an image of oneself. But how could that possibly
take place? God, after all, remains without qualification the Creator
before whose feet the work lies; how then will God be able to find God in
this work? The work does not resemble the Creator, it is not the Creator's image; instead it is the form that the Creator's command takes.
What is decisive is that at the very moment when the Creator has
brought it forth, the work is already torn away from, and alien to, the
Creator; it is no longer the Creator. Even in its living nature the work is
dead, because it is created,[3] conditioned – because, though it arises out

---

[1.] *LB* and Kautzsch, 11, both read "am Himmel," but Bonhoeffer prefers
"im Himmel."

[2.] The German text follows Kautzsch, 11, in preference to *LB*.

[3.] The 1933 edition erroneously reads *geschehenes*, "has happened," instead
of *geschaffenes*, "is created," here and correspondingly *Geschehenes*, "what has hap-

of freedom, it itself is not free but conditioned. Only that which is itself free would not be dead, would not, as a creature, be alien or torn away. Only in that which is itself free could the free Creator behold the Creator.[4] But how can what is created be free? What is created is determined, bound by law,[5] conditioned, not free. If the Creator wishes to create the Creator's own image, then the Creator must create it free. And only such an image, in its freedom, would fully praise[6] God, would fully proclaim God's glory as Creator.

¶At this point the narrative is about us; it is about the creation of humankind. The Bible expresses the essential difference between this work and all God's previous creative activity by the way in which it introduces this work. The Hebrew plural here indicates the significance and sublimity of the Creator's action.[7] It is also to be noted, however, that God does not simply call humankind forth out of nonbeing, as God called forth everything else; instead we are taken up into God's own planning,[8] as it were, and thereby become aware that something new, something that has not yet been, something altogether original, is about to happen.

And God said: Let us make humankind in our image, after our likeness.

Humankind is to go forth from God as the last work, as the new work,

57

---

pened," instead of *Geschaffenes*, "what has been created, a creature," in the next sentence. *HP* reads, "because it is something created, conditioned" (21).

[4.] *EK* adds: ". . . for only what is itself free comes from the origin" (6).

[5.] The German has a play on words: "*Das Geschaffene ist das Gesetzte im Gesetz gebundene*," with *Gesetzte* meaning "set, determined" and *Gesetz* "law." [DSB]

[6.] *EK* reads, "fully, because it could freely, praise" (6).

[7.] *HP* reads, "'Let us make humankind' is an expression of majesty (incorrect!)" (21). Against the view of writers such as Hermann Gunkel (e.g., *Urgeschichte*, 106), Kautzsch argues: "According to the usual interpretation, this plural signifies that God turns to the heavenly beings who surround him. But P [the Priestly document, the source from which this account of creation comes] nowhere shows knowledge of such beings. It is therefore the plural of deliberation with oneself that is used here, in order to emphasize the august importance of this final work of creation" (11, note b). *UK* reads, "Plural *au[c]toris*, plural *Trinitatis* (according to Luther)" (12). *EK* (6) and also *FL* (24) indicate "Luther: Trinity." Cf. Luther in Stiasny's edition, "Trinity" (19–20).

[8.] *UK* reads, "God first *plans* the creation of humankind" (13). *FL* records the same emphasis (24). In the *Confessions*, Augustine connects the plural, "Let us . . . ," in Gen. 1:26 with the Latin term *reformamini* in Rom. 12:2, which corresponds to the Greek term μεταμορφοῦσθε, "be ye transformed" (13.22).

as the image of God in God's work. There is no transition from somewhere else here; here there is new creation. This has nothing whatsoever
to do with Darwin.[9] Quite apart from that issue humankind remains in
an unqualified way God's new, free work. We in no way wish to deny
humankind's connection with the animal world — on the contrary. Our
concern, our whole concern, nevertheless, is that we not lose sight of the
peculiar relation between humankind and God above and beyond this.
The attempt — with the origin and nature of humankind in mind — to
take a gigantic leap back into the world of the lost beginning, to seek to
know for ourselves what humankind was like in its original state[10] and
to identify our own ideal of humanity with what God actually created is
hopeless. It fails to recognize that it is only from Christ that we can know
about the original nature of humankind. The attempt to do that without
recognizing this, as hopeless as it is understandable, has again and again
delivered up the church to arbitrary speculation at this dangerous
point.[11] Only in the middle, as those who live from Christ, do we know
about the beginning.[12]

To say that in humankind God creates the image of God on earth
means that humankind is like the Creator in that it is free. To be sure, it
is free only through God's creation, through the word of God; it is free
for the worship of the Creator. For in the language of the Bible freedom
is not something that people have for themselves but something they
have for others. No one is free 'in herself' or 'in himself' ['an sich']\[13\] —
free as it were in a vacuum or free in the same way that a person may be
musical, intelligent, or blind in herself or in himself. Freedom is not a

---

[9.] Charles Darwin, *The Descent of Man, and Selection in Relation to Sex.* Cf.
UK, "Granting that Darwin was right, that humankind was descended from
animals" (13). See also below, pages 76, 161.

[10.] Cf. *CS (DBW* 1):221–23.

[11.] Cf. Bernhard Bartmann, *Dogmatik*, "Section 75. Grace Before the Fall,"
293–98. For example, "Yet also the later, especially the Greek, fathers thought
. . . of humanity's being in the image of God particularly in terms of reason and
freedom but reason and freedom in the *ideal* sense" (295).

[12.] *FL* reads, "Only when [we] *exist in and through Christ* can we understand
it [*EK*: the "word about being in the image of God" (6)]" (24).

[13.] ["In herself" or "in himself" in the sense of being independent of any
particular context.] [DSB] Cf. Friedrich Gogarten, *Politische Ethik*, ". . . it is not a
freedom in and of itself, not the freedom of being-in-and-of-itself; instead this
freedom occurs always between two people. It is the freedom of being-for-the-
other, of being-from-the-other, at any time" (184). Also see below, 64, passim.

quality a human being has; it is not an ability, a capacity, an attribute of being that may be deeply hidden in a person but can somehow be uncovered.[14] Anyone who scrutinizes human beings in order to find freedom finds nothing of it. Why? Because freedom is not a quality that can be uncovered; it is not a possession, something to hand, an object; nor is it a form of something to hand; instead it is a relation and nothing else. To be more precise, freedom is a relation between two persons. Being free means 'being-free-for-the-other', because I am bound to the other. Only by being in relation with the other am I free.

¶No one can think of freedom as a substance or as something individualistic. Freedom is just not something I have at my command like an attribute of my own; it is simply something that comes to happen, that takes place, that happens to me through the other.[15] We can ask how we know this and whether it is not once again just speculation about the beginning that is part of the fall-out of being in the middle. The answer is that it is the message of the gospel itself that God's freedom has bound itself to us, that God's free grace becomes real with us alone, that God wills not to be free for God's self but for humankind. Because God in Christ is free for humankind, because God does not keep God's freedom to God's self, we can think of freedom only as a 'being free for. . . .' For us in the middle who exist through Christ and who know what it means to be human through Christ's resurrection, the fact that God is free means nothing else than that we are free for God. The freedom of the Creator demonstrates itself by allowing us to be free, free for the Creator. That, however, means nothing else than that the Creator's image is created on earth. The paradox of created freedom remains undiminished. Indeed it needs to be expressed as sharply as possible. Created *freedom* then means — and it is this that goes beyond all God's previous acts and is unique κατ' ἐξοχήν[16] — that God's self enters into God's creation.

¶Now not only does God command and God's word comes to pass; now God enters into creation and so creates freedom. Humankind dif-

59

[14.] The 1933 edition incorrectly reads "flaring up," *aufzuckende. FL* reads, "No ability that can be uncovered [*aufzudeckende*] (through psychoanalysis)" (25).

[15.] In the recapitulation at the start of the sixth lecture, *UK* reads, "Freedom is a form of existence in which the human being lives in his or her entirety" (24); cf. *HP* (24). (Only) *FL* reads, "(Question of theological anthropology)" (28).

[16.] *Par excellence*, preeminently.

fers from the other creatures in that God is in humankind as the very
image of God in which the free Creator looks upon the Creator's own
self. This is what the older dogmatic theologians meant when they spoke
of the indwelling of the Trinity in Adam.[17] In the free creature the Holy
Spirit worships the Creator; uncreated freedom glorifies itself in view of
created freedom. The creature loves the Creator, because the Creator
loves the creature. Created *freedom* is freedom in the Holy Spirit, but as
created freedom it is *humankind's* own freedom. How does this created
existence of a free humankind express itself? In what way does the freedom of the Creator differ from the freedom of that which is created?
How is the creature free? The creature is free in that one creature exists
in relation to another creature, in that one human being is free for
another human being. And God created them man and woman. The
human being is not alone. Human beings exist in duality, and it is in this
dependence on the other that their creatureliness consists.[18] The creatureliness of human beings is no more a quality or something at hand or an
existing entity than human freedom is. It can be defined in simply no
other way than in terms of the existence of human beings over-against-
one-another, with-one-another, and in-dependence-upon-one-another.

¶The "image that is like God"[19] is therefore no analogia entis[20] in
which human beings, in their existence in-and-of-themselves, in their

---

[17.] According to Heinrich Schmid, theologians in the Lutheran orthodox
tradition spoke of the *trinitatis inhabitatio*, or "indwelling of the Trinity" (see
Dogmatik, 163, note 18). Johann Gerhard (1582–1637), Johannes Andreas Quenstedt (1617–1688), and Abraham Calov (1612–1686) in this *inhabitatio* saw a
donum supernaturale, or "supernatural gifts," while David Hollaz (1648–1713)
wished to classify it as among the *dona naturalia*, or "natural gifts." Bartmann
quotes John of Damascus (c. 675–750 C.E.) to the effect that Adam "had the
indwelling God as a dwelling, possessed him as a glorious garment, was clothed
with his grace, rejoiced in the sweet fruit of contemplating him, like any angel,
and fed from this, which is rightly called the 'tree of life'" (*Dogmatik*, 296).

[18.] *UK* (24), *FL* (27), and *EK* (7) confirm that this word is *besteht*, "consist,"
whereas the 1933 edition reads *beruht*, "rests."

[19.] See above, note 2. Bonhoeffer here quotes Gen. 1:26 according to *LB*,
except that he substitutes "God" for "us." [DSB]

[20.] "Analogy of being." *EK* says "therefore no *analogia entis* (the Catholic
view)" (7); cf. *UK* (15). In *Act and Being* Bonhoeffer had taken issue with the
"ontology of the *analogia entis*" of the Catholic Erich Przywara; see *AB* (*DBWE*
2):27, 73–76, 138. To this end he had in particular worked through Przywara's
Religionsphilosophie katholischer Theologie.

being, could be said to be like God's being. There can be no such analogy between God and humankind. This is so in the first place because God — who alone has self-sufficient being in aseity, yet at the same time is there for God's creature, binding God's freedom to humankind and so giving God's self to humankind — must be thought of as one who is not alone, inasmuch as God is the one who in Christ attests to God's 'being for humankind'.[21] The likeness, the analogia, of humankind to God is not analogia entis but *analogia relationis*.[22] What this means, however, is, firstly, that the relatio[23] too is not a human potential or possibility or a structure of human existence;[24] instead it is a given relation, a relation in which human beings are set, a justitia passiva![25] And it is in this relation in which they are set that freedom is given. From this it follows, secondly, that this analogia must not be understood as though humankind somehow had this likeness in its possession or at its disposal. Instead the analogia or likeness must be understood very strictly in the sense that what is like derives its likeness *only* from the prototype, so that it always points us only to the prototype[26] itself and is 'like' it only in pointing to it in this way. Analogia relationis is therefore the relation which God has established, and it is analogia only in this relation which

61

[21.] Cf. *AB* (*DBWE* 2):90–91. "Aseity" means having one's origin in oneself, underived being.

[22.] "Analogy of relationship." Karl Barth in his doctrine of creation, which he began to set forth in the summer semester of 1942, took over from Bonhoeffer the idea of the *analogia relationis* as the key to understanding the image of God in humankind (see *Church Dogmatics* 3/1:228–30) and made it into a basic foundation stone of his anthropology (see *Church Dogmatics* 3/2:220–21 and 323–24). The fifth lecture ended at this point. The sixth is dated by *HP* Dec. 13, 1932 (24).

[23.] "relationship."

[24.] *EK* at this point (7) has the Heideggerian expression " '*Existential' des Daseins*," misspelling Heidegger's German term *Existenzial* (cf. Martin Heidegger, *Being and Time*, 33, 70). Cf. *FL* 29.

[25.] "Passive righteousness." *UK* has "the *analogia relationis* is a passive, a given, relationship" (15), whereas *FL* reads, "*relatio passiva* [space] *justitia passiva* [space] place in relation" (29). Cf. *AB*: "the relation of Dasein to Christ [is] a granted relation (*iustitia passiva!*)" ([*DBWE* 2]:134). The expression is of fundamental significance in Luther's understanding of justification. See especially his *Lectures on Galatians* (1535), *LW* 26:4–358 and 27:4–149 (*WA* 40/1:34–688 and 40/2:1–184). *EK* reads, "sanctitas *passiva*" ("received holiness") (7).

[26.] The 1933 edition incorrectly reads *Vorbild*, "model," instead of *Urbild*, "prototype." *EK* reads "always like this prototype only in that it points to it" (7). All the students' notes have only "*Urbild*."

God has established. The relation of creature with creature is a relation established by God, because it consists of freedom and freedom comes from God.

Humankind in the duality of man and woman, that is, in its likeness to God, is created within the world of the fixed and of the living. And whereas the freedom of human beings over against one another consisted in being free *for* one another, humankind's freedom over against the rest of the created world is to be free *from* it. That means that humankind is its lord; humankind has command over it, rules it. And that constitutes the other side of humankind's created likeness to God. Humankind is to rule — though it is to rule over God's creation and to rule as having been commissioned and empowered to rule by God.

¶Being free from created things is not the same as, say, the ideal of the spirit's being free from nature.[27] On the contrary this freedom to rule includes being bound to the creatures who are ruled. The ground and the animals over which I am lord constitute the world in which I live, without which I cease to be. It is my world, my earth, over which I rule. I am not free from it in any sense of my essential being, my spirit, having no need of nature, as though nature were something alien to the spirit. On the contrary, in my whole being, in my creatureliness, I belong wholly to this world; it bears me, nurtures me, holds me. But my freedom from it consists in the fact that this world, to which I am bound like a master to his servant, like the peasant to his bit of ground [Boden], has been made subject to me, that over the earth which is and remains my earth I am to *rule*, and the more I master it, the more it is *my* earth. What so peculiarly binds human beings to, and sets them over against, the other creatures is the authority conferred on humankind by nothing else than God's word.

¶This is said to us who, being in the middle, no longer know anything about all this and to whom it is all a pious myth or a lost world. We too think that we rule, but the same applies here as on Walpurgis Night: we think we are the one making the move, whereas instead we are being

---

[27.] An echo of the idea of the "dominion of the spirit over nature" which Albrecht Ritschl (1822–1889) developed in his theology. In his *Instruction in the Christian Religion*, section 47, Ritschl speaks of "sonship with God in spiritual freedom and dominion over the world" (240); he also speaks of the "ideal beginnings of the Christian life" (279, note 128). Cf. Bonhoeffer's lecture "Das Recht auf Selbstbehauptung" (The right of self-assertion) on February 4, 1932, in *DBWE* 11:215–26, esp. 221 (*GS* 3:258–69, esp. 264).

moved.[28] We do not rule; instead we are ruled. The thing, the world, rules humankind; humankind is a prisoner, a slave, of the world,[29] and its dominion is an illusion. Technology is the power with which the earth seizes hold of humankind and masters it. And because we no longer rule, we lose the ground [Boden][30] so that the earth no longer remains *our* earth, and we become estranged from the earth. The reason why we fail to rule, however, is because we do not know the world as God's creation and do not accept the dominion we have as God-given but seize hold of it for ourselves. There is no 'being-free-from' without a 'being-free-for'. There is no dominion without serving God; in losing the one humankind necessarily loses the other.[31] Without God, without their brothers and sisters,[32] human beings lose the earth. Already in sentimentally shying away from exercising dominion over the earth, however, human beings have forever lost God and their brothers and sisters. God, the brother and sister, and the earth belong together. For those who have once lost the earth, however, for us human beings in the middle, there is no way back to the earth except via God and our brothers and sisters. From the inception humankind's way to the earth has been possible only as God's way to humankind. Only where God and the brother, the sister, come to them can human beings find their way back to the earth. Human freedom for God and the other person and human freedom from the creature in dominion over it constitute the first human beings' likeness to God.

63

[28.] As Mephistopheles says in Johann Wolfgang von Goethe's *Faust: The Tragedy*, "And you are shoved, though you may think you shove" (Part 1, "Walpurgis Night," v. 4117). [According to central European mythology, Walpurgis Night, April 30, was the night on which witches would assemble to affirm their allegiance to the devil. Fires were therefore lit by the frightened populace to drive them away. Blocksberg, the highest peak in the Harz Mountains, was the legendary place of ancient sacrifice and of such gatherings. This is the location for the witches' sabbath described by Goethe.] [JDEG]

[29.] (Only) *FL* reads "humankind has become the prisoner of what is fixed" (30).

[30.] *Blut und Boden* ("blood and soil") was a slogan of the National Socialist movement. [JDEG].

[31.] In *UK* there follows here, "The first office to which humankind is appointed [*FL* adds "over the world" (3)]: humankind's aseity from the world corresponds to God's aseity from creation" (15); cf. *HP* (26), and an abbreviated indication in *EK* (7).

[32.] The German text has *Bruder*, "brother," alone in each case in this paragraph. [DSB]

BLESSING AND COMPLETION

64 *Vv. 28-31. And God blessed them and said to them: Be fruitful and multiply, and fill the earth and subdue it; and have dominion over the fish in the sea and over the birds under heaven and over every animal that creeps upon the earth. And God said: Behold, I give to you[1] for your food every kind of plant on all the earth that bears its own seed and every kind of fruit-bearing tree that bears its own seed; and to all animals on earth and all birds under heaven and all reptiles that live upon the earth I give every kind of green plant to eat. And so it came to be. And God looked upon everything that he had made, and behold, it was very good. And with evening and morning the sixth day came to be.*

THE BLESSING OF GOD upon humankind is God's promise, God's sure pledge. Blessing involves the choosing of those who are blessed. The blessing is laid upon humankind and remains on it, until it is changed to a curse. Blessing and curse are burdens that God lays upon humankind. They are inherited from one generation to another, often not understood, often uncomprehended. They are altogether real — not magical, to the extent that this implies casting a spell, but real. This blessing — be fruitful, multiply, have dominion, subdue the earth — affirms humankind wholly within the world of the living in which it is placed. It is humankind's whole empirical existence that is blessed here, its creatureliness, its worldliness, its earthliness. What, however, if this very blessing

---

[1.] *LB* says "I have given you"; cf. Kautzsch, "Along with this I allocate all plants to you" (11). Otherwise the text largely follows Luther's translation.

one day changes into a curse?[2] But for the time being this blessing means nothing else than that God saw that God's work was very good.[3] And with morning and evening, there came to be the sixth, the last, day.

> Chap. 2, vv. 1-3. *And on the seventh day God finished the work that God had done and rested on the seventh day from all the work that God had done. And God blessed the seventh day and hallowed it, because on it God rested from the works that God had created and made.*[4]

65

Rest in the Bible really means more than having a rest;[5] it means rest after completing one's work; it means completion. It means the peace of God in which the world lies [liegt];[6] it means transfiguration. It means turning our eyes wholly toward God's being, toward worshiping God. It is after all never the rest of a lethargic god but the rest of the Creator; it is no letting go of the world but the final glorification of the world that gazes at the Creator. Even in God's rest, God of necessity remains the Creator. "My Father is still working, and I also am working."[7] God remains the Creator, but now as the one who has finished the work of creation. We understand God's rest only[8] in the sense that it is at the same time rest for God's creation. God's rest is our rest (as God's freedom is our freedom, God's goodness our goodness). Therefore God hallows the day of God's rest also for Adam and for us, whose heart is

---

[2.] *HP* reads, "The curse of God can take away what God's blessing had given" (26).

[3.] *EK* reads, "The blessing of God lies only upon the dominion that *this* human being exercises" (8).

[4.] Verse 1 (in *LB*, "Thus heaven and earth with their whole host were finished") is lacking. Verse 2 is taken from Kautzsch word for word; *LB* in this verse has the plural "works." Verse 3 corresponds to Luther's translation except for the word "all," which is lacking (*LB*: "from all his works").

[5.] *FL* comments on "God's rest," saying "Our thinking grasps [what is meant is: understands 'rest' as] something for which God needs to apologize" (31).

[6.] Possibly a misreading for *ruht*, "rests."

[7.] John 5:17b.

[8.] The 1933 edition reads *nun*, "now," instead of *nur*, "only." *EK* reads, "only in the sense that it is at the same time the creature's rest. What happens in God's aseity beforehand remains hidden from us. But God's righteousness is our righteousness, and therefore God's rest is our rest" (8). The statements about "aseity" and "righteousness" are also in *FL* (32). *HP* adds "God's holiness is our holiness" (27).

restless until it finds rest in God's rest.[9] To us this rest is wholly a promise, one given to the people of God.[10] To seek too hastily to grasp hold of God's rest for oneself in pious quietism is as much unbelieving presumption as to grumble impudently about the boredom of rest in paradise and thereby defend[11] and glorify unrest and struggle. Such noisy pleasure in one's own vitality may very quickly have to fall silent in the presence of the 'living' God.

66

It is the same day as the day of the Lord's resurrection in the New Testament. It is the day of rest, the day of victory, of dominion, of completion, of transfiguration, the day of worship for us, the day of hope, of looking forward to the day of final rest with God, to the 'rest that belongs to the people [of God]'.[12] All the days of the week have really been created just for the sake of this day. You shall keep the holiday holy[13] and not sleep it away. God's work has been created, we have been created, for the final peace, for the day of the resurrection of Jesus Christ, for the day of the final resurrection and the rest of the Creator with the creatures the Creator has made, "that they may rest from their labor, and their works follow them!"[14]

v. 4a. *This is the history of the genesis of heaven and earth, when they were created.*[15]

[9.] See Augustine, *Confessions* (1,1:31): ". . . inquietum est cor nostrum, donec requiescat in te" ("restless is our heart, until it comes to rest in you").

[10.] Hebrews 4:9: "So then, a sabbath rest still remains for the people of God. . . ." Luther in the Stiasny ed.: "as the Epistle to the Hebrews in an acute and masterly way argues from the 95th Psalm (v. 11) about God's rest" (27–28).

[11.] The 1933 edition, clearly by mistake, reads *vereinigen*, "unite."

[12.] The last two words, "of God," are added in the translation. Cf. Heb. 4:9 and editorial note 10 above. [DSB]

[13.] Exodus 20:8.

[14.] Revelation 14:13b, following Bonhoeffer's translation; *LB* reads, "for their works [NRSV: deeds] follow them."

[15.] Following Kautzsch, 11. Cf. *LB*, "Thus heaven and earth came to be, for they were created."

THE OTHER SIDE[1]

IT WAS LONG AGO REALIZED that what we have here is a second creation   67
story that is quite different from, and substantially older than, the first.[2]
What are we to make of that?[3] What does it mean for our exposition?
When one first looks at both creation stories together, it is plain that the
first and the second accounts are only representations [Darstellungen]
of the same thing from two different sides; indeed it must even be said
that the first without the second, like the second without the first, would
not express what there was to say here. (To be sure, this judgment in turn
arises only from listening to and understanding scripture as a whole.)
The first account is thought out wholly from above, from where God is.

[1.] In the notes of the students who attended the lectures this stands under
the heading, "Second Main Part."

[2.] *UK* reads, "From the Yahwist's source" (16). During the lectures Bonhoeffer used the technical terms of textual criticism. Kautzsch refers to the
source of the "'Yahwist' (called J, because from the beginning it uses the divine
name, Yahweh [*Jahwe* in German] [DSB])" (3). The first, but later, creation story
comes from the source P, the "Priestly document." Kautzsch maintains that J was
written between 900 and 750 B.C.E. and P between 600 and 450 B.C.E. (4, 7). The
French medical doctor Jean Astruc first differentiated two interwoven narratives
in Genesis in 1753 (see Kautzsch, 2). [Later in the eighteenth century J. G. Eich-
horn discovered additional evidence for these narratives as source documents.
The work of these and other scholars culminated in the second half of the nine-
teenth century in the well-known hypothesis of K. H. Graf and Julius Wellhausen
that the Pentateuch was compiled from four source documents of diverse age
and origin.] [JDEG]

[3.] *HP* reads, "The opposition of the sources P and J can be used to demonstrate their relativity" (27). *EK* records the same almost word for word (8).

Humankind is here the final work of God's self-glorification. The world is created for God, for God's honor alone, and humankind is the most precious receptacle, the very mirror of the Creator. It is totally for the sake of God's glory and honor as Creator that everything comes to pass. In spite of the creation of humankind, the world remains the world in the deep,[4] the strange, distant world. The second account by contrast is about the world in its nearness and about the Lord who is near on *earth*, living together with Adam in *Paradise*. The first account is about humankind-for-God, the second about God-for-humankind. The first is about the Creator and Lord, the second about the fatherly God who is near at hand.[5] The first is about humankind as the final work of God, with the whole world created before humankind, the second just the other way around: in the beginning humanity is created, and around humankind, for the sake of humankind, God fashions animals and birds and lets the trees grow. The second account tells the story of human-kind — the first is about what God does; but the second is about the history of humanity with God — the first is about the work of God with humanity; the second is about the God who is near at hand — the first is about the strange God; the second about God in human form, the God of childlike anthropomorphism — whereas the first is about the deity of God. Yet both are only human words, childlike but humble words, about the same God and the same humankind. Hence Genesis 2 [is][6] the other side of Genesis 1 — not an arbitrary but a necessary side, at any rate once the whole has been understood.

68

When Yahweh God made heaven and earth – there was no kind of shrub in the field yet, however, and no kind of herb of the field had yet sprouted; for Yahweh God had not yet caused it to rain on the earth, and there were no human beings yet to till the ground; but a spring of water went up from the earth and watered the whole land (v. 4bff.).[7]

[4.] Cf. Gen. 1:2. [DSB]

[5.] *HP* says, "The second account portrays the gentle fatherly God who is near at hand" (27). The expression *milde*, "gentle," also occurs in *UK* (17).

[6.] In Bonhoeffer's text there is a colon in place of the verb 'is,' which here has been supplied by the translator. [DSB]

[7.] As Kautzsch points out, in v. 4b the Hebrew text reads "earth and heaven, not as in 1:1 and 2:1, the heaven and the earth" (12, note b). Kautzsch renders v. 5 "caused it to rain upon the earth." Otherwise the text largely follows Kautzsch, 12. Instead of "Yahweh God," *LB* always reads *Gott der HErr* [printed in this way],

This corresponds roughly to the state of being "formless and empty" in the first account.[8]

"God the LORD." Cf. *LB*, which reads "and every kind of tree in the field was not yet on earth, and every kind of herb in the field had not yet grown, for God the LORD had not yet caused it to rain on earth, and there were no human beings who tilled the land. But a mist went up from the earth and made all the land damp." (Only) *FL* noted the reference to literature at this point: "Hans Schmidt history-of-religions problem popular lectures" (33). Schmidt's study, *Die Erzählung von Paradies und Sündenfall* (The story of paradise and the fall), appeared in the series "Sammlung gemeinverständlicher Vorträge und Schriften aus dem Gebiet der Theologie und Religionsgeschichte" (Collected popular addresses and essays in the area of theology and the history of religions). By the translation "the rainclouded heaven" Schmidt sought to show that "What is here in mind is the idea of a 'marriage' between heaven and mother earth" (37). Bonhoeffer rejects this thesis, which Schmidt extended to Gen. 1:2 (38); see above, page 38 and editorial note 41.

[8.] Schmidt draws attention to the fact that according to the second account humankind "is created on the wasteland of a still wholly barren earth" (7).

THE HUMAN BEING
OF EARTH AND SPIRIT

---

69   *Then Yahweh God fashioned humankind out of dust from the ground, and*
      blew into its nose the breath of life; so the human being became a living
      being.[1]

HERE WE ARE DIRECTED to the earth in a distinct and exclusive way that is
quite different from before. What is of primary interest here is not at all
the cosmos but our earth and humankind. Here God also receives a very
specific proper name, Yahweh (on the meaning of which there is no
agreement). This is God's real name; that is, it is the name of *this* God,
the God who is being spoken of here. *Elohim* in Genesis 1 is not a proper
name but a generic term and so means roughly 'deity'.[2] One could
suppose that such a proper name is evidence of a very primitive idea of
God and shows that we have no right at all to be speaking here of the
same God whose power chap. 1 has set forth. And yet just at this point

---

[1.] Cf. *LB*, which says "And God the LORD made humankind out of a clod of
earth, and breathed the living breath into its nose. And thus the human being
became a living soul." The text follows Kautzsch, 12. *EK* calls the section "The
Human Being of Dust and Spirit" (8).

[2.] Kautzsch commented that "God (Heb. *'elohim*) everywhere from here
[2:4b] to 3:24 was apparently inserted by an editor who wished thereby to stress
that the Yahweh in 2:4ff. was no other than the *'elohim* who created the world in
ch. 1" (12, note a). Hans Schmidt disagreed with this (5, note 2). Schmidt's interest was in the *separation* of the sources within the section of Genesis from 2:4 to
3:24. His thesis was that the god in the story of the tree of knowledge (and then
in that of the tree of life) is a different god than the one in Genesis 1 — namely
the Canaanite god of fertility. See Hans Schmidt, 29.

one must reply that anthropomorphism in thinking of God, or blatant mythology, is no more irrelevant or unsuitable as an expression for God's being than is the abstract use of the generic term 'deity'. On the contrary, clear anthropomorphism much more plainly expresses the fact that we cannot think of 'God as such' whether in one way or another. The abstract concept of God, precisely because it seeks not to be anthropomorphic, is in actual fact much more so than is childlike anthropomorphism.[3] And we need a proper name for God so that we can think   70 of God in the right way. Indeed the proper name is God as such [an sich]. We have God in no other way than in God's name. This is true today as well. Jesus Christ — that is the name of God, at once utterly anthropomorphic and utterly to the point.[4]

God fashioned humankind out of dust from the ground and blew into its nostrils the breath of life. Here again everything takes place in a very down-to-earth way. The way of speaking is extremely childlike and, for the person who wishes truly to comprehend or to 'know'[5] something, very offensive. How can one talk of God in the same way as one talks about a person who fashions a vessel out of earth and clay?[6] The anthropomorphisms become more and more insupportable: God models or molds with clay, and the human being is fashioned like a vessel out of an earthen clod. Surely no one can gain any knowledge about the origin of humankind from this! To be sure, as an account of what happened this story is at first sight of just as little consequence, and just as full of meaning, as many another myth of creation. And yet in being distinguished as

---

[3.] *EK* reads, "the abstract generic concept can by contrast wrongly be supposed to speak in a *fully* appropriate and legitimate way of God" (8). Cf. Hegel's *Lectures on the Philosophy of Religion*, "the human form of *God becoming a human being* must appear as an essential element of religion in the definition of its object. . . . So-called anthropomorphism [therefore seems to be legitimate]; only the empty specter of absolute abstract essence is what one needs to abjure" (Lasson ed., 12:161, with the words Lasson has added to fill out the text in square brackets). [trans. DSB] In Bonhoeffer's copy of the Lasson edition this has been marked heavily in pencil and with several exclamation marks in the margin.

[4.] The sixth lecture period ended at this point. *HP* dates the seventh period Dec. 20, 1932 (28); *FL* mistakenly dates it Dec. 21 (35).

[5.] Hegel emphasized against Kant that we can *"know"* of God, e.g., the *Lectures on the Philosophy of Religion* (Lasson, 4). See *Internationales Bonhoeffer Forum*, 8:28. Cf. above, page 30.

[6.] Cf. Hans Schmidt, who says that in creating humankind "God works like a potter" (7).

the word of God it is quite simply *the source* of knowledge about the origin of humankind. And now it will also become evident that this account belongs closely with the previous account and forms a unity with it.

To say that Yahweh fashions humankind with Yahweh's own hands expresses two complementary things. On the one hand, it expresses the physical nearness of the Creator to the creature — expresses that it is really the Creator who makes me, the human being, with the Creator's own hands; it expresses the trouble the Creator takes, the Creator's thinking about me, the Creator's intention with me and nearness to me. On the other hand, it expresses also the omnipotence, the utter supremacy, with which the Creator fashions and creates me and in terms of which I am the Creator's creature; it expresses the fatherliness with which the Creator creates me and in the context of which I worship the Creator. That is the true God to whom the whole Bible bears witness.

The human being whom God has created in God's image — that is, in freedom — is the human being who is taken from earth. Even Darwin and Feuerbach could not use stronger language than is used here.[7] Humankind is derived from a piece of earth. Its bond with the earth belongs to its essential being. The 'earth is its mother';[8] it comes out of her womb. To be sure, the ground from which humankind is taken is not the cursed but the blessed ground. It is God's earth out of which humankind is taken. From it human beings have their *bodies*. The body belongs to a person's essence.[9] The body is not the prison, the shell, the

---

[7.] *EK* reads, "To say that humankind is made of earth is to lay stronger emphasis on matter than Darwin/Feuerbach did" (9). Charles Darwin (1809–1882) derived the origin of the species — including the human species — from the process of natural selection in the struggle for existence (*The Origin of Species by Means of Natural Selection*, first published in 1859). For Ludwig Feuerbach (1804–1872) the human being as a sentient being was the starting point for all thought. Cf. Bonhoeffer's characterization in 1931–32 of the way in which Friedrich Nietzsche takes up Feuerbach's doctrine: "The human being is no transcendent imaginary being but the *ens realissimum*," that is, the most real being (*DBW* 11:148 [*GS* 5:187]). [trans. DSB]

[8.] Cf. Sirach 40:1b, which speaks of the earth, "which is the mother of us all" [trans. DSB]; in Bonhoeffer's copy of *LB* the verse is marked with a heavy line in indelible pencil on the inside margin. In the lecture "Thy Kingdom Come" (Nov. 19, 1932), Bonhoeffer quotes the saying exactly (*Preface to Bonhoeffer*, 33 [*GS* 3:274]). Hans Schmidt refers to this biblical passage as well, see 34, note 1, and 38, note 1.

[9.] Cf. Emil Brunner, *God and Man*, 154: "Man is created as a bodily being,

exterior, of a human being; instead a human being is a human body. A human being does not 'have' a body or 'have' a soul; instead a human being 'is' body and soul.[10] The human being in the beginning really is the body, is one — just as Christ is wholly his body and the church is the body of Christ. People who reject their bodies reject their existence before God the Creator. What is to be taken seriously about human existence is its bond with mother earth, its being as body.[11] Human beings have their existence as existence on earth. They do not come from above; they have not by some cruel fate been driven into the earthly world and been enslaved in it.[12] Instead, the word of God the almighty one summoned humankind out of the earth in which it was sleeping, in which it was dead and indeed a mere piece of earth, but a piece of earth called by God to have human existence. "Wake up, you who are sleeping, rise up from the dead, and Christ will give you light"[13] (Eph. 5:14).[14]

72

---

and his bodily nature is a part of his being." Bonhoeffer's copy of Brunner's book bears numerous markings on pages 70–100 (136–78 in the English translation). Bonhoeffer commended this study as reading matter for his seminar "Dogmatic Exercises [Theological Psychology]," which he ran in 1932–33 at the same time as his lecture course on "Creation and Sin" (see *GS* 5:342).

[10.] See Wilhelm Vischer, "Der Gott Abrahams," who claims that to the Hebrews "the human being does not *have* a soul, but on the contrary *is* a soul" (285). Cf. the reference in Ernst Georg Wendel, *Homiletik*, 91.

[11.] *EK* reads, "For the Bible what is to be taken seriously about human beings is their being as body, whereas for the Greeks it is their being as spirit, idea" (9). Friedrich Nietzsche pleads for the I to be honest with regard to the body in *Zarathustra*, in the section "On the Afterworldly," e.g., in the lines: "it was the body that despaired of the earth. . . . It wanted to crash through these ultimate walls — with its head, and not only with its head — over there to 'that world'" (*The Portable Nietzsche*, 143–44).

[12.] Bonhoeffer is here rejecting gnostic ideas; cf., e.g., Reinhold Seeberg, *History of Doctrine* 1:94. On the subject see Hans Jonas, *The Gnostic Religion*: "a pre-cosmic fall of part of the divine principle underlies the genesis of the world and of human existence in the majority of gnostic systems" (62). Cf. also Jonas's paragraphs on the term "cast" or "thrown" (63–65).

[13.] Cf. the NRSV translation: "Sleeper, awake! Rise from the dead, and Christ will shine on you."

[14.] The 1933 edition incorrectly lists this passage as Eph. 5:4. *UK* (19) and *EK* (9) wrote down the correct reference, Eph. 5:14, in their notes. In *LB*, "and rise up," the "and" corresponds to the Greek text. Bonhoeffer used this text in Ephesians as a basis for his baptismal address in October 1932 (*DBW* 11:463–66 [*GS* 4:150–52]). In his copy of *LB* this passage is marked in indelible pencil as a preaching text. Cf. also *AB* (*DBWE* 2):148–49, note 15.

¶This is also what Michelangelo thought.[15] The Adam who rests on the newly created earth is so closely and intimately bound up with the ground on which Adam lies that Adam is, even in this still-dreaming state, a most singular and wonderful piece of earth — but even so still a piece of earth. Indeed it is precisely in this state of nestling [Hingeschmiegtsein][16] so closely to the blessed ground of the created earth that the whole glory of the first human being becomes visible. And in this resting on the earth, in this deep sleep of creation, the human being now experiences life through being physically touched by the finger of God. It is the same hand that has made the human being that now, as though reaching from afar, tenderly touches and awakens the human being to life. God's hand no longer holds the human being in its grasp; instead it has set the human being free, and the creative power of that hand turns into the yearning love of the Creator toward the creature. The hand of God in this picture in the Sistine Chapel discloses a greater knowledge about the creation than does much profound speculation.

73

And God blew into the human being's nostrils the breath of life; so the human person became a living being. Here body and life merge completely. God breathes the spirit of God into the body of the human being. And this spirit is life; it brings the human being to life. Other life is created through God's word, but in the case of human life God gives of God's own life, of God's own spirit. Human beings do not live as human beings apart from God's spirit. To live *as a human being* means to live as a body in the spirit. Flight from the body is as much flight from being human as is flight from the spirit. The body is the form in which the spirit exists, as the spirit is the form in which the body exists. All this is said only about humankind, for only in the case of human beings do we know about body and spirit.[17] The human body differs from all non-

---

[15.] Karl Barth refers to Michelangelo's painting of the creation of Adam in the Sistine Chapel in the Vatican in *The Epistle to the Romans*, 249.

[16.] *HP* copied down the sentence fairly fully using this word (29). *UK* recorded a slightly different word in German (*angeschmiegt* for *hingeschmiegt*) that has no significant difference in meaning (19). The 1933 edition incorrectly reads *Hingegebensein*, "state of surrendering to." Karl Barth in his *Church Dogmatics* quotes the incorrect wording of 1933 and criticizes it (3/1:245).

[17.] *UK* reads here: "'The bodily is the end of God's ways.' So an older theologian once said" (16). This is a saying of Friedrich Christoph Oetinger's (see below, page 121). Its mention at this point is also noted by *FL* (35) and *HP* (30).

human bodies[18] in that it is the form in which the spirit of God exists on earth, just as it is altogether identical with all other life in being earth-like. The human body really does live only by God's spirit; that is what constitutes its essential being.[19] God as such is glorified [Gott verherr-licht sich] in the body, that is, in the body that has the specific being of a human body. That is why where the original body in its created being has been destroyed, God enters it anew in Jesus Christ, and then, where this body too is broken, enters the forms of the sacrament of the body and blood. The body and blood of the Lord's Supper are the new reali-ties of creation promised to fallen Adam. Because Adam is created as body, Adam is also redeemed as body [and God comes to Adam as body],[20] in Jesus Christ and in the sacrament.

Humankind created in this way is humankind as the image of God. It   74 is the image of God not in spite of but precisely in its bodily nature. For in their bodily nature human beings are related to the earth and to other bodies; they are there for others and are dependent upon others. In their bodily existence human beings find their brothers and sisters and find the earth. As such creatures human beings of earth and spirit are 'like' God, their Creator.[21]

[18.] *EK* says, "The human body differs from the vegetative body. . . ." (9).

[19.] In German nouns such as *Geist*, whether meaning "Spirit" or "spirit," are spelled with an initial capital letter. In these paragraphs Bonhoeffer seems to slide from the idea of God's spirit to that of the human spirit and back. [DSB]

[20.] The notes taken by *UK* (20) and *EK* (9) make it likely that the clause standing in the brackets was inadvertently omitted in the 1933 edition.

[21.] *HP* (30) and *FL* (36) here refer back to the "*analogia relationis*" (cf. above, page 65). [Because Bonhoeffer so consistently speaks of Adam as *Mensch*, "human being," rather than as *Mann*, "man," here and in the section that follows (up to the point of the creation of woman), pronouns referring to Adam have been translated as referring to human beings in general, not just male human beings. Thus when "he" or "him" refers to "Adam," it has been translated vari-ously as "Adam" or "the human being," or "humankind."] [DSB]

THE CENTER OF THE EARTH

75   *And Yahweh God planted a garden in Eden towards the east and put in it
the human being God had made. And Yahweh God made grow out of the
earth all kinds of trees that were delightful to see and good to eat and the
tree of life in the center of the garden and the tree of the knowledge of good
and evil. And a river flowed out of Eden to water the garden, and from
there divided into four main rivers. The first is named Pishon; it flows
around the whole land of Havilah, and there one finds gold. And the gold
of the land is precious; and one finds bdellium resin and shoham stone
there. The second river is named Gihon; it flows around the whole land of
the Moors [Mohrenland]. The third river is named Hiddekel; it flows on
this side of Assyria. The fourth river is the Phrates. And Yahweh God took
the human being and put the human being in the garden of Eden to till it
and keep it. And Yahweh God commanded the human being, saying: You
shall eat from every kind of tree in the garden, but from the tree of the
knowledge of good and evil you shall not eat; for on the day you eat from it
you shall die.*[1]

[1.] The text follows *LB* throughout, but the rendering of the words for Havilah, bdellium resin, shoham stone, Gihon, and Phrates (Euphrates in *LB*) follows
Kautzsch, 12–13. Kautzsch explains: "*Bedolah, budulhu* in Assyrian, is probably
the Greek *bdellion* [Latin and English bdellium], a precious aromatic resin.
Shoham stone is either beryl or a type of onyx" (12, note g). [The phrase "land of
the Moors" is an anachronism, as "Moors" usually refers to the people of north-
west Africa from the eighth century C.E. on. The Hebrew literally reads "land of
Cush" (NRSV), which in the Old Testament is generally Ethiopia or Nubia, the
land to the south of Egypt. "Hiddekel" transliterates the Hebrew. Cf. KJV. NRSV
reads "Tigris."] [DSB]

HOW CAN ONE SPEAK of the first earth, earth in its youth, except in the language of fantasy [Märchen]? God prepares an exceedingly magnificent garden for the human being [der Mensch][2] created with God's own hands.[3] What else would a person from the desert think of here but a land with magnificent rivers and trees full of fruit? Precious stones, rare odors, gorgeous colors surround the first human being. The fruitful   76 land in the distant east, between the Euphrates and the Tigris, of which so many wonderful things were being told — perhaps that was the place, the garden of the first human being.

¶Who can speak of these things except in pictures? Pictures after all are not lies; rather they indicate things and enable the underlying meaning to shine through.[4] To be sure, pictures do vary; the pictures of a child differ from those of an adult, and those of a person from the desert differ from those of a person from the city. One way or another, however, they remain true, to the extent that human speech and even speech about abstract ideas can remain true at all — that is, to the extent that God dwells in them.

In complete consistency with the framework of the picture, the story is told how the human being was put into this garden to live in it, and how in the center [Mitte][5] of the garden stood two trees: one the tree of life and the other the tree of the knowledge of good and evil. The destiny of humankind is now to be decided in relation to these two trees.[6]

[2.] See editorial note 21 at the end of the previous section.

[3.] Cf. the beginning of the quotation from John of Damascus in Bernhard Bartmann, *Dogmatik*: "With his body he [Adam] lived in an exceedingly divine and glorious place; with his soul, however, he resided in a sublime and utterly glorious domain, for he had the indwelling God as his dwelling" (296). (For the end of the quotation see above, page 64, editorial note 17.) Concerning what follows, *UK* writes: "(The imagination of someone from the orient!)" (20).

[4.] In *EK* there follows: "(cf. Luther's letter to his son Hansie.)" (9). The same reference is made by *HP* (31). Luther in a letter written from the Koburg Castle on June 19, 1530, pictures the kingdom of heaven for his four-year-old son: "I know of a pretty, beautiful, [and] cheerful garden. . ." (*LW* 49:323 [*WA-BR* 5:377–78, no. 1595]).

[5.] Bonhoeffer uses this word *Mitte* to mean two different things. I have used the English word "middle" to translate Bonhoeffer's text where it refers to time and the English word "center" to translate *Mitte* where it refers to place, including the "center" that God provides as a limit. [DSB]

[6.] *HP* reads, "Not humankind but the two strange trees stand, and remain, at

We remain wholly in the world of pictures, in the world of the magical, with spells that are effected through forbidden contacts with sacred objects.[7] We hear about trees of miraculous power, about enchanted animals, about fiery angel figures, the servants of a God who walks in this, God's enchanted garden. We hear about this God's mysterious deeds, about the creation of the woman from the man's rib — and in the midst of this world is the human being, the intelligent creature [der kluge], who knows the surrounding world, who freely gives names to it, and before whom the whole animal kingdom appears in order to receive their names. The human being is naked and not ashamed, speaks with, and has to do with, God as though they belonged to each another, talks with the beasts in the fields and lives sumptuously and with delight 77 [herrlich und in Freuden][8] in the enchanted garden — and then reaches out for the fruit of an enchanted tree and in that moment is displaced from paradise. This is a myth, a childlike, fanciful picture of the dim and distant past [Vorzeit] — so says the world. This is God's word; this is an event at the beginning of history, before history, beyond history, and yet in history; this is a decision that affects the world; *we ourselves* are the ones who are affected, are intended, are addressed, accused, condemned, expelled; *God, yes God,* is the one who blesses and curses; it is *our* primeval history [Urgeschichte],[9] truly our own, every individual person's beginning, destiny, guilt, and end — so says the church of Christ.

Why contend for the one assertion at the expense of the other? Why not see that all our speaking of God, of our beginning and end, and of our guilt *never* communicates these things themselves but always only pictures of them? Why not see that in both instances, with these ancient magical images as well as with our technical, abstract images, God must reach out to us, and that God must teach us if we are to become wise [klug]?

---

the center of the garden" (31). *UK* (20) and *FL* (36) are similar, and *EK* is almost word for word the same (9).

[7.] *UK* uses the technical term "taboo" (20) for what Bonhoeffer spells out here.

[8.] The German expression is a familiar one, included in the collection of quotations made by George Büchmann (1822–1884), which Bonhoeffer quotes from Luke 16:19, as *HP* attests precisely (31). The 1933 edition incorrectly reads *Frieden,* "peace," for *Freuden,* "joy, enjoyment, delight."

[9.] The 1933 edition has *Vorgeschichte,* "prehistory" — a misreading of Bonhoeffer's text. That Bonhoeffer did say "*Urgeschichte*" is attested by *EK* (9).

¶The exposition of what follows must therefore seek to translate the old picture language of the magical world into the new picture language of the technical world. This must always be done, however, on the basis of the presupposition that, whether in the one language or the other, *we* are the ones intended to be addressed. We must be open and prepared to be addressed by what was said at that time about human beings in that magical picture of the world. To be sure, we differ from the people who thought in terms of that worldview in that Christ has appeared, whereas they were waiting; but we are *the same* as they were in that — whether in hope or in fulfillment — we can live only through Christ as people who have been lost and, whether in hope or in fulfillment, have been graciously pardoned.

In the center of the garden stand two trees with particular names that connect them to human existence in a peculiar way: the tree of life and the tree of the knowledge of good and evil. To the latter is attached the prohibition against eating of its fruit and the threat of death. *Life, knowledge, death* — these three things are spoken of here as connected with one another, and it is important to understand this connection. Historical research seems to show that the stories of the tree of life and of the tree of knowledge originally came from different sources.[10] But that is all very uncertain. Our concern is the text as it presents itself to the church of Christ today.[11]

We begin with the tree of life. It follows from the context that humankind was not expressly forbidden to eat from this tree. Indeed this tree first gains its particular significance only after humankind has fallen prey to death by eating from the tree of knowledge. Before that, life is not something problematic or to be sought after or snatched at; instead it is just there, as a given life, indeed life before God.

¶For that reason the tree of life is in this passage mentioned with such little ceremony. *It was at the center;* that is all that is said about it. The life that comes from God is at the center; that is to say, God, who gives life, is at the center. At the center of the world that has been put at Adam's disposal and over which Adam has been given dominion is not Adam him-

78

[10.] *EK* has here: "Cf. H. Schmidt 'Die Paradiesgeschichte'" (9). Hans Schmidt saw in Gen. 2:4–3:24 two stories, each with a tree, interwoven with each other. Kautzsch makes a similar conjecture (12, note e).

[11.] Cf. above, pages 22–23 (from the paragraph beginning "Theological exposition. . .").

self but the tree of divine life. Adam's life comes from the center which is not Adam but God; it revolves around this center constantly, without ever trying to take possession of this center of existence. It is characteristic of humankind that human life constantly revolves around its own center, but that it never takes possession of it. And this life that stems from the center, which God alone possesses, remains unassailed as long as humankind does not let itself be pushed off the track from another side. Adam is not, in temptation, to touch the tree of life, to seize hold of the divine tree at the center. There is no need at all to forbid [verboten] Adam — who would in no way understand the prohibition [Verbot] — to do this. Adam has life.

Adam has life, however, in a particular way.[12] In the first place, *Adam* really possesses it and is not merely possessed by it. In the second place, Adam has life in the unity of unbroken obedience to the Creator — has life just because Adam lives from the center of life, and is oriented toward the center of life, without placing Adam's own life at the center. The distinctive characteristic of Adam's life is utterly unbroken and unified obedience, that is, Adam's innocence and ignorance of disobedience.

¶The life that God gave to humankind is not simply part of the make-up [eine Beschaffenheit], a qualitas,[13] of humankind; instead it is something given to humankind only in terms of its whole human existence. Human beings have life from God and *before* God. They receive it; they receive it, however, not as animals but as human beings. They possess it in their obedience, in their innocence, in their ignorance; that is, they possess it in their freedom. The life that human beings have happens in an obedience that issues from freedom. So while it cannot occur to Adam directly to lay hands on the tree of life, because Adam already has life, the tree of life can nevertheless come indirectly under danger from elsewhere. It can be endangered by the freedom in the unbroken unity of obedience in which Adam has life. This means that it can be endangered by the tree of the knowledge of good and evil. *In what way?*

The tree of the knowledge of good and evil, just like the tree of life, stands at the center of the garden. But as soon as this tree is pointed out, a special word of God is immediately attached — the prohibition against eating from it and the threat of death as soon as human beings transgress this commandment.

[12.] *EK* has "in contrast to the animals" (10).
[13.] "Quality," "property," or "attribute." [DSB]

How is Adam to grasp what death is, what good and evil are, indeed even what a prohibition is,[14] living as Adam does in unbroken obedience to the Creator? Can any of this mean anything else than empty words to Adam? Certainly Adam cannot know what death is, what good and evil are; but Adam understands that in these words God confronts Adam and points out Adam's limit [Grenze].[15] It is we who ask: How can Adam, who does not know about good or evil, who is innocent and ignorant, understand the word of God that addresses Adam as a prohibition? The prohibition contained two complementary aspects. On the one hand it indicated that Adam was human, was free (free 'for' and 'from') — it is Adam, the human being, who is addressed concerning Adam's own human existence, and Adam understands this. On the other hand it indicates to this human being who is addressed as a free person their limit or boundedness, that is, the human being's creature-liness. The prohibition addresses Adam concerning Adam's freedom and creatureliness and binds Adam to this existence, the existence that belongs to Adam's own being. The prohibition means nothing other than this: Adam, you are who you are because of me, your Creator; so now be what you are. You are a free creature, so now be that. You are free, so be free; you are a creature, so be a creature. And this "— so be . . ." is not a second thing besides the first but something always given already in and along with the first and guaranteed by the first. It is about being human — about the human existence that Adam receives from God at any given time — that Adam is addressed.[16]

80

[14.] Hans Schmidt argues, the "ability to distinguish between what is 'good' and what is 'bad' in the sense of what is 'morally perfect' and what is 'sinful'" is already "presupposed" at that moment "when a prohibition, with its demand to be observed, confronts human beings" (21 and note 1). Bonhoeffer refutes this argument in what follows.

[15.] *Grenze* is usually translated as "limit" in this book. As such it sometimes means a creaturely limit that cannot be surpassed and sometimes a prohibition that may not be transgressed. It is translated "boundary," however, when used together with spatial terms such as "center" and in phrases like "transgressing a boundary." Occasionally *Grenze* and its cognates are also translated "limit or boundedness," "limit or constraint," "limitedness" and "unlimitedness." [DSB]

[16.] Cf. above, pages 42–43, concerning how with God the "indicative," "you are," and the "imperative," "so be," are one. At the end of this paragraph, the conclusion of the seventh lecture period, *HP* has "Creation: the Tree of Life. Sin: somehow the tree of knowledge. Here is the diacritical point. . . ." (33). *EK* continues, "at which one must see how creation and sin stand together" (10). Cf. *UK*

This singular interrelatedness, which is basically only the interrelatedness of freedom and creatureliness, is expressed here in the picture language of the Bible in that the tree of knowledge, the forbidden tree that denotes the human being's boundary, stands at the center. *The human being's limit is at the center of human existence,* not on the margin; the limit or constraint that people look for on the margin of humankind is the limit of the human condition, the limit of human technology, the limit of what is possible for humanity. The boundary that is at the center is the limit of human *reality,* of human *existence as such.* Knowledge of the limit or constraint on the margin is always accompanied by the possibility of failing to know any internal limit.[17] Knowledge of the boundary at the center means knowing that the whole of existence, human existence in every possible way that it may comport itself, has its limit.

81

¶There where the boundary — the tree of knowledge — stands, there stands also the tree of life, that is, the very God who gives life.[18] *God is at once the boundary and the center of our existence.* Adam knows that. But Adam knows it in such a way that this knowing is only an expression of Adam's existence from the center — Adam's being oriented toward the center; it is an expression of Adam's creatureliness and freedom. Adam's knowing is embedded in Adam's freedom for God, in unbroken obedience to God; it is *knowledge arising from the freedom of the creature, knowl-*

(21–22); and *FL* has an echo of it (37). *HP* dates the eighth lecture period as Jan. 10, 1933 (33). In the recapitulation at the beginning of the period, *FL* has the following, which is emphasized with a line in the margin: "*the relationship with God and the moral relationship not to be torn apart*" (39). *UK* has "The unity still obtains: what God gives is bound to be" (23); *HP* is similar (33).

[17.] Compare Bonhoeffer's phrase "the possibility of failing to know any internal limit" with his exposition of idealist philosophy in his inaugural lecture of July 31, 1930: "In that I limit my possibilities in thought . . . in the very possibility of making a limit I demonstrate the infinity of my possibilities. . . ." ("Man [*sic*] in Contemporary Philosophy and Theology," *NRS* 60 [*DBW* 10:368 (*GS* 3:74)]). In Bonhoeffer's copy of Hegel's *Philosophy of Religion,* he marked the following passage with a colored pencil (and an exclamation mark in the margin): ". . . Plato [in the Dialogue *Philebus,* 26] declared the *peras,* the boundary that limits itself by itself, to be superior to the *apeiron,* the boundless" (Lasson ed., 12:148). [trans. DSB] Cf. *Internationales Bonhoeffer Forum* 8:81–82 and 14. [For a brief discussion of the point involved in Hegel's doctrine of the infinite, see W. T. Stace: *The Philosophy of Hegel,* 142–49.] [JDEG]

[18.] The 1933 edition reads "the very Lord [*Herr selbst*]." This is shown to be an error by *HP,* who has "the God who gives life" (34) and *UK,* who has "the very God [*Gott selbst*]" (23).

edge in life, knowledge in ignorance. Thus Adam cannot know evil, cannot conceive it, and cannot know or conceive death either. But Adam knows the limit of human beings because Adam knows God. Adam does not know the boundary as something that can be transgressed; otherwise Adam would know about evil. Adam knows it as the given grace that belongs to his creatureliness and freedom. Adam also knows, therefore, that life is possible only because of the limit; Adam lives from this boundary that is at the center. Thus Adam understands this prohibition and the threat of death only as a renewed gift, as the grace of God. The limit is grace because it is the basis of creatureliness and freedom; the boundary is the center. Grace is that which holds humankind over the abyss of nonbeing, nonliving, not-being-created, and Adam can think of all this nothingness only in terms of the given grace of God.

¶Thus not a word in the story up to this point hints at the possibility of understanding the prohibition differently, say as a temptation. The *prohibition* in paradise is the *grace* of the Creator toward the creature. God tempts no one.[19] Only the Creator knows what the tree of the knowledge of *good* and *evil* is up to this point; Adam does not yet know it. As one who lives in the unity of obedience Adam does not comprehend that which is two-sided [das Zwiefache];[20] as one who lives in the unity of the knowledge of God as the center and the boundary of human life Adam cannot conceive of the breaking apart of that knowledge into good and evil. Adam knows neither what good nor what evil is[21] and lives in the strictest sense *beyond good and evil*;[22] that is, Adam lives out

82

[19.] Cf. the exposition of the sixth petition of the Lord's Prayer (Matt. 6:13) in Martin Luther's *Small Catechism*: "God indeed tempts no one. . ." (*Book of Concord*, 347). *UK* reads, "otherwise he [Adam] would already have fallen, because no human being would be able to resist, were God to tempt" (24). *FL* has very much the same (20).

[20.] *Zwiefach* means strictly "twofold, double" — like the two views one can take of a prohibition or like "the tree of knowledge of good and evil." Cf. what follows. [DSB]

[21.] Cf. Friedrich Gogarten, *Politische Ethik*, who says that the human being "who lets God be his God, as Adam does in Paradise, . . . knows nothing about good and evil" (72).

[22.] *Beyond Good and Evil* is the title of a work that Friedrich Nietzsche wrote in 1885–86. The idea is present already in many places in *Also sprach Zarathustra* (1883–84), e.g., in the section "Before Sunrise" (*The Portable Nietzsche*, 277–78): ". . . all things have been baptized in the well of eternity and are beyond good and evil."

of the life that comes from God, before whom a life lived in good, just like a life lived in evil, would mean an unthinkable falling away.

¶Good and evil, tob and ra,[23] thus have a much wider meaning here than good and evil in our terminology. The words tob and ra speak of an ultimate split [Zwiespalt][24] in the world of humankind in general that goes back behind even the moral split, so that tob means also something like "pleasurable" [lustvoll] and ra "painful" [leidvoll] (Hans Schmidt).[25] Tob and ra are concepts that express what is in every respect the deepest divide [Entzweiung][26] in human life. The essential point about them is that they appear as a pair, that in being split apart [in ihrer Zwie-spaltigkeit] they belong inseparably together. There is no tob, nothing that is pleasurable/good/beautiful, without its being always already immersed in ra, in that which is painful/evil/base/false [Unechte]. And what is painful/evil — in this wide sense — does not occur without a glimmer of desire for pleasure [Lust],[27] which is what makes pain so completely pain. That which is good, in the sense of tob, is for us always only something that has been torn from evil, that has passed through evil, that has been conceived, carried, and borne by evil. The luster of the pleasurable/good is its origin in evil, in its overcoming of evil, to be

83

[23.] *Tob* and *ra* are Hebrew words, each having a range of meanings. *Tob* means "good, pleasing, pleasant, delightful, delicious, happy, glad, joyful," while *ra* means "bad, evil, disagreeable, displeasing, unpleasant, harmful." (See *The New Brown-Driver-Briggs-Gesenius Hebrew and English Lexicon.*) Hence *tob* can be translated by the German *lustvoll*, which means either "pleasurable" or "joyful," and *ra* by *leidvoll*, which means either "painful, suffering" or "sorrowful." [DSB]

[24.] *Zwiespalt* means literally "a state of being split into two" and so "split, rift, cleavage, disruption, conflict, strife, dissension." [DSB]

[25.] Cf. Hans Schmidt, according to whom the words *tob* and *ra* "in their original concrete sense mean not 'good' and 'evil'" but that "which gives sensual pleasure and its opposite: they mean 'pleasurable' and 'painful'" (26). *UK* adds the pair of ideas, "joy" [*Freude*] and "unhappiness" (24), and *FL* adds "happiness" and "unhappiness" (40). Cf. Friedrich Nietzsche, *Zarathustra*, in the section "The Drunken Song": "my unhappiness, my happiness is deep" (*The Portable Nietzsche*, 433) and above all in the section "On the Afterworldly": "Good and evil and pleasure and pain . . . " (*The Portable Nietzsche*, 142 [trans. altered DSB]).

[26.] [*Entzweiung* means literally "dividing/separating or being divided/separated into two."] [DSB] Cf. Hegel, *The Christian Religion*, in the section "The Representation of the Fall," 159: "The highest disunion, the distinction between good and evil, . . . is certainly knowledge." Cf. also *Internationales Bonhoeffer Forum* 8:131.

[27.] *Lust* can also be translated "joy, delight, desire" or "lust." [DSB]

sure, but in the same way that a child overcomes the mother's womb, that is, in such a way that the good is enhanced [geadelt] by the greatness of the evil from which it has torn itself. To us Ignatius is 'greater' than Francis, Augustine is greater than Monica, Hagen is greater than Siegfried.[28]

In the same way, however, 'evil' is enhanced by the 'good' from which it comes; pain is enhanced by the pleasure out of whose depths alone it has become possible. No real evil wholly lacks the luster of the good. We have no utter [schlechthin] evil, nothing that is utterly painful, in human beings. Where there is utter evil with no good to enhance it, where baseness itself takes form, there human beings have lost their humanity and we call them sick; where that which is utterly painful has managed to lay hold of human beings, so that pleasure has been wholly destroyed in pain, there the sickness of mind called melancholia has overwhelmed human beings and they are no longer human.[29] Healthy human beings in pain are borne up and nourished by what brings pleasure; in their experience of pleasure they are churned up by what is painful, in good by evil, in evil by good. They suffer from an inner split [Zwiespalt].

This describes *us*; it is we who have eaten from the tree of knowledge, not Adam. But we must go on and enquire further in order to understand the import of what the Bible says about the tree of knowledge: ". . . as soon as you eat from it you must die." The tree of knowledge is the *tree*   84 *of death*. It stands immediately next to the tree of life, and *the tree of life is endangered only by this tree of death*. Both trees are still untouched and untouchable; both constitute the boundary and the center. Whoever grasps at life must die; "those who want to save their life will lose it."[30] Only those who have lost it, however, will grasp at it. And those who have attained the knowledge of good and evil, who live as people who are split apart within themselves [im Zwiespalt], have lost their life.

¶Why have they lost life? We have said that what is pleasurable/good is immersed in what is painful/evil, and vice versa. But just what is

---

[28.] The steeliness of will of Ignatius of Loyola (1491–1556) contrasts with the gentleness of Francis of Assisi (c. 1181–1226). Augustine tells us about his pious mother Monica especially in the ninth book of his *Confessions*. Hagen is the murderer of Siegfried in the *Nibelungenlied*, a Middle High German epic poem.

[29.] "Melancholia" or "depression" as a technical term in psychiatry stands for the depressive emotional disorder that those who suffer from its severe forms experience as an unendurable condition.

[30.] Cf. Matt. 16:25, Luke 9:24. *UK* alone has here "Why does the one who reaches out for what is good deserve death?" (25).

painful in pleasure? It is that in all pleasure a person desires eternity, but knows that pleasure is transient and will end. That is not a knowing that comes from a prior knowledge now applied to every pleasurable event; it is something that the depth of pleasure itself discloses to us if we listen to it: a thirst, a craving [Sucht],[31] for eternity, precisely because pleasure is not eternal but instead has fallen prey to death. On the other hand we ask: What pleasure is there in pain? It is that in the depth of pain a person feels pleasure in transience, pleasure in the obliteration of apparently endless pain, pleasure in death.[32]

What is the evil in good? It is that the good dies. What is the good in evil? It is that the evil dies. What is the state of being divided or torn apart into tob and ra in the world and in humankind? It is the pain and the pleasure with which a human being dies. A human being who knows about tob and ra knows immediately about death. Knowing about tob and ra itself constitutes death. Humankind dies from knowing good and evil. Humankind is dead in its own good and in its own evil. Death in terms of transience is not the death that comes from God. What does it mean to be dead? It does not mean the abolition of one's being a creature. Instead it means no longer being able to live before God, and yet having to live before God. It means standing before God as an outlaw, as 85 one who is lost and damned, but not as one who no longer exists. It means receiving life from God no longer as grace coming from the center and the boundary of one's own existence but as a commandment that stands in one's way and with a flaming sword denies one any way of retreat.

¶Being dead in this sense means to have life not as a gift but as a *commandment*. But from this commandment no one can escape, not even by

---

[31.] *Sucht* means "a craving" or "an obsessive, uncontrollable, or insatiable desire."

[32.] See Nietzsche, *Zarathustra*, in the section "The Drunken Song": "Pleasure [*Lust*] wants itself, wants eternity, wants recurrence, wants everything eternally the same. . . . Woe entreats: Go! Away, woe! . . . *Woe implores, 'Go!'* . . . . All pleasure wants the eternity of all things. . . . — *what* does pleasure not desire! It is thirstier, heartier, hungrier, more terrible, more secretive than all woe; it wants *itself*, it bites into *itself*, the ring's will wrestles in it [*des Ringes Wille ringt in ihr*]. Pleasure . . . *wants deep, wants deep eternity*" (*The Portable Nietzsche*, 434–36). [trans. altered DSB] [Nietzsche here poetically pictures *Lust* (pleasure, lust) as a snake biting its own tail and so forming a "ring" or circle. The verb *ringt* means "wrestles, strives" or "forms a ring."] [JDEG]

choosing oneself to die, for to be dead is itself to be subject to the commandment to live. *To be dead means to-have-to-live.* That irks our natural way of thinking. Being dead is not deliverance, salvation, or the final possibility of fleeing; instead flight into death is flight into the most terrible bondage to life. The *inescapable nature of life as a commandment* — to know that is *to know death.*

The *commandment to live* demands from me something that I am not in a position to fulfill. It obliges me to live out of myself, out of my own resources, and I am unable to do that. Just this, however, is the commandment that burdens those who know about *tob* and *ra.* They are obliged to live out of their own resources, and they do so, yet are unable to do it. *They do so* by living out of their own inner split, by living with their own good that comes out of evil and by their own evil that comes out of good, by deriving the strength of pain from pleasure and the strength of pleasure from pain. Humankind lives in a circle; it *lives* out of its own resources; it is alone. Yet *it cannot live,* because in fact it does not live but in this life is dead, because it *must* live, that is, it *must* accomplish life out of its own resources and just that is its death (as the basis at once of its knowledge and of its existence!).[33] Humankind whom God's commandment confronts with a demand[34] is thrown back upon itself and now has to live in this way. Humankind now lives only out of its own   86
resources, by its knowledge of good and evil, and thus is dead.

After all this, it is now at last quite clear that the tree of life comes to be in danger only where the tree of death has had its effect. It is clear why the prohibition was attached to the tree of death but not to the tree of life — or, to put it the other way around, why the tree to which the prohibition was attached has to be the tree of death. There is still one thing that remains quite unclear, however: how this deed that[35] opened up

---

[33.] A philosophical distinction made since Gottfried Wilhelm von Leibniz (1646–1716), to whose formulation of the problem in his *Monadology* — the inquiry after the *principium rationis sufficientis* ("the principle of sufficient reason") — Martin Heidegger refers in his *The Essence of Reasons* (11–33). Cf. Immanuel Kant, "Preface" to *Critique of Practical Reason*: "Though freedom is certainly the *ratio essendi* [basis of being] of the moral law, the latter is the *ratio cognoscendi* [basis of knowledge] of freedom" (4, note 1).

[34.] According to *HP* (37), *UK* (26), and *FL* (46), in his (eighth) lecture Bonhoeffer said: "who transgress God's commandment." It is more probable that the text at this point was altered by Bonhoeffer than that it was misread.

[35.] *HP* reads, "this death that. . ." (37).

and created this split-apart world of ours for us came about at all. The
world that has been torn apart into tob and ra is known only in death.
And Adam knows nothing of this world. To Adam it remains hidden in
the tempting fruit of the tree of knowledge. What Adam knows is that
the secret of humankind's limit, of the life of the human being, is in
God's keeping.

At this point, however, we need to remind ourselves again that this is
not a tale about some primeval human being that hardly affects us. If it
were only a tale like that, our main task would be to give rein to our imagination so that it would transport us to this fairyland beyond tob and ra.
Every such game of imagination would altogether discount our actual
situation; indeed it is possible only in the split-apart world in which
human beings suppose that they could somehow still escape from themselves. What is important to understand, however, is that this story
claims us not as listeners with the gift of imagination but as human
beings who, no matter how much they stretch their imaginations and all
their other mental or spiritual powers, are simply unable to transport
themselves to this paradise 'beyond good and evil', 'beyond pleasure
and pain'; instead, with all their powers of thinking, they remain tied to
this torn-apart world, to antithesis, to contradiction. This is so because
our thinking too is only the expression of our being, of our existence,
which is grounded in contradiction. Because we do not exist in a state of
unity, our thinking is torn apart as well.

87   ¶Instead of sanctioning this impossibility [of transporting ourselves to
that fairyland beyond],[36] however, and instead of being allowed to
judge what the Bible calls good by our idea of what is good and on that
basis to criticize what the Bible says here about what is beyond good and
evil, we are confronted by this Adam who disturbs us and criticizes us.
This is so just because Adam is a human being like us and Adam's history is our history, with the one decisive difference, to be sure, that for us
history begins where for Adam it ends. Our history is history through
Christ, whereas Adam's history is history through the serpent. But precisely as those who live and have their history through Christ alone we
are enabled to know about the beginning not by means of our own imagination but only from the new center, from Christ. We have this knowledge as those who by faith have been set free from the knowledge of

---

[36.] Section in brackets added by translator. [DSB]

good and evil, from death, and who by faith alone are able to make Adam's image their own.[37]

[37.] The end of the eighth lecture. *HP* dates the ninth Jan. 17, 1933 (37). From the comprehensive recapitulation at the beginning of the ninth lecture period *HP* recorded the following: "The existence of human beings who live between good and evil stands at any given time in relation to death, because they understand what it means to be transient. [*UK* reads, "Human beings who know that they are transient know of their death but only as a release, not as a punishment. They understand it wrongly. Human beings must live" (27).] The Greek knows of death as the cessation of the imperative to live. In suicide a person escapes from the demand that one must live. [*FL* reads, "suicide a possible way of bringing pain to completion in pleasure" (47).] The good that is always related to evil is not God's good. The person who has eaten from the tree of knowledge, who knows about good and evil, has fallen away from God. Before Adam ate, being good or evil did not in any way exist for the human being; Adam had not yet fallen away. So it is now with us; we are between good and evil and so stand between two possible states of having fallen away. This is not Hegel's divine knowledge of what is good and evil. Unity is grounded in faith alone. Faith is the truly good thing in God's eyes [*das wirklich Gute Gottes*]" (37f.). (This final phrase is later important in Bonhoeffer's *The Cost of Discipleship*.) [JDEG] *FL* reads "[according to] Hegel human beings have God's knowledge of good and evil. To wish to live on the basis of one's own good is . . . not good" (48). Cf. Hegel's *The Christian Religion* regarding Gen. 3:22a ("Behold Adam has become like one of us"): ". . . The confirmation of the fact that knowledge of good and evil belongs to the divinity of man is placed on the lips of God . . ." (159–60).

THE POWER OF THE OTHER

88   *And Yahweh God*[1] *said: It is not good that the human being [Mensch]*
should be alone; I will make a helper who is a suitable partner.[2] *So out of*
the ground Yahweh God formed all the beasts of the field and all the birds
of heaven and brought them to the human being to see what they would be
called; and whatever the human being called the living creatures, so they
were named. The human being gave names to all cattle and all the birds of
heaven and all the beasts of the field; but God found no helper who was a
partner suitable for the human being. So Yahweh God let a deep sleep fall
upon the human being, and when sleep had come, God took a rib and filled
out its place with flesh. Then Yahweh God formed into a woman the rib he
had taken from the human being and brought her to the human being.
Then the human being said: This at last is bone of my bones and flesh of my

---

[1.] Kautzsch regularly reads "Yahweh God," and Bonhoeffer follows him in
this regard. In the 1933 edition "God" was inadvertently omitted here.

[2.] ["A helper who is a suitable partner" translates "*ein Beistand . . . wie er für*
ihn paßt" (literally: "a helper . . . who fits or suits him"). Normally *Beistand* means
"help, support, helper, assistant, supporter." The original Hebrew word *'ezer*
means "help, succor" and by extension "one who helps, helper." The NRSV renders this as "a helper as his partner."] [DSB] Cf. *LB*, which, instead of *Beistand*,
emphasizes the gender of the "helper who is a partner" by using the word *Gehil-*
fin, "female helper, assistant": ". . . make a helper [*Gehilfin*], who will be around
him. Then when God the LORD had made all the different animals in the field
and all the different birds under heaven, he brought them to the human being,
. . . but for the human being no helper [*Gehilfin*] was found who would be there
around him."

flesh. She shall be called woman [Männin],[3] *because she was taken out of man [Mann]." That is why a man [Mann] will leave father and mother and cleave to his woman [Weib], and they will be one flesh. And they were both naked, the man and his woman, and they were not ashamed.*[4]

AT THIS POINT the text all at once, with no apparent relation to what has gone before, tells us how woman [Weib] came to be. No doubt in terms of narrative technique it is a mistake that the woman has not heard God's prohibition, for no intrinsic significance of any kind is attached to this circumstance. Yet the story does have its own special significance in just this place. Let us keep in mind that the tree of life was mentioned first, not yet as something which was desired, or to which any prohibition was attached, but as the *tree around whose fruit everything in the end revolves.* We saw how it was first placed in danger by the tree of knowledge; now more and more links are added to the chain, increasing the danger, and making it ever more threatening. After the tree of knowledge comes the creation of the woman, and, finally, it is the serpent that leads to the act of grasping at the tree of knowledge and of life. The incomprehensibility of this deed makes the author of the story, with exceptional profundity, look at, and take up, everything conceivable in connection with this deed in order to make it more comprehensible — or, more exactly, to make clear its incomprehensibility. It is clear that for the author the creation of the woman belongs already to the prehistory of the fall.[5]

89

[3.] The word *Männin* (formed by adding a feminine ending to the masculine *Mann*, "man") was coined by Luther to render the Hebrew *ishshah*, "woman," who is made from *ish*, "man." [JDEG]

[4.] In vv. 18a and 24-25 the text follows *LB*; in vv. 18b-23 it follows Kautzsch, 13.

[5.] *FL* reads, "it is superficial reasoning to take this as a basis for speaking about marriage as an order of creation. . . ." (49); *HP* says, "One may not speak of the institution of marriage here. It is the story of human community as such" (38). Cf. *UK* (27–28). Kautzsch, in the introduction to the section on "Paradise and the Creation of the Woman" (Gen. 2:4b-25), speaks of "God's order" and of "marriage" (12). [The German term *Schöpfungsordnung*, translated here as "order of creation," was a misused concept in Bonhoeffer's time. Whereas Martin Luther had maintained that marriage or the family (like the state) is a natural order of creation that confronts us with ethical obligations, some German Protestants used the concept to justify nationalist and even National Socialist ideas about the demands of the nation or even the race. See the section "Ethics Based on Orders of Creation" below, 148ff.] [JDEG]

"It is not good that the human being should be alone; I will make a helper who is a suitable partner."

The first person is alone. Christ also was alone; we also are alone. But everyone is alone in his or her own way. Adam is alone in anticipation of the other person, of community [Gemeinschaft]. Christ is alone because he alone loves the other person, because Christ is the way by which the human race has returned to its Creator. We are alone because we have pushed other people away from us, because we have hated them. Adam was alone in hope, Christ was alone in the fullness of deity,[6] we are alone in evil, in hopelessness.

God creates a suitable partner, a helpmate, for Adam. It is not good that Adam should be alone. To what end does the human being who lives in God's keeping need a helper who is a partner? The answer becomes clear only if we continue to reflect on the story in its context. Elsewhere in the Bible God alone is a partner, a help to human beings.[7] So when the text here speaks of the woman *in this way*, it must mean something quite unusual. That also becomes evident from what the story depicts. God first of all forms animals out of the ground from which God has taken humankind. According to the Bible human beings and animals have the same kind of body! Perhaps the human being would find a helper who is a suitable partner among these brothers and sisters — for that is what they are, the animals who have the same origin as humankind does. The peculiar feature here is that evidently it is precisely the human being who must know whether or not this could provide a helper who is a suitable partner. Whether one of the creatures that are led before the human being would be a helper and partner depends on whether the human being would call it such. There sits wise Adam, at once calling all the animals by name and letting them pass by — the fraternal world of animals that has been taken from the same ground as has the human being. It was Adam's first occasion of pain that these brothers and sisters whom Adam loved did not fulfill the human being's own expectation. They remained a strange world to Adam; indeed they remain, for all their nature as siblings, creatures subjected

[6.] Colossians 2:9. *HP* reads, "Christ [was alone] in the fullness of hope" (38).

[7.] [The image of God as a partner, a help [*ein Beistand, eine Hilfe*] is seen, for example, in Exod. 18:4; Deut. 33:7, 26, 29; Pss. 33:20, 70:5, 115:9-11, 121:1-2, 124:8.] [DSB] *UK* reads, "When it is understood like this, we see what an honor it is to be a helper" (28); *FL* reads much the same (50).

to, named by, and ruled over by, Adam. The human person remains alone. As far as I know, nowhere else in the history of religions have animals been spoken of in terms of such a significant relation. At the point where God wishes to create for the human being, in the form of another creature, the help that God is as God — this is where the animals are first created and named and set in their place.

¶Yet Adam is still alone. What has come out of the ground remains alien to humankind. Now the strange thing happens that Adam must fall into a deep sleep. What the human being is unable to achieve or find while awake God does for the sleeping human being. Thus Adam essentially does not know how it happens. But Adam knows that God has made use of the human, has taken a piece of the sleeping human body, and has formed the other person from it. And it is with a true cry of joy[8] that Adam recognizes the woman [Weib]: "This at last is bone of my bones and flesh of my flesh. She shall be called woman [Männin], because she was taken out of man."

¶Thus Adam understands the uniqueness of this creature that God has shaped with the contribution Adam has made, out of human flesh, but Adam sees what Adam has done for the other wholly in the light of God's gift. That Eve[9] is derived from Adam is a cause not for pride, but for particular gratitude, with Adam. Adam does not infer from it any claim for himself; instead Adam knows that he is bound in a wholly new way to this Eve who is derived from him. This bond is best described in the expression: he now belongs to her, because she belongs to him. They are now no longer without each other; they are one and yet two.[10] And the two becoming one is the real mystery that God has initiated by what God did to sleeping Adam. They have from their origin been one, and only in becoming one do they return to their origin. But this becoming one never means the merging of the two or the abolition of their crea-

[8.] Hans Schmidt deduces that the first concern in the creation of the woman is help in working the ground (6, 12) and speaks of Adam "exulting with joy" (13, 29).

[9.] Bonhoeffer at this point begins suddenly to speak of "the woman" as "Eve," despite the fact that the text will not call her that until the point of the expulsion from the garden in Gen. 3:20. [JDEG]

[10.] *FL*, in his record of the recapitulation at the beginning of the tenth lecture period, has: "Being free and being a servant — Being man and being woman. Exactly the same as being [made] one by Christ in the church" (53). The allusion to Gal. 3:28 was also recorded in *HP* (41).

tureliness as individuals.[11] It actualizes to the highest possible degree
their belonging to each other, which is based precisely on their being different from each other.[12]

In what way then is Eve a "helper who is a partner" to Adam? In terms
of the whole context this can only mean that the woman becomes the
helper who is a partner of the man [Mann] in bearing the limit imposed
upon him. What does this mean? Adam was alone. In the prohibition
Adam was addressed — as we have seen — as a human being [auf sein
Menschsein], in his human freedom and creatureliness.[13] Adam had
these gifts, because Adam received them in unbroken obedience — and
received them in daily converse with the Creator. Adam knew of
humankind's boundedness, but only in the positive sense that to Adam
the idea of transgressing against the boundary was unthinkable. Adam
lived his life, to be sure, within this boundary, but Adam could still not
really love this life in its boundedness. Instead, between love and hate,
Adam lived as one who received the divine gift with pure faith and sight.
The Creator knows that this free life as a creature can be borne within its
limit only if it is loved, and out of unfathomable mercy the Creator
creates the helper who is a partner suitable for a human being. The
helper who is a partner had to be at once the embodiment of Adam's
limit and the object of Adam's love. Indeed love for the woman was now
to be the human being's[14] very life (in the deepest sense of the word).

¶*Limit* and *life* constitute the inviolable, inaccessible center of paradise around which Adam's life circles. This center *takes on form* and by

---

[11.] *UK* reads, "The original creatureliness of the individual is a category
that belongs to Christianity in contrast to the Greek myth (Plato's Banquet)"
(30). [The Greek word *sumposion* meant a drinking party or banquet.] [DSB] In
Plato's dialogue *The Symposium*, the comic poet Aristophanes tells how the first
human being was created as a round creature with four arms and four legs and
afterwards divided into two (189e–190e). Kautzsch refers to the "famous Platon-
ic" myth (13, note d). *FL* adds: "[The] *individual* is specifically Christian (discovered by Kierkegaard)" (53).

[12.] According to *UK*, Bonhoeffer dealt with the question "How can Adam
speak about father and mother?" at this point at the end of his ninth lecture on
Jan. 17, 1933 (29). See the end of this section from page 100. What now follows
Bonhoeffer presented in his tenth lecture, on Jan. 24, 1933.

[13.] See above, page 85.

[14.] Here, where one might expect Bonhoeffer to begin using the term
"man" [*Mann*], he continues to speak of "the human being" (*der Mensch*). [JDEG]

the hand of God the Creator becomes Adam's helper who is a partner. Knowing the other person as God's creature, simply as the other, as the other who stands beside me and constitutes a limit for me, and at the same time knowing that the other person is derived from me, from my life, and so loving the other and being loved by the other because the other is a piece of me — all that is for Adam the bodily representation of the limit that should make Adam's limit easier for Adam to bear. In other words, love for a person helps one to bear the limit. The other person is the limit that God sets for me, the limit that I love and that I will not transgress because of my love. This means nothing other than that both people, while remaining *two* as creatures of God, become *one* body, that is, belong to one another in love. By the creation of the other person freedom and creatureliness are bound together in love. That is why the other person is once again grace to the first person, just as the prohibition against eating from the tree of knowledge was grace.[15] In this common bearing of the limit by the first two persons in community, the character of this community as the church is authenticated.[16]

¶This means, however, that one thing is quite certain, namely that at the point where love for the other is obliterated, a human being can only hate the limit. A person then desires only, in an unbounded way, to possess the other or to destroy the other. For now the human being insists on that human being's own contribution to, and claim upon, the other, insists that the other is derived from oneself; what the human being until now accepted humbly at this point becomes a cause for pride and rebellion. That is our world. The grace of the other person's being our helper who is a partner because he or she helps us to bear our limit, that is, helps us to live before God — and we can live before God only in community [Gemeinschaft] with our helper — this grace becomes a curse. The other becomes the one who makes our hatred of God ever more passionate, the one because of whom we can no longer live before God, and who again and again becomes a judgment against us. As a result marriage and community inevitably receive a new and different meaning. The power of the other which helps me to live before God now becomes the power of the other because of which I must die before God.

93

[15.] See above, page 87.

[16.] See below, pages 100–101. Eph. 5:30-32. In the recapitulation at the beginning of the tenth lecture, *HP* recorded, "Close relation between the concept of the church and original creatureliness" (42).

The power of life becomes the power of destruction, the power of community becomes the power of isolation, the power of love becomes the power of hate.[17]

"That is why a man [Mann] will leave father and mother and cleave to his woman [Weib], and they will be one flesh." One could say that at this point the storyteller plainly stumbles. How can Adam, who knows nothing of father and mother, say such a thing? One could also call this saying "the storyteller's own practical application"[18] or put forward similar ways of looking at it. Deep down, however, we recognize a basic fact that until now has been kept more in the background and that now unintentionally, as it were, breaks out into the open. The Adam who speaks like this is we ourselves, we who have fathers and mothers, we who know the uniqueness of belonging to one another in the love of man and woman but for whom this knowledge has been wholly spoiled and destroyed by our guilt. This statement is not a justification for running away from the worldly order [Ordnung],[19] that is, from the ties one has with one's father and mother; instead it is the only possible way in which to describe the depth and seriousness of belonging to one another.[20] This ultimate belonging to one another is, however, unquestionably associated with human sexuality. Quite plainly sexuality expresses the two complementary sides of the matter: that of being an individual and that of being one with the other. Sexuality is nothing but the ultimate possible realization of belonging to each other. It has here as yet no life of its own detached from this, its purpose.

¶The community of husband and wife [Mann und Frau] is a community of love that is accepted as given by God and that glorifies and worships God as the Creator. It is therefore the church [Kirche] in its original form. And because it is the church, it is a community bound with an eternal bond. Such statements for us do not mean the glorifica-

94

[17.] *HP* reads, "The protest against this breaking apart [of the limit and love] from each other is the community of the church" (44). *UK* reads, "That is why the community with others that remains intact is the church" (31–32).

[18.] Bonhoeffer is quoting Kautzsch (13, note e), on "That is why" in Gen. 2:24.

[19.] Here Bonhoeffer is not speaking of an "order of creation." Cf. above, note 5. [DSB]

[20.] *UK* says, "Man and woman belong together, even when that means breaking other ties" (29).

tion of marriage as we know it; instead they point out that at any rate for us the bond between husband and wife does not partake of this unambiguous reality, and that the most questionable of all the church's official functions may be precisely its role in officiating at marriage. Sexuality has torn the community of love completely to pieces, so that it has turned into an obsessive desire [Sucht] that affirms itself and denies the other as God's creature. This community which is based upon the claim that the one makes by reason of one's share in the other — of one's rib in the other, of the other's being-derived-from-oneself — plainly fails to glorify the Creator in such a way that the Creator may again do the work of creation with the unknowing, sleeping human beings, Adam and Eve. Instead of such a community glorifying the Creator there is a reaching out to grasp the strength and glory of the Creator for oneself — a raising to unconscious awareness [bewußtlosen Bewußtheit] of one's own ego, a begetting and giving birth by one's own power, in an awake but delirious state [im Wachsein des Rausches]. Nevertheless this profound destruction of the original human condition does not abrogate one thing: that in its deepest sense the community of husband and wife [Mann und Frau] is destined to be the church (Eph. 5:30-32).

"And they were both naked, the man and his woman, and they were not ashamed." 95

Shame arises only out of the knowledge of humankind's dividedness [Entzweiung], of the world's dividedness in general, and thus also of one's own dividedness. Shame expresses the fact that we no longer accept the other as God's gift but instead are consumed with an obsessive desire for the other; it also expresses the knowledge that goes along with this that the other person too is no longer content to belong to me but desires to get something from me. Shame is a cover in which I hide myself from the other because of my own evil and the other person's evil, that is, because of the dividedness that has come between us. Where one person accepts the other as the helper who is a partner given by God, where one is content with understanding-oneself-as-derived-from and destined-for-the-other, in belonging-to-the-other, there human beings are not ashamed. In the unity of unbroken obedience one human being stands naked before another, uncovered, revealed in body and in soul, and is not ashamed. Shame arises only in a split-apart world [in der Welt des Zwiespalts]. Knowledge, death, sexuality — the relation

between these three primal words of life is what is at issue here and in
what follows.[21]

[21.] The notes taken during the lecture show that the ninth lecture ended at
this point. The tenth lecture must have been on Jan. 24, 1933. Bonhoeffer
began it by expanding on what it meant to be a *Beistand,* or "helper" (see above,
pages 98–100, and editorial note 12). Then he reminded his hearers of the difference between the first and second accounts of creation. *HP* has: "1st creation
account concerning God and creation — 2nd creation account concerning
humankind, which stands in the center" (44). (Only) *FL,* evidently with regard
to the first creation account, reads, "before God the creation of the human
being [*Mensch*] and [his] woman is a [unique] act" (54). Then follows the exposition of Gen. 3:1-3.

THE PIOUS QUESTION[1]

And the serpent was more cunning than all the animals in the field that   96
Yahweh God had made, and it said to the woman: Did God really say, You
shall not eat from every kind of tree in the garden? And the woman said to
the serpent: We do eat from the fruit of the trees in the garden; but of the
fruit of the tree in the center of the garden God has said, Do not eat from it,
and do not even touch it, lest you die.[2]

THE PROHIBITION AGAINST EATING from the tree of knowledge, the
creation of Eve, and the serpent are to be understood as all links in one
chain, linked together for a common assault upon the tree of life. All
come from God the Creator, and yet now, strangely, they form a common front with humankind against the Creator.[3] The prohibition that
Adam has heard and obeyed as grace becomes the law that provokes
wrath in human beings and in God; the woman who was created to be a
man's helper who is a suitable partner and to give him the strength to

---

[1.] [The German word *fromme* means "pious, devout, godly, religious." Like
the English word "pious," it sometimes retains its original positive meaning but
mostly conveys a negative meaning.] [DSB] *HP* (44) and *UK* (32) recorded the
heading just as: "The Question."

[2.] The biblical text follows *LB.*

[3.] Cf. Hans Schmidt: "Here one can imagine as an echo of a still earlier,
totemistic religion [earlier even than the fertility religion of the god Baal] also
the animal that is clever beyond human knowledge and wages a struggle against   26
the god of the holy grove. [With reference to Gen. 3:14-19:] The first thing the
god is intent on doing in intervening against the human couple is to cast an effec-
tive spell to disrupt the alliance that he discovers they have with this animal in
opposing him."

bear his boundary leads him astray; the serpent, one of God's creatures, even becomes an instrument of evil.

¶How does this come about? To this question the Bible gives no answer, or at any rate no unequivocal or direct answer, but only a peculiarly indirect one. Simply to blame the devil as God's enemy for bringing all this about would be to vulgarize and distort the biblical account completely. This is just what the Bible, for very definite reasons, does not say. Likewise to blame the freedom of human beings to do good or evil as something that human beings use only in the wrong way would be to misinterpret the context completely. The characteristic and essential thing about the biblical narrative by contrast is precisely that the whole course of events takes place in the world God has created and that no diaboli ex machina[4] are set in motion to make this incomprehensible event understandable or to dramatize it.

¶The *twilight* [Zwielicht][5] in which what has been created and what is evil appear here cannot in any way be made an unmixed light without destroying something that is decisive. The ambiguity of the serpent, of Eve, and of the tree of knowledge as creatures of God's grace and yet as the place where the voice of evil is heard must be preserved as such; it must on no account be crudely simplified and its two aspects be torn apart to make it unambiguous. For precisely this twilight, this ambiguity, in which the creation here stands constitutes the only possible way for human beings in the middle to speak about this event — and the Yahwist too was a human being in the middle. Only in this way is it possible to maintain two complementary concerns: truly to lay all the guilt on human beings and at the same time to express how inconceivable, inexplicable, and inexcusable that guilt is.

[4.] Literally, "devils out of the machine." This is an expression of Bonhoeffer's formulated by analogy with *deus ex machina* ("the god from the machine"). The latter term refers to the figure in the theater of classical antiquity who appeared suddenly with the aid of a mechanical contrivance and solved problems by means of a "supernatural" miracle.

[5.] The German word *Zwielicht* means "twilight," the half-light between day and night. But *Zwie-*, like "twi-" in "twilight," is a prefix that literally means "two," and Bonhoeffer uses the word in the sense of a mixture of light from different sources, as when artificial light is switched on in the streets at twilight. The point here is the ambiguous nature of such a dual or double light. See also note 12 below. And cf. above the use of *das Zwiefache* and *Zwiespalt*, pages 87–89. [DSB]

¶The Bible does not seek to impart information about the origin of evil[6] but to witness to its character as guilt and as the unending burden that humankind bears. To pose the question about the origin of evil as something separate from this is far from the mind of the biblical author. Yet when the question is posed in the way that the biblical author poses it, the answer cannot be unequivocal or direct. It will always contain two sides [das Doppelte]: that I as a creature of God have done what is completely opposed to God and is evil, and that just for that very reason this constitutes guilt and indeed inexcusable guilt. It will therefore never be possible simply to blame the devil who has led one astray; instead this same devil will always be precisely in the place where I, as God's creature in God's world, ought to have been living and did not wish to live. It is, of course, just as impossible to accuse creation of being imperfect and to blame it for my evil.[7] The guilt is mine alone: I have committed evil in the midst of the original state of creation. The complete incomprehensibility of this act is expressed in Genesis 3 by the fact that an evil force does not suddenly and manifestly break its way into creation from somewhere or other; instead this evil is completely veiled in the world of creation, and it takes place in creation through humankind. If an account of the fall of Lucifer had preceded this, as Catholic theology and as Luther too would have it,[8] then Adam, as the first human being to fall victim to this Lucifer, would in principle be exonerated. But it is precisely in accord with the completely down-to-earth nature of the biblical account that what prepares the way for the fall and the fall itself take place in the midst of what has been created, and in this way the fall's complete inexcusability is expressed as plainly as possible.

"The serpent was more cunning than all the animals in the field." The text does not state simply that the serpent is the devil. The serpent is a creature of God, but it is more cunning than all the others. Nowhere in

98

[6.] (Only) *FL* reads, "that is speculation" (55).

[7.] *HP* reads, "Precisely because evil happens in paradise, the guilt of God's creature is inexplicable" (45). Cf. *UK* (33).

[8.] In Bernhard Bartmann's *Dogmatik*, "Sect. 71. The Fall of the Angels. The Devils," 275–79, precedes "Sect. 72. The Creation of Humankind," 280–83. 275: "This Satan [who appears in the Old Testament] may well be the *snake in Paradise*." Luther, in the Stiasny ed., 53: "But on which day the fall of the angels happened, whether on the second or the third day of creation, is uncertain." Luther refers to Luke 10:18.

the entire story is the devil introduced in bodily form.[9] And yet evil takes place; it takes place through humankind, through the serpent, through the tree. At first it is only God's word itself that is taken up again. The serpent asks: Did God really say, You shall not eat from every kind of tree in the garden? It does not dispute this word, but opens the eyes of the human being to a depth of which the human being has until now been unaware, a depth from which one would be in a position to establish or to dispute whether a word is God's word or not. The serpent itself at first only poses the possibility that perhaps the human being has in this regard misheard, as God could not possibly have meant it in that way. God, the good Creator, would surely not impose something like that on God's own creature; that would surely be to limit God's love.

99 ¶The decisive point is that through this question the idea is suggested to the human being of going behind the word of God and now providing it with a human basis — a human understanding of the essential nature of God. Should the word contradict this understanding, then the human being has clearly misheard. After all, it could only serve God's cause if one put an end to such false words of God, such a mistakenly heard command, in good time.

¶The question is thus one that is put by a forked tongue, for it plainly wants to be thought of as coming from God's side. For the sake of the true God, so it appears, it wants to cause the given word of God to fall [zu Fall bringen]. In this way the serpent purports somehow to know about the depths of the true God beyond this given word of God — about the true God who is so badly misrepresented in this human word. The serpent claims to know more about God than the human being who depends on God's word alone. The serpent knows of a more exalted God, a nobler God, who has no need to make such a prohibition. It wants to be somehow itself the dark root from which the visible tree of God then first stems. And from this strongly held position the serpent now fights against the word of God. It knows that it has power only where it purports to come from God and to represent God's cause. Only as the pious serpent is it evil. In posing its question it derives its existence from the power of God alone, and it is able to be evil only where it

---

[9.] "In bodily form" translates "*in seiner Leibhaftigkeit.*" In German "*der Leibhaftige*" is an expression that means "the devil incarnate" but avoids using the word "devil." [DSB]

is pious. So now it purports to be the power that stands behind God's word and from which God then draws God's own power.

¶The question that the serpent posed was a perfectly pious one. But with the first pious question in the world, evil appears on the scene. Where evil shows itself in its godlessness, it is altogether powerless; at that point it is just a bogeyman [Kinderschrecken], something we have no need to be afraid of. Indeed evil does not concentrate its power at that point at all; instead it there most often diverts attention away from the other place where it really wishes to break through. And in this latter place it is veiled in the garb of piety. The wolf in sheep's clothing, Satan in the form of an angel of light[10] — that is the figure that is in keeping with evil. Did God really say . . . ? — that is the utterly godless question.[11] Did God really say that God is love, that God wishes to forgive us our sins, that we need only believe God, that we need no works, that Christ died and was raised for our sakes, that we will have eternal life in the kingdom of God, that we are no longer alone but upheld by God's grace, that one day all grieving and wailing shall come to an end? Did God really say: You shall not steal, you shall not commit adultery, you shall not bear false witness. . . . ? Did God really say this to me? Or does it perhaps not apply to me in particular? Did God really claim to be a God of wrath toward those who do not keep God's commandments? Did God really demand the sacrifice of Christ — the God whom I know better, the God whom I know to be the infinitely good, all-loving Father? This is the question that appears so innocuous but through which evil wins its power in us and through which we become disobedient to God. Were the question to come to us with its godlessness unveiled and laid bare, we would be able to resist it. But Christians are not open to attack in that way; one must actually approach them with God, one must show them a better, a prouder, God than they seem to have, if they are to fall.

¶What is the real evil in this question? It is not that a question as such is asked. It is that this question already contains the wrong answer. It is

100

[10.] *UK* reads, "The snake is 'the wolf in sheep's clothing' [cf. Matt. 7:15], 'Satan in the cloak of an angel' (2 Corinthians 11)" (34). Cf. 2 Cor. 11:14: "Satan disguises himself as an angel of light."

[11.] Bonhoeffer uses this text to great effect in his address on "The Church and the Peoples of the World," which he delivered at the crucial Life and Work ecumenical conference at Fanø, Denmark, in September 1934 (*NRS* 289-90) [*DBW* 13:298-99]. It was at this conference that the ecumenical movement aligned itself with the Confessing Church in Germany, even if only for the moment. [JDEG]

that with this question the basic attitude of the creature toward the Creator comes under attack.[12] It requires humankind to sit in judgment on God's word instead of simply listening to it and doing it. And this is achieved by proposing that, on the basis of an idea, a principle, or some prior knowledge about God, humankind should now pass judgment on the concrete word of God.[13] But where human beings use a principle, an idea of God, as a weapon to fight against the concrete word of God, there they are from the outset already in the right; at that point they have become God's master, they have left the path of obedience, they have withdrawn from being addressed by God. In other words, in this question what is possible is played off against reality [Wirklichkeit], and what

---

[12.] *HP* at the end of the tenth lecture says, "The creature is expected to go back behind the creation. That is what is evil about the question" (47). The eleventh lecture period was dated Jan. 31, 1933. (On Monday, Jan. 30, 1933, the President of the Reich, Paul von Hindenburg — who died in 1934 — appointed Adolf Hitler Chancellor of the Reich.) At the beginning of this eleventh lecture *HP* has, "The twilight [*Zwielicht*, see above, editorial note 5], the light of Lucifer and the light of the creation. In this twilight the fall takes place. The snake speaks wholly out of this twilight" (47); "The 'really' brings on the dual light" (48). *UK* (34) and *FL* (58) read much the same; the latter also records the meaning of the word 'Lucifer' as "Light-bearer." See below, page 140.

[13.] German idealism, as expressed by Johann Gottlieb Fichte and Georg Wilhelm Friedrich Hegel, postulated the idea of an eternal gospel in which Christ was an *Idee*. As such the gospel needed to become concrete repeatedly in the present, and this meant that its content changed. Karl Barth opposed idealism, insisting that *the* event of the gospel was Jesus Christ "once for all." See, for example, Barth's 1929 address on "Fate and Idea in Theology," with which Bonhoeffer would have been familiar. While the gospel had to be preached concretely in each contemporary situation, the historical context did not determine its content. Bonhoeffer followed Barth in this regard, but went even further in his insistence on the concreteness of Christian proclamation. In his lectures on Christology he rejected the idea of Christ as "timeless truth" or a "universally available idea" and spoke instead of Christ "as Word . . . spoken in the concrete moment" (*CC* 50). Likewise in July 1932, in his address to a Youth Peace Conference in Czechoslovakia on "A Theological Basis for the World Alliance," he rejected the notion of the church preaching "timeless principles" and spoke of the need to declare the word of God with the authority of Christ "here and now, in the most concrete way possible" (*NRS* 162) [*DBW* 11:332]. This conviction was repeatedly affirmed through Bonhoeffer's involvement in the church struggle against Nazism and against those among "the pious" who, under the influence of Fichte and Hegel, relativized the claims of the gospel vis-à-vis Nazism. See John de Gruchy, ed. *Dietrich Bonhoeffer: Witness to Jesus Christ*, 13–24. [JDEG]

is possible undermines what is reality. In the relation of human beings to God, however, there are no possibilities: there is only reality.[14] There is no "let me first . . . ";[15] there is only the commandment and obedience.

For the first human being, who lives entirely within this reality, being addressed with regard to what might be possible — namely, to disobey the word of God — is equivalent to being addressed with regard to freedom, the freedom in which that human being belongs wholly to God. The first human being can be addressed in this way only when this possibility of disobeying God is veiled in the reality of 'being for God'. It is only because the question is asked in a such way that Adam understands it as a new possibility of 'being for God' that it can lead him to 'being against God'. The possibility of Adam's *own* 'wanting-to-be-for-God', as Adam's own discovery, is the primal evil in the pious question of the serpent.

¶It is not a piece of stupidity but the very pinnacle of the serpent's cunning that the serpent so crudely exaggerates when it asks the question: "Did God really say — 'You shall not eat from every kind of tree in the garden'?" In this way the serpent has Eve on its side from the outset and compels her to acknowledge . . . No, God naturally did not say that. And already this reaction, in which Eve is made to qualify something with regard to a word of God — even though it has been misconstrued to her — must throw her into the greatest confusion. Indeed it must make her aware, for the first time, of the fascination of passing judgment on the word of God. By means of what is obviously false the serpent will now also bring about the downfall of what is right. May we be on our guard against such cunning exaggerations of God's commandment. 102 Evil[16] is certainly at work in them.

The serpent's question, then, proves to be *the* satanic question κατ'

[14.] (Only) *FL* has, "Possibility [is] no mode of reality" (57). Bonhoeffer decisively banishes the category of "possibility" from theological thought, e.g., in his inaugural lecture on July 31, 1930, "Man [*sic*] in Contemporary Philosophy and Theology," *NRS* 64–65, 69 (*DBW* 10:373, 378 [*GS* 3:78 and 84]). Cf. *AB* (*DBWE* 2): "The question about the possibility of faith can only be answered through its reality" (133). In *AB* the category of 'possibility' from idealist philosophy is countered by the theological category of 'eschatological possibility': "to-let-oneself-be-defined by means of the future" (159). "Reality" was also to become a key concept in Bonhoeffer's *Ethics*. [JDEG]

[15.] Luke 9:61.

[16.] *FL* has "Evil itself. . . " (59). The 1933 edition has "the Evil One."

ἐξοχήν, *the* question that robs God of God's honor and seeks to lead human beings astray from the word of God. Against this question, which under the appearance of being pious attacks God as the ultimate presupposition of all existence, human beings can defend themselves in no other way than with an ἄπαγε Σατανᾶς.[17]

¶Eve's answer remains on the level of ignorance. She does not know about evil; she does not recognize it. Therefore all she is able to do is to repeat the given commandment and state it correctly. And that is a great deal: she holds fast to the commandment. But in doing this she allows herself to become involved in this clever conversation. It has somehow struck a spark within her. The old order still remains intact, however. Humankind cannot go behind God's word. The tree of knowledge and the tree of life remain untouched.

[17.] "Lead away, Satan." Cf. ὕπαγε, σατανᾶ in Matt. 4:10: "Begone, Satan" according to *LB*. The Greek in Matt. 4:10 occurs also in Matt. 16:23 and Mark 8:33. [Bonhoeffer clearly meant to quote the expression as it occurs in these passages from Matthew and Mark; he either misquoted the Greek or, much more likely, his manuscript was miscopied here.] [DSB]

Sicut Deus[1]

And the serpent said to the woman: You will not die at all. Instead God
knows that on the day you eat from it your eyes will be opened, and you will
be like God and know what good and evil is.

THE FIRST PART of the conversation is over. But Eve's answer does not forbid the serpent from trying again. So the conversation continues — the first conversation *about* God, the first religious, theological conversation.[2] It is not common worship, a common calling upon God, but a speaking about God, about God in a way that passes over, and reaches beyond, God. Inasmuch as Eve has let herself become involved in this

---

[1.] "Like God." Karl Barth speaks of "that passionate desire: *Eritis sicut deus!*" in *The Epistle to the Romans*, 236 passim.

[2.] Cf. Karl Barth, *The Epistle to the Romans*: "*Eve* — and we must honour her as the first 'religious personality'. . ." (247). [Cf. also Bonhoeffer's *Ethics*: "The knowledge of good and evil seems to be the goal of all ethical reflection. The first task of Christian ethics is to invalidate this knowledge. . . . Already in the possibility of the knowledge of good and evil Christian ethics discerns a falling away from the origin. Humankind at its origin knows only one thing: God. . . . The knowledge of good and evil indicates something as having preceded it: the separation [*Entzweiung*] of humankind from its origin. In the knowledge of good and evil humankind does not understand itself in the reality of the particular character received from its origin, but instead in terms of its own possibilities, its possibility of being good or evil. It knows itself now as something apart from God, something outside of God. . . . The knowledge of good and evil thus involves being separated [*Entzweiung*] from God. Humankind knows about good and evil only in opposition to God" (17–18, cf. 29 [*DBW* 6:301–2]).] [Trans. altered DSB]

conversation, the serpent can now risk the real attack. It speaks about God, speaks indeed with the attitude of having a deep knowledge of the secrets of God; that is, it speaks in a pious way. This mask of piety, however, is now taken off in an open attack. *Did* God really say. . . ? Yes, God *did* say. . . . But *why* did God say it. . . ? That is how the conversation proceeds. God said it out of envy. . . . God is not a good but an evil, cruel God; be clever, be cleverer than your God and take what God begrudges you. . . . God did say it, yes indeed, you are right, Eve, but God lied; God's word is a lie . . . for you will not die at all. . . . That is the ultimate possible rebellion, that the lie portrays the truth as a lie. That is the abyss that underlies the lie — that it lives because it poses as the truth[3] and condemns the truth as a lie. "You will not die at all. Instead God knows that on the day you eat from it your eyes will be opened, and you will be like God and know what good and evil is."

¶It had been the very Creator who had said that this tree would impart knowledge; the only difference is that the Creator had decreed death for this deed, whereas the serpent links it with the promise of being-*sicut-deus*. And to anticipate something that is to be spelled out only later: for humankind to become-sicut-deus as the serpent promises can mean nothing but what the Creator calls death. It is true that humankind becomes sicut deus through the fall; but human beings who are sicut deus human beings can no longer live — they are in a state of death. That means that the serpent, in all its attempt to pretend that God's truth is a lie, can never escape this truth. On the contrary, even in its lie the serpent *must* grant that this truth is valid; the serpent too speaks of the death of humankind, but only in another form. But more on this later.[4]

We stand here at the last point to which the biblical author brings humankind, before the abyss comes and the inconceivable, infinite chasm opens up. The chain of events — a chain that starts with God's prohibition, continues with the creation of the woman and goes on to the serpent's question, events that link up together in the struggle against the tree of life — here reaches its end. In what does this final step toward the inconceivable consist? For at this point we need to state once more[5] that it can in no way lead to what is conceivable but strictly and

---

[3.] Cf. Friedrich Gogarten, *Politische Ethik*: "A lie always has only a stolen existence: it steals existence for itself from the truth" (42).

[4.] See below, page 135.

[5.] Cf. above, page 95.

only toward the inconceivable. This very step has to leave the inconceivable wholly inconceivable and unpardonable.

"You will not die at all." "You shall die." These two statements mark the cleavage that now splits the world apart for Adam. Statement stands against statement. This goes beyond his power of comprehension; for how is he to know what a lie is? Truth against truth — God's truth against the serpent's truth. God's truth tied to the prohibition, the serpent's truth tied to the promise, God's truth pointing to my limit, the serpent's truth pointing to my unlimitedness — both of them truth, that is, both originating with God, God against God. And this second god is likewise the god of the promise to humankind to be sicut deus. God against humankind sicut deus; God and humankind in the imago dei versus God and humankind sicut deus. Imago dei — humankind in the image of God in being for God and the neighbor, in its original creatureliness and limitedness; sicut deus — humankind like God in knowing out of its own self about good and evil, in having no limit and acting out of its own resources, in its aseity,[6] in its being alone. Imago dei — bound to the word of the Creator and deriving life from the Creator; sicut deus — bound to the depths of its own knowledge of God, of[7] good and evil. Imago dei — the creature living in the unity of obedience; sicut deus — the creator-human-being who lives on the basis of the divide [Zwiespalt] between good and evil. Imago dei, sicut deus, agnus dei[8] — the human being who is God incarnate, who was sacrificed for humankind sicut deus, in true divinity slaying its false divinity and restoring the imago dei.

105

How can Adam understand the serpent's sicut-deus-promise? At any rate not as the diabolical promise of death and of rebellion against the Creator. As one who is altogether ignorant of the possibility of evil he can understand the promise in no other way than as the possibility of being more pious, more obedient, than he is in his imago-dei-structure. Sicut deus — for Adam that can only be a new possibility within the given possibility of being a creature in the imago dei. It can only mean a new, deeper kind of creaturely being. *That* is how he is bound to understand the serpent.

¶To be sure, Adam sees that the new, deeper kind of creatureliness

---

[6.] "Underived being."
[7.] The 1933 edition reads "in."
[8.] "Lamb of God."

must be won at the cost of transgressing the commandment. And this very fact must focus his attention. Adam is in fact *between* God and God, or better, between God and a false god [Götze],[9] in a situation in which the false god portrays itself as the true God. But what else does the false god represent to Adam but the primordial possibility[10] for creaturely being? What else can the false god do but merely point out Adam's dependence upon the Creator and usher Adam anew into it? What can this promise — that being-sicut-deus will be a deeper kind of being-for-God — accomplish other than to enable Adam to hold fast to the given reality of the Creator and the Creator's word all the more firmly? What can the false god be to him other than the final and the most profound pointer to the only true word of God, to God the Creator? What is the false god to Adam other than the ultimate grace with which God binds humankind to God? What else is the pious conversation of Eve with the snake but the final sealing of the right that the Creator alone has over humankind? How then can Eve's answer be anything else but praise for the incomparable, incomprehensible grace of the Creator, praise that now breaks out from the *ultimate* depth of her creatureliness and her freedom for God and the neighbor?

106

[9.] "False god" or "idol"; Bonhoeffer means both at the same time. [DSB]

[10.] The German text reads *Unmöglichkeit*, "impossibility," but this hardly makes sense in the context. Ilse Tödt has suggested that it makes more sense if one reads *Urmöglichkeit*, "primordial possibility," i.e., that Bonhoeffer's manuscript may well have been miscopied here. [DSB]

THE FALL

And the woman saw that it would be good to eat from the tree and that it   107
was beautiful to look at, and that it was an enjoyable [lustiger][1] tree to be
desired because it would make one wise, and she took of its fruit and ate
and also gave of it to her husband [Mann], and he ate.

INSTEAD OF ANY REPLY, instead of any further theological discussion with
the serpent, what now follows is — the deed. We ask, what has happened?
In the first place what has happened is that the center has been intruded
upon, the boundary has been transgressed. Now humankind stands in
the middle, with no limit. Standing in the middle means living from its
own resources and no longer from the center. Having no limit means
being alone. To be in the center and to be alone means to be sicut deus.
Humankind is now sicut deus. It now lives out of its own resources,
creates its own life, is its own creator; it no longer needs the Creator, it
has itself become creator, inasmuch as it creates its own life. Thereby its
creatureliness is eliminated, destroyed. Adam is no longer a creature.
Adam has torn himself away from his creatureliness. Adam *is* sicut deus,
and this "is" is meant with complete seriousness — not that Adam feels
this, but that Adam is this. Losing *the limit* Adam has lost *creatureliness*.
Adam as limitless or boundless [Der grenzenlose Adam] can no longer
be addressed with regard to Adam's creatureliness.

¶This faces us with a fact that is central: creatureliness and the fall are

---

[1.] Luther's translation. The word *lustig* is derived from *Lust*, which means
"pleasure, joy, delight, desire" and sometimes "lust," but itself means "enjoyable,
amusing, merry, jolly, happy, funny, fun." [DSB]

not related to each other as if the fall were a creaturely act that could not abolish creatureliness but at most merely modify it or make it less good [deteriorisieren].[2] On the contrary, the fall *really* makes the creature — humankind in the imago dei — into a creator-sicut-deus. In the first place, then, the right to address humankind sicut deus with regard to creatureliness no longer exists. Moreover it is no longer possible to recognize such human beings in their creatureliness, just because of their being sicut deus. From now on no human assertion can be made about human beings that fails to bear in mind, and to take into specific account, their being sicut deus. The reason for this is that such an assertion would have to come from beyond humankind; but humankind in its unlimitedness allows no such beyond out of which anything could be stated about it. Humankind's being sicut deus after all *includes* precisely its not wanting to be a creature. God alone can address humankind in a different way; that is, God alone can address humankind with regard to its creatureliness that can never be abrogated. And God does that in Jesus Christ, in the cross, in the church. Only as the truth that is spoken by God, and that we believe in for God's sake despite all our knowledge of reality, does God speak of the creatureliness of humankind.[3]

In what does humankind's being sicut deus consist? It consists in its own attempt to be for God, to have access to a new way of 'being-for-God', that is, in a special way of being pious.[4] Indeed this piety was supposed to consist in humankind's going back behind the given word of God to procure its own knowledge of God. This possibility of a knowledge of God that comes from beyond the given word of God is humankind's being sicut deus; for from where can it gain this knowledge if not from the springs of its own life and being? Thus for their knowledge of God human beings renounce the word of God that approaches

[2.] From the Latin *deterior,* "less good, inferior." Cf. Adolf von Harnack, *History of Dogma,* concerning the doctrine of original sin in Thomas and Duns Scotus (6:297–305). Bernhard Bartmann, *Dogmatik,* begins "Section 80. Consequences of Original Sin" with the thesis: "Through original sin humankind have deteriorated in body and soul" (312). At the beginning of his exposition he cites the definition of Trent (Council of Trent 1545–1563) "'that the whole Adam . . . *secundum corpus et animam in deterius commutatum fuisse'*" ("experienced a deterioration in body and soul").

[3.] End of the eleventh lecture period. *HP* dates the twelfth Feb. 7, 1933 (53).

[4.] *HP* reads, "[Humankind *sicut deus*] believes that it has discovered a new way of being pious, being obedient, one that is contrary to the commandment of the revealed God and in accordance with the hidden God" (53).

them again and again out of the inviolable center and boundary of life; they renounce the life that comes from this word and grab it for themselves. They themselves stand in the center. This is disobedience in the semblance of obedience, the desire to rule in the semblance of service, the will to be creator in the semblance of being a creature, being dead in the semblance of life.[5]

How have things come to such a state? We shall answer this question biblically, in the following way. First, we shall once again indicate the chain of events that is now in retrospect to be understood as leading up to the deed. Second, we shall point to the infinite chasm that lies between the end of this chain of events and the deed itself. And, third, we shall correct the question itself by extricating the theological question from the speculative one and answering it.

1. It is in principle never wrong to recall the chain of events that have preceded an evil deed. Everything depends, however, on never making the chain of events itself responsible for the deed, extending it no further than the point where the chasm opens, where it becomes completely incomprehensible how the evil could have been done. Only by way of showing this incomprehensibility may the deed be retrospectively related to the chain of events preceding it. At the beginning of this particular chain of events stands the prohibition that is laid upon Adam. It points out to Adam his creatureliness and his freedom, which can be understood only as a freedom for God. Thus this very prohibition could only have made the grace of the Creator all the more apparent to Adam. But being addressed in this way with regard to his creatureliness and his freedom made the distance between the Creator and the creature all the more evident and so also had to emphasize the creature's distinct existence.

¶Adam's awareness of his own distinct being is then enormously intensified by the creation of woman from Adam's rib.[6] The boundary within which Adam lives has now taken on bodily form. To be sure, Adam

---

[5.] *FL* reads, "to be *sicut deus* = to be dead" (65), and comments: "Proof?" *HP* (53) and *UK* (37) also make the equation, from which it follows that in Gen. 2:17 God did not state what was untrue. Hans Schmidt is able to think of the god of this narrative — who for Schmidt is Baal — as "consciously stating what is untrue; for the snake is quite right: the word 'on the day on which you eat from the tree, you must die,' is not true. For it is not fulfilled" (30).

[6.] The creation of the woman follows as a second "stage" after the prohibition given to Adam, according to *UK* (37) and *HP* (54).

loves this form of limit that the other, different person now constitutes; Adam also knows a piece of himself to be in it, however, so that the boundary in this bodily form alerts Adam to what Adam can rightfully claim as his own and so, in turn, to his own being.

110   ¶Humankind's limit has drawn nearer, but for that reason has become all the more sharply defined. But this very revelation of the limit in bodily form, in the love he has for the other person, would have brought Adam an ever deeper knowledge of the grace of the Creator. With the creation of woman, humankind's limit has advanced into the midst of the created world. This, to be sure, did not increase the danger of transgressing against the limit; on the contrary it lessened it, for Adam would now be obliged to worship God as his only Creator all the more fervently. Nevertheless it is clear that if between the creature and the Creator the boundary were to be transgressed, then this would coincide with the transgression of the boundary within creation. Every transgression of the boundary would at the same time injure the creatureliness of the other person. Violating the tree of life would at the same time violate the other person. But how can one speak of danger at the point where an unbroken unity of obedience would make impossible any idea that the given limit could be transgressed and where the limit was known only as grace?

To this must now be added a final point.[7] It was pointed out to the human beings that their obedience and the object of that obedience were two very different things, and that they would be under no necessity at all to let their obedience be determined by this particular object; their obedience to God would not have to consist in refraining from eating the fruit. This means that they are now made particularly aware of their freedom in unbroken obedience as something *in addition to* their creatureliness; indeed their freedom is set over against their creatureliness as a second, different entity. Yet their freedom is made out to belong to their creatureliness, so that to exercise it would be nothing other than service, the service they owe God. At this point the human beings have an ultimately clear knowledge of themselves as they stand before God. We ask, once more: Why does the created world at this point not break out in rejoicing, thanks, and praise to the Creator of a kind that never ends and never wants to end? Why does this not mean new power for a new obedience?

[7.] *UK* reads, "3rd stage" (38); cf. *HP* (54).

Eve falls first. She falls as the weaker one, as the one who is partly   111
taken from the man. But there is no excuse for her fall; she is fully her
own person. Yet the culmination of the story is Adam's fall. Only when
Adam falls does Eve fall wholly, for the two are after all one. Adam falls
because of Eve, and Eve falls because of Adam; the two are one. They are
two and yet one also in their guilt. They fall together as one, yet each carries the whole burden of guilt alone. God created humankind as man
and woman — and humankind fell away from God as man and as woman.

How could it happen that Adam did not regard Eve's deed as a last
sign pointing to the one who created him? He was not even able to
understand what Eve had done. He was still only able to understand it as
another infinite reinforcement of the serpent's word that pointed out to
him his creatureliness and freedom for God. "And he ate."[8]

2. There are three things to establish. *First*, that the act was something
inconceivable and hence inexcusable. Nothing in the nature of
humankind or of creation or of the serpent can be uncovered as a basis
on which to explain this event. No theory of posse peccare or of non
posse peccare[9] is able to comprehend the fact that the deed was done.
Every attempt to make it understandable merely takes the form of an
accusation that the creature hurls against the Creator. *Second*, however,
from a human point of view this deed is final; it cannot be abrogated.
Otherwise Adam would be able to absolve himself from his guilt. Then
his guilt would not be guilt, and Christ would have died in vain.[10] *Third*,
this deed by human beings whom God created as male and female is a   112
deed done by humanity [der Menschheit]; no human being can absolve
himself or herself from it. The guiltiness of the deed becomes immeasurable inasmuch as no one commits the deed in isolation, but each

---

[8.] *HP* reads, "The chain of events ends with the statement, 'and Adam ate'"
(54–55). *UK* adds, "Wholly incomprehensible, contingent, irrational reality!"
(38). *FL* has the same (66).

[9.] "To be able to sin" and "not to be able to sin." The differentiation
between *posse peccare* or *posse non peccare* (as applying before the fall), *non posse
non peccare* (after the fall), and *non posse peccare* (the eschatological prospect) was
developed by Augustine in his dispute with Pelagius. Cf. Adolf von Harnack, *History of Dogma*, on Augustine (4:175–80). See also *AB* (*DBWE* 2):145–46.

[10.] Cf. Gal. 2:21. (Only) *FL* says "Luther: the fact that Christ has died per-
suades human beings that they are irredeemable" (66). The third point that now
follows is lacking in the student notes. Cf. the section "'Adam' as I and as
Humanity" in *AB* (*DBWE* 2):144–47 and *CS* 73–74 and 218–20 (*DBW* 1:71–72
and 241–46).

bears guilt for what the other has done. Adam falls through Eve, and Eve through Adam. This does not mean, however, that the other person thereby relieves me of my burden; instead I am infinitely burdened with the guilt of the other.

Because the fall of humankind is both inconceivable and finally inexcusable in God's creation, the word *disobedience* fails to describe the situation adequately. It is rebellion, the creature's stepping outside of the creature's only possible attitude, the creature's becoming creator, the destruction of creatureliness, a defection, a falling away [Sturzen] from being safely held as a creature. As such a defection it is a *continual* fall, a *dropping* into a bottomless abyss, a state of being let go, a process of moving further and further away, falling deeper and deeper. And in all this it is not merely a *moral lapse* but the destruction of creation by the creature. The extent of the fall is such that it affects the whole created world. From now on that world has been robbed of its creatureliness and drops blindly into infinite space, like a meteor that has torn itself away from the core to which it once belonged.[11] It is of this fallen-falling world that we must now speak.

3. The question why there is evil is not a theological question,[12] for it presupposes that it is possible to go back behind the existence that is laid upon us as sinners. If we could answer the question why, then *we* would not be sinners. We could blame something else. So the 'question why' can never be answered except by the statement 'that' which burdens humankind so completely.

113   The theological question is not a question about the origin of evil but one about the actual overcoming of evil on the cross; it seeks the real forgiveness of guilt and the reconciliation of the fallen world.

[11.] Cf. "The Madman" in Friedrich Nietzsche's *The Gay Science*: "Are we not continually plunging downward? And backward, sideways, forward, in all directions? Is there still any up or down? Do we not wander as though through an endless nothing? Do we not feel empty space breathing upon us?" (*The Portable Nietzsche*, 95). [trans. altered, DSB] In Bonhoeffer's copy, this passage is marked (*Werke*, Part 1, vol. 5, 163).

[12.] *HP* reads, "The Why is a speculative question" (55); cf. *UK* (39) and *FL* (70).

THE NEW THING

Then the eyes of them both were opened, and they became aware that they   114
were naked; and they sewed fig leaves together[1] and made themselves an
apron.[2]

"THE END OF GOD'S WAYS is bodily existence."[3] The text does not say:
Then they came to know and recognized what good and evil are; instead
it says: Then their *eyes* were opened and they saw that they were naked.
Are we really to understand from this that after all the whole story is
about the question of the origin of love between man and woman? That
eating from the tree of knowledge was the great, proud, liberating act of
humankind through which it won for itself the right to love and create
life? Was the knowledge of good and evil essentially the new knowledge
of the child who has become an adult?[4] Was Adam's only mistake in the

---

[1.] According to Kautzsch, 14. *LB* has "plaited figleaves. . . ."

[2.] *LB* and Kautzsch both read "aprons."

[3.] The often quoted words about "the end of God's ways/works" are to be
found in Friedrich Christoph Oetinger in several places, sometimes formulated
with "ways," sometimes with "works." (Oetinger was an eighteenth-century
theosophist in Württemberg.) See Elisabeth Zinn's doctoral dissertation that
appeared in 1932, *Die Theologie des Friedrich Christoph Oetinger:* "Bodily existence
[corporeality] is the end of God's ways" (177), and "Corporeality is the end of
God's works" (152). Cf. B. F. C. Oetinger, *Sämtliche Werke* (1:3, 27–28). Bonhoeffer's copy of Hans Lilje, *Das technische Zeitalter,* is marked where these words
are quoted (48). In the lecture course Bonhoeffer quoted these words here for
the second time, the first time being in the lecture on the creation of
humankind. See above, page 78, editorial note 17.

[4.] Hans Schmidt, 27, infers *inter alia* on the basis of Deut. 1:39 that a child

end that he did not rush immediately from the tree of knowledge to the tree of life to eat its fruit as well?

¶What is correct in all this is that what is essentially at issue here is the problem of sexuality.[5] The knowledge of good and evil is for Adam, who lives in unity, an impossible knowledge of duality, of the whole as torn apart. This duality is comprehensively expressed in the terms tob and ra,[6] or in our language pleasurable-good and painful-evil.[7] And precisely the fact that pleasurable and good are so closely related deprives the moralistic interpretation of any weight. In this split [gespaltenen], fallen world the pleasurable has in the end as much seriousness about it as the 'good', inasmuch as both alike have fallen out of their original unity. Both exist only in duality and find no way back to unity.

This breaking apart [Entzweiung] into tob and ra expresses itself first of all in Adam's relation to Eve. Eve, the other person, was the limit given to Adam in bodily form. He acknowledged this limit in love, that is, in the undivided unity of giving himself; he loved it precisely in its nature as a limit for him, that is, in Eve's being human and yet 'being another human being'. Now he has transgressed the boundary and come to know that he has a limit. Now he no longer accepts the limit as God the Creator's grace; instead he hates it as God begrudging him something as Creator. And in the same act of transgressing the boundary he has transgressed the limit that the other person represented to him in bodily form. Now he no longer sees the limit that the other person constitutes as grace but as God's wrath, God's hatred, God's begrudging. This means that the human being no longer regards the other person with love. Instead one person sees the other in terms of their being over against each other; each sees the other as divided from himself or herself. The limit is no longer grace that holds the human being in the unity of creaturely, free love; instead the limit is now the mark of dividedness. Man and woman are divided from each other.

"is not yet capable" of knowing about *tob* and *ra*, "because its senses have not yet been awakened." Cf. also the concluding section of *Act and Being*, "The Definition of Being in Christ by Means of the Future: The Child" (*DBWE* 2:157–61).

[5.] Cf. Hans Schmidt, according to whom "The knowledge at issue here is the awakening of the sexual sense, and in the opinion of the narrator it is that *alone* and nothing but that" (22). According to Schmidt, the god who appears in the story of the tree of knowledge is a fertility god (29).

[6.] See above, page 88 and editorial note 23.

[7.] *HP* (56) and *UK* (39) add "beautiful . . . ugly." *FL* also has "beautiful" (67).

¶This means two things. First it means that the man claims his share of the woman's body or, more generally, that one person claims a right to the other, claims to be entitled to possess the other, and thereby denies and destroys the creaturely nature of the other person. This obsessive desire [Sucht] of one human being for another finds its primordial expression in sexuality. The sexuality of the human being who transgresses his or her boundary is a refusal to recognize any limit at all; it is a boundless obsessive desire to be without any limits. Sexuality is a *passionate hatred* of any limit. It is extreme lack of respect for things-as-they-are [Unsachlichkeit];[8] it is self-will, an obsessive but powerless will for unity in a divided [entzweiten] world. It is obsessive because it knows of a common *human being*[9] from the beginning; it is powerless because in losing his or her limit a human being has finally lost the other person. Sexuality seeks to destroy the other person as a creature, robs the other person of his or her creatureliness, lays violent hands on the other person as one's limit, and hates grace.[10] By destroying the other person one seeks to preserve and reproduce one's own life. Human beings create by destroying; in sexuality the human race preserves itself while it destroys. Unbridled[11] sexuality is therefore destruction κατ᾽ ἐξοχήν; it is a mad acceleration of the fall, of the downward drop. It is affirming oneself to the point of self-destruction. Obsessive desire [Sucht] and hate, tob and ra — these are the fruits of the tree of knowledge.

From this dividedness, however, there now follows a second thing, humankind's covering itself up. Human beings with no limit, in their hatred and in their obsessive desire, do not show themselves in their

116

[8.] I.e., the opposite of *Sachlichkeit*, "respect for things as they are." [DSB]

[9.] The 1933 edition here erroneously reads, "for the sake of a common *human being*."

[10.] Concerning the terms "destruction" and "hatred" cf. Nietzsche's "definition of love," "the only definition worthy of a philosopher," in *Ecce Homo*: "Love — in its means, war; at bottom, the deadly hatred of the sexes" (267).

[11.] The 1933 edition reads, "Unbridled like uncreative [*wie unschöpferische*] sexuality." The additional words contradict the context and are possibly a misreading of "merely selfish" [*nur ichsüchtige*]. Cf. *CS* (*DBW* 1), which speaks of sin as the will "to affirm only oneself [*nur sich selbst*]" (248); cf. also *AB* (*DBWE* 2), which refers to Luther's definition of "sin as egocentricity [*Ichsucht*]" (147). Cf. Bonhoeffer's "The Theology of Crisis," where he likens such egocentricity to "the theological insight of the Reformers, which they expressed in terms of the *cor curvum in se, corrupti mentis*," in which human beings "are their own creator and lord, . . . indeed the center of their world of sin" (122).

nakedness. Nakedness is the essence of unity, of not being torn apart, of being for the other, of respect for what is given, of acknowledging the rights of the other as my limit and as a creature. Nakedness is the essence of being oblivious of the possibility of robbing others of their rights. Nakedness is revelation; nakedness believes in grace. Nakedness does not know it is naked, just as the eye does not see itself or know about itself. Nakedness is innocence.

¶Covering oneself up is the essence of a world split into tob and ra; hence in the world of tob and ra even revelation must veil itself. It is therefore a most profoundly contradictory state of affairs that human beings who are rid of all limits are, after all, compelled to point out their limit without wanting to do so, inasmuch as they cover themselves up and feel shame. In their shame human beings acknowledge their limit. This is the peculiar dialectical nature of a world that is torn apart, that human beings live in it without a limit, and so as one, yet always with hatred against the limit, and so as divided, and are ashamed in their nakedness. The shame of human beings is an unwilling pointer to revelation, to the limit, to the other, to God. For that reason the persistence of shame in the fallen world constitutes the only — even though an extremely contradictory — possibility of a sign pointing to original nakedness and the sanctity of this nakedness. This is not because shame in itself is something good — that is the moralistic, puritanical, and totally unbiblical interpretation[12] — but because it is compelled to give unwilling witness to the fallen state of the ashamed.[13]

That church dogmatics has sometimes seen the essence of original sin in sexuality[14] is not as absurd as Protestants have often declared on the

117

[12.] This opposes such interpretations as that of Hermann Gunkel, *Urgeschichte*: "Only one must not here suppose that there is a connection between sin and the *feeling of shame* [*Schamgefühl*] between the sexes; after all everyone who observes children knows that bashfulness [*Schamhaftigkeit*] is a virtue and in no way a consequence of sin" (61).

[13.] Hans Schmidt, 22, sees in the statement that the human beings "now sew large leaves together and make loincloths that each fastens around the body" an "artistic stroke" which simply emphasizes the awakening of the sexual sense. At this point the twelfth lecture period ended. *HP* dated the thirteenth period Feb. 14, 1933 (58).

[14.] See the overview of doctrinal statements in Bernhard Bartmann, *Dogmatik* (vol. 1, sect. 79, "The Transmission of Original Sin by Procreation," 310–12), to which Bonhoeffer referred in *CS* (*DBW* 1):244–45, note 4. (Only) *FL* adds "Augustine / original sin sexuality" (69). Hans Schmidt finds in the

basis of a moralistic naturalism.[15] Knowing about tob and ra is not to begin with an abstract knowledge of ethical principles; on the contrary it starts out as sexuality, that is, as a perversion of the relation of one human being to another.[16] And as the essence of sexuality consists of creating in the midst of destroying, so the dark secret of the nature of humankind, essentially conditioned by original sin, is preserved from generation to generation in the course of continuing procreation.[17] The protest that appeals to the natural character of sexuality is unaware of the highly ambivalent character of every so-called 'natural' aspect of our world.[18] The way in which sexuality is sanctified is by being restrained by shame, that is, by being veiled, and by the calling [die Beru-

118

"Augustinian interpretation" that sees "sin in its primordial form as *concupiscentia* [sensual desire]," a disastrous misconstruing of what was originally intended in Genesis 3 (52).

[15.] Cf. Adolf von Harnack, *History of Dogma*, 5:219, note 1: "It is perhaps the worst, it is at any rate the most odious, consequence of Augustinianism, that the Christian religion in Catholicism is brought into particularly close relations to the sphere of sex." In Harnack's view, this was more dangerous, more poisonous than the "'ancient naturalism [*antike Naturalismus*]'" (220, note 1). Along this line Bonhoeffer already in *The Communion of the Saints* spoke of "the devastating effect" of this on the doctrine of original sin; see *CS* (*DBW* 1):224 (concerning Genesis 3), 242–43 (concerning Augustine). Bonhoeffer still was saying much the same in the summer of 1932 in his lectures "Das Wesen der Kirche"("On the essence of the church")(*DBW* 11:264, note 165 [*GS* 5:242]). The new understanding of "good and evil" in Gen. 2:17 that Bonhoeffer expounded in 1932–33, however, led him to another view.

[16.] *HP* sets the words, "*Sexuality: Perversion of the Relation of One Human Being to Another!*" prominently at the beginning of the thirteenth lecture (58). See below, page 171.

[17.] Cf. the description of "inheritance" in Hans Schmidt, who claimed that the deuteronomical history book knew of "the people's *bond of guilt* — certainly not in the sense of a purely natural inheritance that was handed on through the generations but nevertheless in the sense of a burden that was common to fathers and their children, to forefathers and the children of their children." Against this background "people read the story of the first parents as a story of the origin of 'inherited guilt' [*Erbschuld*]" (48–49).

[18.] Cf. Schmidt, "in its oldest meaning the story speaks in trembling awe of the holy secret of sexuality. As soon as God came to be conceived of wholly in the sense of the religion of Israel, and the titanic aspect of the activity of the primordial human being behavior was recast in terms of sin, naturalness was lost" (52) in speech about love. According to Schmidt, in Genesis 3 the concept of "sin" does not appear anywhere (49).

fung] of the community of marriage, which is under this restraint, to be in church. The deepest reason for this is that human beings have lost their creaturely nature; this has been corrupted by their being sicut deus. The whole created world is now covered in a veil; it is silent and lacking explanation, opaque and enigmatic. The world of human beings who are sicut deus is ashamed along with them and hides itself from their view.

THE FLIGHT

And they heard the steps of Yahweh God,[1] who was walking in the garden, for the day had turned cool. And Adam hid himself with his woman from the face of Yahweh God beneath the trees in the garden. And Yahweh God called Adam and said to him: Where are you? And he said: I heard the sound of your steps in the garden, and I was afraid, for I am naked, and so I hid myself. And God said: Who told you that you are naked? You have not eaten from the tree from which I commanded you – You shall not eat from it – have you? So Adam said: The woman whom you made my companion gave to me from the tree, and I ate. Then Yahweh God said to the woman: Why did you do this? The woman said: The serpent beguiled me; that is why I ate.

ADAM, AS ONE WHO KNOWS *tob* and *ra* and has fallen from unity into dividedness, can no longer stand before the Creator. Adam has transgressed the boundary, and now he hates his limit. Indeed Adam denies the limit, as one who is sicut deus — limitless, boundless [grenzenlos]. But just as Adam, in shame, against Adam's own will, has to acknowledge the other person, so against Adam's own will Adam admits to the Creator that Adam is fleeing from his Creator, hiding from God. Adam does not boldly confront God; instead when Adam hears God's voice, Adam hides. What a strange delusion of Adam's, both then and today, to

---

[1.] *LB* reads, ". . . heard the voice of God the LORD. . . ." *LB* reads "voice" and Kautzsch reads "walking" (14) wherever "steps" occurs in the text here translated. The third edition of Kautzsch's translation read, with the addition in brackets, "noise [of the steps]" ([1909] 1:11). Otherwise the text corresponds to *LB.*

suppose that one could hide from God — as though the world were opaque to God to the same extent that it appears veiled, hidden, and opaque to us after we have fallen out with it!

¶Humankind, which has fallen away from God in a precipitous plunge, now still flees from God. For humankind the fall is not enough; its flight cannot be fast enough. This flight, Adam's hiding away from God, we call conscience.[2] Before the fall there was no conscience. Only since humankind has become divided from the Creator are human beings divided within themselves. Indeed it is the function of conscience to make human beings flee from God and so admit against their own will that God is in the right; yet, conscience also lets human beings, in fleeing from God, feel secure in their hiding place. Thus humankind, instead of realizing that it really is in flight, is deluded by conscience into believing that its flight is a triumphal procession and that all the world is in flight before it. Conscience chases humankind away from God into its secure hiding place. Here, far away from God [in der Gottesferne],[3] humankind itself plays the role of being judge and in this way seeks to evade God's judgment. Humankind now lives truly out of the resources of its own good and evil, its own innermost dividedness from itself.[4] Conscience means feeling shame before God; at the same time one conceals one's own wickedness in shame, humankind in shame justifies itself — and yet, on the other hand, at the same time there is in shame an unintentional recognition of the other person. Conscience is not the voice of God within sinful human beings; instead it is precisely their defense against this voice. Yet precisely as a defense against this voice, conscience still points to it, in spite of all that human beings know and want.

Adam, where are you . . . ? This word of the Creator calls the fleeing Adam away from his conscience to stand before his Creator. Humankind is not permitted to remain alone in its sin; God speaks to Adam and halts him in his flight. Come out of your hiding place, out of your self-reproach, out of your cover-up, out of your secrecy, out of your self-

---

[2.] Cf. Bonhoeffer's view of conscience in *AB* (*DBWE* 2):138–43. Here Bonhoeffer opposed the idea of "Luther's religion as a religion of conscience," which Bonhoeffer saw represented by Karl Holl, Emanuel Hirsch, and Friedrich Brunstäd. [See also Bonhoeffer's discussion of conscience in *E* 242–47.] [JDEG]

[3.] *Gottesferne* is a term that Bonhoeffer later used in *[The Cost of] Discipleship*.

[4.] See above, pages 87–89.

torment, out of your vain remorse.[5] Confess who you are, do not lose yourself in religious despair, be yourself. Adam, where are you? Stand before your Creator. This challenge goes directly against the conscience.   121
The conscience says: Adam, you are naked, hide yourself from the Creator; you dare not stand before God. God says: Adam, stand before me. God slays the conscience. Adam in fleeing must realize that he cannot escape from his Creator. We have all had the dream in which we want to flee from something horrible and yet cannot flee from it. That dream is one that repeatedly rises up out of the subconscious as knowledge of this, the true situation of fallen humankind. The same thing is now expressed in Adam's answer: I am naked, and so I hid myself. Adam tries to excuse himself with something that accuses him. He tries to flee further and yet knows that he has already been apprehended. I am sinful, I cannot stand before you. As though one could use sin itself as an excuse — the inconceivable folly of humankind! Just because you are a sinner, stand before me and do not flee.

¶Adam, however, still fails to stand; instead he answers: The woman whom you made my companion gave to me from the tree, and I ate. He confesses his sin, but in the very act of confessing it he seeks to flee again. You gave me the woman, not I; I am not guilty, you are guilty. The ambiguous twilight [Zwielicht][6] of creation and sin is turned to account. The woman was after all your creature; it is your own work that brought about my fall. Why did you bring forth an imperfect creation? What can I do about it? So instead of standing before God, Adam falls back on the trick learned from the serpent of correcting what is in God's mind, of appealing from God the Creator to a better god, a different god.[7] That is, Adam tries once again to escape. The woman takes to flight with him, pointing, as she does so, to the serpent — which means that she actually points to the serpent's Creator. Adam has not come to stand before God;

[5.] Cf. *AB* (*DBWE* 2) "(*contritio activa!*)" (139); cf. *DBW* 9, where in a statement written in 1926 Bonhoeffer claims that Luther rejected the view that one "could squeeze contrition out of oneself" (367).

[6.] See above, page 104, editorial note 5.

[7.] According to the heretical teaching of Marcion, who was excommunicated by Rome in 144 C.E., the God to whom the New Testament witnesses could not be the same as the Creator of the world about whom the Old Testament speaks. Bonhoeffer's teacher Adolf von Harnack (1851–1930) in his 1921 book *Marcion* advanced the point of view that one could not learn what is Christian from the Old Testament (138). See below, pages 156–57.

he has not confessed. He has appealed to his conscience, to his knowledge of good and evil, and on the basis of this knowledge accused his
Creator. He has not recognized the grace of the Creator that shows itself
122   precisely in that God calls Adam and does not let him flee. Instead
Adam sees this grace only as hate, as wrath, a wrath that inflames his
own hate, his rebellion, his desire to get away from God. Adam keeps on
falling [bleibt im Fallen]. The fall drops with increasing speed for an
immeasurable distance.

CURSE AND PROMISE

Then Yahweh God said to the serpent: Because you have done this, cursed 123
are you among all cattle and among all animals in the wild. You shall
creep[1] upon your belly and eat the ground as long as you live. And I am
going to put enmity between you and the woman, and between your seed
and her seed. Her seed shall trample your head underfoot, and you will bite
him in the heel. And to the woman God said: I am going to bring upon you
much pain when you come to be with child; you shall bear children with
pain, and your desire shall be for your man, and he shall be your master.
And to Adam he said: Because you have listened to the voice of your woman
and have eaten from the tree about which I commanded you and said, You
shall not eat of it, cursed is the ground because of you; in toil[2] you shall
grow food on it for yourself all your life long. Thorns and thistles it shall
bear for you, and you shall eat the plants of the field. In the sweat of your
face you shall eat your bread, until you again become the dust[3] from which
you were taken. For you are dust, and dust you shall become.

WE DRAW NEAR TO THE END. God speaks to Adam, to fallen, unreconciled,
fleeing Adam, by way of curse and promise. Adam is upheld alive in a
world between curse and promise, and the last promise allows him to
return to the earth from which he was taken, allows him to die. Paradise

---

[1.] *LB* says, "Upon your belly shall you go."

[2.] *LB* says, *mit Kummer*, "with sorrow/trouble/worry."

[3.] *LB* says, "become earth . . . ," and "earth" instead of "dust," both here and
in the following sentence. Kautzsch translates the Hebrew word as "ground" or
"dust" (15). Otherwise Bonhoeffer's text mostly follows *LB*.

is destroyed. "Alas, alas, you have destroyed it, destroyed the beautiful world with a mighty fist [Faust]. It falls down, it collapses in ruin. . . . O mighty one among the sons of earth, build it again, more splendid than before; build it again in your heart!"[4] This is just what does not apply here. On the contrary, what is said to Adam is: You must now live in this destroyed world; you cannot escape from it. Live in it, between curse and promise.

¶The curse and the promise are proclaimed over Adam's life in his fallen state in terms of four great ideas: enmity with the serpent, the pain of childbirth, the toil of work, and death.[5] Curse and promise are applied with reference to the same thing. The curse is the Creator's affirmation of the world that has been destroyed. That humankind must live in the fallen world, that humankind gets what it wants, that as the being who is sicut deus it must live in its sicut deus world — that is the *curse*. That humankind *is allowed* to live in this world and that it will not be deprived of the word of God, even though that word be the word of the God of wrath, the God who expels, who pronounces a curse — that is the *promise*. Thus Adam lives between curse and promise.

Curse and promise are in the first place eternal enmity with the serpent, with the power of pious godlessness, in which humankind is placed. Humankind in the world that has been destroyed, humankind between God's curse and promise, is faced with temptation. It does not possess the word of God in peace and tranquillity; instead it hears that

---

[4.] *FL* (71) and *HP* (61) both read: "Faust I." Bonhoeffer's quotation is from Johann Wolfgang von Goethe's *Faust*, Part 1, verses 1607–11 and 1617–21 (178–79). [trans. DSB] In this passage, the words are sung by the choir of invisible spirits that accompanies Mephistopheles. Adolf von Harnack, *History of Dogma*, cites the verses beginning with "Alas! Alas!," omitting only the two verses beginning "O mighty one among the sons of earth" (1617–18), which Bonhoeffer here includes.

[5.] Bonhoeffer here seems on the verge of saying what some recent biblical scholars have argued, that God is not literally cursing Adam and Eve here, but announcing, proclaiming, declaring the consequence of what they have done. See, for example, Phyllis Trible, who has argued that "Though the tempter (the serpent) is cursed, the woman and the man are not. But they are judged, and the judgments are commentaries on the disastrous effects of their shared disobedience" ("Eve and Adam: Genesis 2–3 Reread," 80). As Gene Tucker concludes, "neither is cursed directly, but the circumstances of their lives bear the marks of disobedience, guilt and estrangement" ("The Creation and the Fall: A Reconsideration," 119). [JDEG]

word again and again in the distorted form of the pious question that misrepresents it. Humankind conducts itself not in peace but with enmity and struggle against God. In this fate under the curse, however, humankind is given the promise of victory, a victory that has to be fought for and has to be won again and again, but one in which it tramples the serpent's head underfoot. To be sure, this battle leaves humankind wounded, for the serpent, though defeated, still bites it in the heel. The battle for the word of God marks humankind with scars. Human beings are to be no superhuman heroes. Instead they are to be locked in dogged battle, knowing victory again and again but also being wounded again and again; that is how things are to be for every member of the human race. It is in this sort of battle, which humankind takes upon itself as curse and as promise and in which it fights to the end, that it is allowed to live.

The new thing[6] that the tree of knowledge brought upon Adam and Eve was shame and obsessive desire. The visible sign of this sundering [Entzweiung] of the original unity between man and woman, of the innermost rupture in the community between them, is the suffering that the woman bears as the fruit of the communion with the man that she so obsessively desired. Indissolubly united with the new thing, with the pleasure of obsessive desire, is pain. Tob and ra, the pleasurable and the painful, enter into human life like two siblings who belong together. The knowledge of pain increases pleasure, and the knowledge of pleasure increases pain. It is the woman's humiliation that she has to bear children with pain, that she is bound to desire the man yet has to serve him with pain. She has gotten her way; in being sicut deus she may belong to Adam. But this very belonging is now, at one and the same time, both curse and promise. Humankind must drink to the dregs its new sicut-deus knowledge of tob and ra. Inasmuch as humankind does that, however, it may live and indeed *does live* before God in the world that has been destroyed; it lives between God's curse and promise.

In its enmity with the serpent, humankind's *relationship with God* comes under the law of tob and ra, of curse and promise, and becomes divided. The fate pronounced on the woman embraces curse and promise, tob and ra, in the *community* of man and woman. Now, thirdly, the word directed to Adam proclaims the destruction and dividedness of the original relation between humankind and *nature* and the alienation

[6.] See above, page 121 (heading).

125

that takes its place. The arable ground [Der Acker] — for whose fruits Adam has until now needed only to stretch out his hand, the ground that provided what he needed — the soil [der Boden], the earth, the land is cursed on account of Adam's act.[7] It comes to mean for Adam worry, woe, toil, an enemy. The other created things rebel against humankind-sicut-deus, against the creature that thinks it can live out of its own resources. They exclude and withdraw from it; they become mute, enigmatic, and unfruitful. With the fall of humankind, however, they themselves, as creatures made subject to humankind, fall into dividedness as well; they become nature without a master and thus in rebellion and despair, nature under the curse, accursed ground. That is our earth. Cursed, it is cast out of the glory of its created state, out of the unambiguous immediacy of its speech and its praise of the Creator into the ambiguity of utter strangeness and enigma. The trees and the animals, which once immediately represented God's word as the Creator, now in often grotesque ways point instead as though to the incomprehensibility and arbitrariness of a despot who is hidden in darkness.

¶Thus the *work* that human beings do on the ground that is cursed comes to express fallen humankind's state of dividedness from nature; that is, work too falls under the curse. At the same time, however, it comes to express an obsessive [suchtige] nostalgia for the original unity; that is, work stands under the promise that humankind is still allowed to live alongside nature, from which it was taken and to which it belongs as a sibling. So the fruit of the field becomes both the bread that we eat with tears and yet at the same time the bread of grace of the one who upholds, who allows human beings to go on living on the accursed ground and remain true to their mother, the earth,[8] even though she stands under God's curse. Human beings at work live between curse and promise, between tob and ra, pleasure and pain, but they live before God the Creator.

[7.] Bonhoeffer echoes here the tradition of the "fall of nature" that can be found from Theophilus and John Chrysostom to Martin Luther, who wrote in his "Lectures on Genesis 1–5": "And what of thorns, thistles, water, fire, caterpillars, flies, fleas, and bedbugs? . . . The earth does not produce anything of this kind on its own, but because of Adam's sin. . . . Now the entire creation in all its parts reminds us of the curse that was inflicted because of sin" (*LW* 1:208–9, 204). [JDEG]

[8.] Cf. Bonhoeffer's 1929 essay, "Grundfragen einer christlichen Ethik" (Basic questions for a Christian ethic), *DBW* 10:345 (*GS* 5:179).

The world is changed and destroyed in that human beings in their dividedness can no longer live with God, with one another, and with nature; yet, in this dividedness between tob and ra, they also cannot live *without God*, without one another, and without nature. They do live in a world that is under a curse. Yet just because it is *God's* curse that oppresses it, the world is not wholly God-forsaken; instead it is a world that even under God's curse is blessed and in its enmity, pain, and work is pacified, a world where *life is upheld and preserved*.[9] Preserved for what? To what end? Verse 19 says it unmistakably: "until you again become the earth from which you were taken. For from earth you were taken, and earth you shall again become."[10] Fallen Adam lives on his way to death. His life is a life that is preserved on its way to death. Why? Because by eating the fruit of the tree of knowledge Adam as a human-being-sicut-deus has ingested [hineingegessen][11] death into himself. Adam is dead before he dies. The serpent was right: You will be like God; you will by no means die, that is, die the death that means ceasing to exist. But the Creator was also right: On the day that you eat from it you shall die, that is, die the death that means being sicut deus. Let us look closely into this extraordinary twilight: the serpent which brings about the fall of humankind with its lie is compelled to tell God's truth. Humankind-sicut-deus is dead, for it has cut itself off from the tree of life; it lives out of its own resources, yet it cannot live. It is compelled to live, yet it cannot live. That is what death means.

At this point, however, the enmity against the serpent, the painful community of man and woman, and the ground that is cursed turn into divine compassion for humankind in its inability to live in its state of disruption [Zwiespalt]. Human beings can live only when they are preserved in this state of disruption; but they live only on the way to death. They cannot escape from life. The final and most terrible of curses that

---

[9.] The verb *erhalten* means "to uphold" or "to preserve." While the former translation brings out Bonhoeffer's wordplay with "fall(en)," the latter has been used because it points toward Bonhoeffer's movement away from "orders of *creation*" (*Schöpfungsordnungen*) to what he called "orders of *preservation*" (*Erhaltungsordnungen*). [DSB]

[10.] Bonhoeffer here does not quote from his own version of the text at the top of the section (see above, page 131); instead he follows *LB* more closely. [DSB]

[11.] *HP* (64) and *FL* (73) agree here. The 1933 edition has *hineingenommen*, "included."

oppresses humankind is death, having to return to dust. Yet now death becomes for human beings, who live because they are preserved in compassion, a promise held out to them by the God of grace. Adam cannot but understand this death, this turning into dust, as the death of his present existence in death, his being *sicut deus.* The death of death — that is the promise this curse carries. Adam understands this death of death to mean sinking back into the nothingness out of which God created the world. To him the final promise is nothingness, nothingness as the death of death. For this reason Adam sees his life as preserved for nothingness. After all, how should Adam, who has fallen from faith, know that the real death of death is never nothingness but only the living God, indeed that there is no such thing as nothingness, that the promise of the death of death never means nothingness but only life, Christ himself? How should Adam know that, in this promise of death, already the end of death, the resurrection of the dead, was being spoken of? How could Adam hear announced already in the peace of death, and returning to mother earth, the peace that God wishes once more to conclude with the earth, the peace that God wishes to establish over a new and blessed earth in the world of the resurrection?[12]

[12.] *FL* adds, "peace in Jesus Christ" (73), as does *HP* (65) and *UK* (44).

THE MOTHER OF ALL
THAT LIVES[1]

And Adam called his woman [Weib] Eve,[2] because she is a mother of all   128
that lives.[3]

THERE IS WILD EXULTATION, defiance, audacity, and triumph when Adam
now gives to his woman, the very woman on whom this curse has fallen,
the name the mother of all that lives. It is as though, like Prometheus, he
boastfully insists on his claim to have pulled off a robbery against his
Creator;[4] and now, with his booty, this woman of his to whom he is
bound in a new way, in defiance of the heavy fate that the curse has laid
upon them both, he renounces all ties with the Creator. Eve, fallen as
she is, is the ancient mother of humankind with whom all pleasure and
all pain began. She is the first of those who know; all her children — as
those who also know, those who are afflicted with pleasure and pain —

[1.] The students' notes indicate that the fourteenth lecture began at this
point, on Feb. 21, 1933.

[2.] *LB* "Heva."

[3.] *LB* and Kautzsch (15) both say, "of all who live." The students' notes confirm that Bonhoeffer said "of all that lives." Hans Schmidt regularly has "mother
of all that lives" (see 17, 32–33, 38 note 1, 52).

[4.] In comparing the two story lines, which he has separated as coming from
two different original sources, Hans Schmidt states that it seems that in the story
about the tree of life "the act by the human beings is understood in a more
Promethean, heaven-storming way than in the other story [the story that refers
to a tree of knowledge], for the word that the man says concerning his wife
sounds like a word full of unbowed defiance, like a proud cry of exultation over
the godlike ability to give children life" (34).

look back to her full of gratitude and of reproach. To Adam she is the symbol of the new life that has been torn from the Creator and is now endured [dahingelebte][5] in passion and pain [in Leidenschaft].[6] The extraordinary thing, however, is that in Adam's words there is something almost like an undertone of deep thanks which he offers to the Creator for the curse. What a strange contradiction: to give thanks to the Creator that humankind is upheld and preserved in this world that is far away from God, thanks to the Creator that humankind may be sicut deus, thanks to the Creator just because even humankind-sicut-deus, with all its defiance and audacity, does not get away from its Creator! Eve, the fallen, wise mother of humankind — that is the one beginning. Mary, the innocent, unknowing, mother of God — that is the second beginning.

[5.] The verb *dahinleben* means "to live a life of poor quality." [DSB]

[6.] There is a wordplay on *Leidenschaft* here. Ordinarily this German word means sexual or other "passion," but etymologically it means what causes *Leiden*, "suffering." Both meanings are intended here. Cf. the two meanings of "passion" in phrases like "sexual passion" and "the passion of Jesus." [DSB]

GOD'S NEW ACTION

And Yahweh God made cloaks of skin for Adam and for his woman and   129
clothed them with these.[1]

THE CREATOR IS NOW the preserver; the created world is now the fallen
but *preserved world*. In the world between curse and promise, between *tob*
and *ra*, good and evil, God deals with humankind in a distinctive way.
"He made them cloaks," says the Bible. That means that God accepts
human beings for what they are, as fallen creatures. God affirms them in
their fallenness. God does not expose them to one another in their
nakedness; instead God covers them. God's action accompanies
humankind on its way. The decisive point, however, is that God's action
is now one that orders and restrains. It does not break the new laws that
now apply to the earth and humankind after the fall; it participates in
them. At the same time, however, by participating in them, it imposes on
them restraint and order [Ordnung]; that is, it points to the wickedness,
the fallen state, of those laws. By making cloaks for human beings God
shows them that it is their wickedness that makes this necessary. By what
God does, God *restrains* their obsessive passion [Sucht] but does not
destroy them. God's way of acting to preserve the world is to affirm the
sinful world and to show it its limits by means of order.

¶None of these orders,[2] however, has in itself any eternal character,
for all are there only to uphold or preserve life. Adam's life, as we have

---

[1.] *LB* reads, "skins and clothed them." The text here follows Kautzsch, 15.
[2.] See above, page 95, note 5.

already pointed out, is preserved until it finds its end in death; our life is preserved only until it finds its end in — Christ. All orders of our fallen world are God's orders of preservation that uphold and preserve us for Christ. They are not orders of creation but orders of preservation.[3] They have no value in themselves; instead they find their end and meaning only through Christ. God's new action with humankind is to uphold and preserve humankind in its fallen world, in its fallen orders, for death — for the resurrection, for the new creation, for Christ. Humankind remains between tob and ra, remains split [im Zwiespalt]; even with its tob-good it remains beyond God's good. With its whole existence [Dasein], split as it is between tob and ra, it remains far away from God, continuing to drop downward [im Sturz], in the fallen and falling world. For just this reason humankind is in the twilight. And because it is in the twilight, all human thinking about creation and the fall (including the biblical author's own thinking) is restricted to this twilight — to the extent that it remains thinking that is down to earth and does not resort to fantasy. That is why human beings speak of paradise and of Adam's fall in the way that the Bible speaks of it. Humankind after all cannot find its way back behind its split state to unity; it is no longer able so unambiguously to distinguish the light of Lucifer, the light-bearer, from the light of God.[4] Humankind remains in the twilight, and God affirms it in this, its new sicut-deus world, by upholding and preserving it there.

[3.] Reporting on the meeting of the Intermediate Department for Ecumenical Youth Work on April 29–30, 1932, Bonhoeffer wrote that the idea of an order of creation "was a dangerous and a fallacious basis. The concept of 'orders of preservation' from God should be introduced in place of orders of creation" (*NRS* 180 [*DBW* 11:324 (*GS* 1:129)]). This is what Bonhoeffer had argued at the conference. Cf. the seminar "Gibt es eine christliche Ethik?" from the summer semester 1932 (*DBW* 11:312 [*GS* 5:292]) and his lecture on July 26, 1932, "A Theological Basis for the World Alliance?" (*NRS*, 157–73, N.B. 165–68 [*DBW* 11: 327–44, N.B. 335–38 (*GS* 1:140–58, N.B. 149–51)]). After 1933, when he saw that this new term was being dangerously misused, he no longer used it (Bethge, *Dietrich Bonhoeffer*, 355, 378; "The Challenge of Dietrich Bonhoeffer's Life and Theology," 42). [Also see Wayne Whitson Floyd, Jr., "The Search for an Ethical Sacrament: From Bonhoeffer to Critical Social Theory," *Modern Theology* 7, no. 2 (January 1991): 175–93; and "Christ, Concreteness and Creation in the Early Bonhoeffer," *Union Seminary Quarterly Review* 39, nos. 1 and 2 (1984): 101–14.] [JDEG]

[4.] See above, page 107, and editorial note 10.

The Tree of Life[1]

And Yahweh God said: Look, Adam has become like one of us and knows   131
what good and evil are. But now, lest he stretch out his hand and pluck
from the tree of life as well, and eat, and live for ever! So Yahweh God ban-
ished him from[2] the garden of Eden to till the ground [Acker][3] from
which he was taken, and drove Adam out and placed the cherubim in front
of the garden of Eden with a naked, whirling sword, to guard the way to the
tree of life.

THE WHOLE STORY moves toward its end in these verses. The significance
of the tree of life — of which, curiously enough, so little has been said
until now — becomes really clear at last. Indeed it becomes plain that the
whole story has really been about this tree. The Adam who had received
his life from God and who lived from the center, where this tree stood,
could not have thought of touching this tree. Only the tree of knowledge
could place the tree of life in danger. In what way? It could do so inasmuch as the fruit of the tree of knowledge, the knowledge of good and
evil, was the death of humankind — inasmuch as humankind-sicut-deus
is not living but dead humankind — that is, inasmuch as Adam reaches

---

[1.] *HP* (66), *UK* (44), and *FL* (74) all have as a heading for the section on vv.
22-24: "*Sicut Deus* the Outcast."

[2.] *LB* reads, "Then God the LORD let him go out of . . ."; Kautzsch renders
the text, "Then Yahweh God sent him forth out of the garden of Eden" (15).

[3.] Here, as in vv. 14-19, Bonhoeffer chooses *Acker*, "arable ground or land."
LB has "field"; Kautzsch has *Boden*, "ground/soil" (15). Otherwise the text generally follows *LB*.

out for the tree of life only after having fallen subject to death in order after all not to have to die in being-sicut-deus.

¶There can at this point be no more doubt that the serpent was right in the promise it made. The Creator confirms the truth of that promise: Humankind has become like one of us. It is sicut deus. Humankind has got what it wants; it has itself become creator, source of life, fountainhead of the knowledge of good and evil. It is alone by itself, it lives out of its own resources, it no longer needs any others, it is the lord of its own world, even though that does mean now that it is the solitary lord and despot of its own mute, violated, silenced, dead, ego-world [Ichwelt].

Humankind knows, however, what it has lost in being sicut deus: humankind-sicut-deus cannot live without enmity between it and the serpent, that is, without God, cannot live without another human being, cannot live without the other creatures. In conscience and in remorse one human being constantly seeks to imagine the presence, the reality, of another in his or her life. Humankind accuses itself, torments itself, and glorifies itself only in order to lie its way out of the dreadful loneliness of a solitude in which no voice echoes to its own.[4] Humankind knows about the life it has lost. It knows that it *must die.*

¶But humankind is not sicut deus for nothing; even out of this knowledge of their death human beings still derive for themselves a gruesome pleasure that they may die, that they are free to dispose of their own lives. Humankind recognizes that for it death consists in having to live before God without the life that comes from God; it recognizes that precisely as sicut deus it is condemned to live without life. But having fallen subject to death, it constantly perverts this knowledge into pleasure that it may die. One can express this ultimate reality of Adam's death only by means of such a paradoxical statement. Wanting to live, being unable to live, having to live — that is the way in which humankind-sicut-deus is dead. And this life of Adam's is now a continuing, renewed rebellion against this existence [Dasein]; it is a quarrel with life, a grasping at the

---

[4.] In *AB*, in the section entitled "Definition of 'Being' in Adam," Bonhoeffer cited Eberhard Grisebach's *Gegenwart* (564–65): "Limits are placed upon me, therefore, through the experience of conscience, from myself and never but through myself, but I never am provided a genuine limit from without. That is [. . .] just the astounding thing about conscience, that human beings hear only themselves in an ultimate and frightful isolation and therefore believe that they are hearing themselves . . . as God" (*DBWE* 2:143). Cf. also Bonhoeffer's inaugural lecture on July 31, 1930, "Man [*sic*] in Contemporary Philosophy and Theology" (*NRS* 66–67 [*DBW* 10:376 (*GS* 3:82)]).

life that would put an end to *this* life, that would be the new life. What Adam wants under any circumstance is *to live*. Indeed Adam is allowed to live in the world that God preserves. But Adam is wise and knows that this life is precisely life on the way to death, and thus itself is death. And now Adam's obsessive desire for life is boundless; an indescribable thirst for life seizes hold of Adam in the state of death that being sicut deus constitutes.

¶This thirst takes a strange form. For what causes despair in Adam's   133
situation is just this, that Adam lives out of Adam's own resources, is imprisoned within Adam, and thus can want only Adam, can hanker only after Adam; for Adam has indeed become Adam's own god, the creator of Adam's own life. When Adam seeks God, when Adam seeks life, Adam seeks only Adam. On the other hand it is just this solitude, this resting in oneself, this existing in and of oneself, that plunges Adam into an infinite thirst. It is therefore essentially a desperate, an unquench-able, an eternal thirst that Adam feels for life. It is essentially a thirst for death; the more passionately Adam seeks after life, the more completely he is ensnared by death. That is why Adam's thirst for life is perverse. Pining away as Adam is without life, Adam wants death; perhaps death may give Adam life. Adam then and today, to the extent that Adam understands Adam as Adam, does not want eternal life; instead Adam wants death, wants to die — which of us wants to live forever? Yet in this very act of dying Adam hopes to rescue his life from the bondservice and drudgery [Frohn][5] of having to live without life. Thus Adam flees from life and seeks to grasp life at the same time, as one who at one and the same time is fleeing from God and craving [Sucht] for God. Adam wants to be sicut deus — and at the same time to grasp at the tree of life. But such grasping at that tree is now finally barred to Adam. Adam is sicut deus, but as such in a state of death. Adam has eaten from the tree of knowledge, but the thirst that its fruit has given Adam for the tree of life remains unquenched.[6]

[5.] The modern spelling of this word is *Fron*. It is reminiscent of the German feudal system and means "bondservice, compulsory service" and in conse-quence also "drudgery." [DSB]

[6.] Cf. the triad in Bonhoeffer's lecture "Thy Kingdom Come: The Prayer of the Church for God's Kingdom on Earth" from November 19, 1932: "Death, loneliness, and desire — these are the three powers that enslave the earth" (*Pref-ace to Bonhoeffer*, 35 [*GS* 3:275]; cf. "We live on the cursed ground [*Acker*]" (*Preface to Bonhoeffer*, 32 [*GS* 3:273]).

¶And from now on the boundary that separates paradise from the ground on which Adam toils will be just there: where the tree of life stands. "God drove Adam out, and placed the cherubim in front of the garden of Eden with a naked, whirling sword, to guard the way to the tree of life." The boundary has not shifted; it is where it always was, at the tree of life in the center, where no one may set foot. But Adam now stands in another place. The limit is no longer in the center of Adam's life; instead it assails Adam from outside. Adam keeps on running up against it; it is always in the way. The German fairy tales about Sleeping Beauty and about the swirling flame[7] differ from what is reported here in that no one encroaches beyond the whirling naked sword of the cherubim and remains alive. The tree of life is guarded by sentinels[8] of death; it remains inviolable, divinely unapproachable. But Adam's life outside the gate is a constant attack on the kingdom from which he is shut out. It is a flight, a search to find upon the ground that is cursed what he has lost — and then a desperate raging again and again against the sentinels who keep watch with the whirling sword. That the sentinel's sword whirls and is sharp is something the biblical author does not say without reason. Adam knows that; Adam discovers that again and again. But the gate stays shut.

134

[7.] Hermann Gunkel, *Genesis*, refers to "the swirling flame that envelops Brunhilde" (25) in Richard Wagner's *Valkyrie*, in which Wagner takes up ancient Nordic ideas.

[8.] It is clear that *Mächte*, "powers," printed in the 1933 edition both here and two sentences later, resulted from a reading error. *HP* (68), *UK* (46), and *FL* (76) show that Bonhoeffer used the word *Wächter*, "sentinels." Kautzsch comments that cherubs are among other things "sentinels that keep watch at holy places" (15, note f).

CAIN

And Adam knew his woman Eve, and she became pregnant and gave birth   135
to Cain.[1]

THIS VERSE IS AN INTRINSIC PART of the preceding story. Adam and Eve, the human beings sicut deus who have fallen into death, demonstrate their new community in a new way. They become the proud creators of new life. But this new life is created in the community of human beings and death that is characterized by obsessive desire. Cain is the first human being who is born on the ground that is *cursed*. It is with Cain that history begins, the history of death. Adam, the one who is preserved for death and consumed with thirst for *life*, begets Cain, the *murderer*. The new thing about Cain, the son of Adam, is that as sicut deus he himself lays violent hands on human life. The human being who may not eat from the tree of life grasps all the more greedily at the fruit of death, the destruction of life. Only the Creator can destroy life. Cain usurps for himself this ultimate right of the Creator and becomes the murderer. Why does Cain murder? Out of hatred toward God. This hatred is great. Cain is great; he is greater than Adam, because his hatred is greater, and that means that his obsessive desire for life is greater. The history of death stands under the sign of Cain.

The end of Cain's history, and so the end of all history [das Ende der Geschichte überhaupt], is Christ on the cross, the murdered Son of God. That is the last desperate assault on the gate of paradise. And under the

---

[1.] These words begin v. 1, as in *LB*. Kautzsch says, "The end of this verse is uncertain [textually and in meaning]" (16, note a).

whirling sword, under the cross, the human race dies. But Christ lives. The trunk of the cross becomes the wood of life [zum Holze des Lebens],[2] and now in the midst of the world, on the accursed ground itself, life is raised up anew. In the center of the world, from the wood of the cross, the fountain of life springs up. All who thirst for life are called to drink from this water, and whoever has eaten from the wood of this life shall never again hunger and thirst.[3] What a strange paradise is this hill of Golgotha, this cross, this blood, this broken body. What a strange tree of life, this trunk on which the very God had to suffer and die. Yet it is the very kingdom of life and of the resurrection, which by grace God grants us again. It is the gate of imperishable hope now opened, the gate of waiting and of patience. The tree of life, the cross of Christ, the center of God's world that is fallen but upheld and preserved — that is what the end of the story about paradise is for us.

> Once more God opens the gate
> to fair Paradise today;
> no angel now bars the way.
> Glory to God, who is great,
> and praise and honor, we say.[4]

[2.] Cf. Rev. 22:2, where the Greek phrase ξύλον ζωῆς can be rendered either as "tree of life" or as "wood of life." Cf. also Rev. 22:1, which speaks of "the fountain of life" mentioned in the following lines of Bonhoeffer's text. Revelation 22:1-5 was a favorite passage of Bonhoeffer's, as shown by the frequency with which he expounded it at Finkenwalde in 1935–37. See *DBW* 14:770-77. [DSB]

[3.] Cf. John 4:14.

[4.] *FL* reads, "Luther" (77). Bonhoeffer apparently quoted from memory the last stanza of the hymn "Lobt Gott, ihr Christen alle gleich" ("Praise God, you Christians, all alike"), whose author was Nikolaus Herman (1500–1561). In its printed version the song has "cherub" instead of "angel." See *Evangelisches Gesangbuch für Brandenburg und Pommern* 13, v. 5; *Evangelisches Gesangbuch* 27, v. 6.

MARTIN RÜTER AND ILSE TÖDT

EDITORS' AFTERWORD
TO THE GERMAN EDITION

THE EXPOSITION OF GENESIS 1–3 that Dietrich Bonhoeffer gave in the winter semester of 1932–33 is characterized by silence before the ἄρρητον[1], or concentration on the unutterable word of God.   137

Between the planning and the delivery of this course of lectures, Bonhoeffer's life took a turn. After this turn the theological findings to which Bonhoeffer came, including those that he was able to relate to work he had done previously, appear in a new light.

I

In the first section of this Afterword we shall look at the lecture course as it was planned *before* this turn, as still a continuation of Bonhoeffer's previous academic work.

Theological Anthropology

The subject area that lies between dogmatics and ethics in theology is anthropology. It was this area that Bonhoeffer chose for his inaugural lecture as a *Privatdozent* in systematic theology. In the great hall of the University of Berlin he declared "that on the one hand a century of inventors, who have built a new world on the ground of the old, and on the other hand a lost war, must put before us the question of man in a

---

[1.] Bonhoeffer translated this word at the beginning of his course of lectures on Christology in 1933 as "the inexpressible," as Luther had done in 2 Cor. 12:4 (in *LB* Paul in paradise hears ἄρρητα ῥήματα, "inexpressible words")(*CC* 27 [*GS* 3:167]).

new and more acute form." This question was one of "the most passionately raised questions of contemporary philosophy."[2]

The creation stories in Genesis are the basic texts in theological anthropology. On the basis of Genesis 1–3 the young *Privatdozent* could continue to investigate the burning question posed by his inaugural lec138   ture. Because it was the practice at the university to settle the theme of every lecture course during the semester before it was to be delivered, Bonhoeffer already in the summer of 1932, or even before, must have decided on the theme of the course of lectures he was to deliver in the winter semester of 1932–33.

Ethics Based on Orders of Creation

Another question was of great topical interest in theology at the time, "the theme of ethics, which has stepped into the foreground in an unexpectedly prominent way. The question now is just how and on what basis ethics should be founded: should it be based on the doctrine of creation or of reconciliation or of sanctification?"[3]

At the beginning of the 1930s the world economy was in severe recession. The constitutional democracies seemed unable to cope with the ferment of social and political discontent. In Germany moreover the democratic political structure had been set up as a result of a world war whose outcome was for a long time experienced as a national humiliation. In this situation of intense insecurity, people who wished to be more than mere pawns of fate were looking for a secure basic orientation and direction for their lives.

Protestant theology in the German-speaking part of Europe met this quest by pointing to God's inviolable creation and its 'orders'. At an ecumenical conference in Berlin in April 1932, which Bonhoeffer had organized, Professor Wilhelm Stählin presented a set of theses that "provided a justification of war between the nations" [die Kampfesaufgabe der Völker] on the basis of the orders of creation. Bonhoeffer made a counter-proposal that introduced the concept of "'orders of preservation'

[2.] "Man [*sic*] in Contemporary Philosophy and Theology" (*NRS* 50, 52 [*DBW* 10:357–58, 360 (*GS* 3:62–84)]).

[3.] Bonhoeffer at the beginning of his course of lectures, "Jüngste Theologie" ("Modern theology"), which ran parallel with the lectures on "Schöpfung und Sünde" ("Creation and sin") in 1932–33 (*GS* 5:305).

from God."[4] He cautioned against the argument that God's command was to be discovered in certain given orders regarded as having been created by God and so as 'very good'. For in principle everything could be justified in that way — including "the division of man into nations [Völker], national struggles, war, class struggle, the exploitation of the weak by the strong, the cut-throat competition of economics." What people appeal to as an order of creation seems to be "eternal"; in this fallen world in which "creation and sin are so bound up together that no human eye can any longer separate the one from the other," however, all such orders are subject to change. God's orders of preservation by contrast "obtain their value [Wert] wholly from outside themselves, from Christ, from the new creation." And a commandment of Christ "is limited by nothing else, by no so-called 'orders of creation'."[5]

139

Thus when he announced the lecture course as one that would deal with "Schöpfung und Sünde" ("Creation and sin"), Bonhoeffer did so with a thesis to which he had given some thought, one with which he could move into the theological debate about the basis of ethics. When it came to the actual delivery of the lectures, however, his concept of the "order of preservation" was to play only a subsidiary role.

An Ethical versus a Biological View of Humankind

In "an attempt to document the *exegetical evidence*" concerning Genesis 1–3, Bonhoeffer's lectures on "Schöpfung und Sünde" ("Creation and sin") expanded the exposition in his dissertation *The Communion of Saints* about "the fundamental social relations [Grundbeziehungen] of humankind in its primal state [Urständlichkeit]." In this he had referred to "the medieval symbolism for the Fall [which] puts a tree in the center, with the serpent coiled round it, and on either side the man and the woman, separated by the tree from which they disobediently ate. That the narrator [of Genesis 1–3] sees sexuality as the power which now

---

[4.] See Bonhoeffer's report in the periodical *Die Eiche*, edited by Friedrich Siegmund-Schultze, in 1932 (*NRS* 179–80 [*DBW* 11:323–24 (*GS* 1:128f.)]). Cf. also the debate with the idea of orders of creation in Bonhoeffer's 1932 seminar, "Gibt es eine christliche Ethik?" ("Is there a Christian ethic?") (*DBW* 11:312 [*GS* 5:291–92]).

[5.] From Bonhoeffer's lecture "A Theological Basis for the World Alliance?" given at the ecumenical youth conference on peace in Ciernohorské Kúpele on July 26, 1932 (*NRS* 165, 166, 167 [*DBW* 11:335–38 (*GS* 1:149–51)]).

the narrator [of Genesis 1–3] sees sexuality as the power which now stepped between human beings had a devastating effect upon the doctrine of original sin." The young doctoral student stressed the importance of the idea that because community with God and with humankind *"is destroyed by moral [ethische] failure it clearly has moral character originally."*[6]

One section of the dissertation dealt with 'original sin'. Just as Reinhold Seeberg and especially Adolf von Harnack, Bonhoeffer's teachers in Berlin, had done in their histories of dogma, so Bonhoeffer too focused above all on Augustine. "The licentious times in which Augustine lived caused him to be horrified at the overwhelming power that *concupiscentia*[7] has in the world." Bonhoeffer saw this as the reason for Augustine's preoccupation with the biological and natural. But he regarded the bringing of this physical aspect into the doctrine of original sin as a false step; it had prevented Catholic theologians from attaining "an ethical view of mankind." "It was *Luther* who put all the weight on man's ethical guilt, and overcame the biological view of the race [Gattung] which had been derived from the notion of physical reproduction [die Idee der Zeugung]. In the 'willing of the I' ['Ichwillen'] he found the essence of original sin, that is, in a personal ethical act."[8] For Bonhoeffer as a student working for his doctorate under the 'voluntarist' Seeberg, ethics was connected with the 'will'; sin appeared to him to be an evil will that destroyed community by its "egocentric tendency [ichsüchtig Richtung]."[9] It seemed quite clear that "For Christian thinking good and evil are qualities of the will."[10]

In his lectures during the summer semester 1932, Bonhoeffer took up the point of view that he had been developing until then: "The doctrine of 'original sin' along with the idea that results from it of the transmission [of original sin] by procreation is a poor attempt to do justice to the

---

[6.] *CS* 41–42 (*DBW* 1:223–24); italics in the original but not in the English translation.

[7.] "(Sensual) desire, concupiscence."

[8.] *CS* 76 (*DBW* 1:243–45); italics in the original German text.

[9.] *CS* 81 (*DBW* 1:247). Here Bonhoeffer is in agreement with Seeberg.

[10.] *CS* 81 (*DBW* 1:73, continuation of note 2). This sentence comes from Bonhoeffer's repudiation of Max Scheler's defense of the idea of original guilt; cf. *DBW* 1:246. Bonhoeffer took up a similar position on the doctrine of original sin in *Act and Being,* especially in the section "'Adam' as I and as Humanity" (*DBWE* 2:144–47).

actual condition of sinful existence. It also does damage to the humanity
of human beings."[11] In the seminar he also conducted during this summer semester, Bonhoeffer assigned the fall, as well as good and evil, to
the area of ethics — as unequivocally as he had done in his dissertation:
"According to Gen. 1–3 the conscience is to be identified with the knowledge of good and evil. . . . This knowledge leads to self-justification. God
alone can be 'like God'. Ethics may therefore never seek to base itself on
conscience. . . . To be sure, Gen. 1–3 is legend [Legende]. But there is
truth in *this* legend."[12]

By the time Bonhoeffer came to expound Genesis 1–3 during the fol-   141
lowing semester, however, he no longer saw humankind simply within
the limits of what was spiritual and ethical.

Theological Exposition

Bonhoeffer's announcement of his lecture course as a "theological
exposition" showed that he wished to stay true to Karl Barth's method.
In 1922, in the foreword to the new edition of his *Epistle to the Romans*,
Barth had declared: "If I have a 'system', then it is limited to a recognition of what Kierkegaard called the 'infinite qualitative distinction'
between time and eternity, and to my regarding this as possessing negative as well as positive significance: 'God is in heaven, and thou art on
earth'.[13] The relation between *such a* God and *such a* man, and the relation between *such a* man and *such a* God, is for me the theme of the Bible
and the essence of philosophy."[14]

Was *Creation and Fall* then Bonhoeffer's Old Testament equivalent to
Barth's exposition of the epistle to the Romans?[15] In agreement with
Barth, Bonhoeffer affirmed in the winter semester of 1931–32 that

---

[11.] Bonhoeffer's lecture course, "Das Wesen der Kirche" ("The essence of
the church") (*GS* 5:242) [not included as part of Bonhoeffer's lecture in *DBW*
11]. [trans. DSB]

[12.] Bonhoeffer's seminar, "Gibt es eine christliche Ethik?" ("Is there a
Christian ethic?"), as reconstructed by Otto Dudzus from the notes of one student, Wolf-Dieter Zimmermann; Dudzus became one of Bonhoeffer's students
only in 1933 (*GS* 5:294–95). Cf. *DBW* 11:308 and editorial note 22. Zimmermann's notes on this part of the seminar have not been included in *DBW* 11.

[13.] Barth is quoting Eccles. 5:2.

[14.] Barth, *Epistle to the Romans*, 10.

[15.] James Burtness makes this comparison in *Internationales Bonhoeffer
Forum*, 6:172.

"Theology really begins with a *petitio principii.*"[16] Theology in Barth's sense has its basis in God's turning to humankind, something that human beings can only "pray for." Would Adolf von Harnack, who like others in Berlin regarded Karl Barth's theology with suspicion, have seen such a procedure as scientific or scholarly? Almost imploringly von Harnack had written in 1929 to Bonhoeffer, his erstwhile student, that theological existence was being "threatened by contempt for scientific theology and by unscientific theologies. Those who stand by the standard of genuine science must therefore hold it high with all the more conviction."[17]

142   After Bonhoeffer encountered Barth's writings in the summer of 1925, he remained Barth's independent but nevertheless resolute ally. In the Genesis lectures Bonhoeffer wished to offer what was unusual in Berlin and indeed was regarded there with suspicion: a basic, "postcritical" exposition of scripture.[18] The students at Berlin were evidently aware of the provocative nature of the title Bonhoeffer gave to the lecture course when he announced it.[19]

Bonhoeffer saw that in Karl Barth the church — and not just "individual piety" — becomes "once again the presupposition of theology." This agreed with his own conviction that the church stands "before the bracket within which theology is done."[20] Bonhoeffer characterized theological exposition in the same way during and after the delivery of

---

[16.] From Bonhoeffer's lectures, "Die Geschichte der systematischen Theologie des 20. Jahrhunderts" ("The history of systematic theology in the twentieth century") (*DBW* 11:202) [*GS* 5:221]. *Petitio principii* means "a begging of the question"; in traditional logic it denotes a logical fallacy that presumes to prove something on the basis of a premise that has yet to be demonstrated. The literal meaning of *petitio* is "a requesting, application, claim" and that of *principium* is "groundwork, foundation, first principle."

[17.] Letter of December 22, 1929 (*DBW* 10:160–61) [*GS* 3:20]. Also see *DB-E*, 52.

[18.] The label "post-critical" is how Rudolf Smend characterized Karl Barth's method of exposition in the title of his contribution to *Parrhesia*, the *Festschrift* commemorating Barth's eightieth birthday. On Bonhoeffer's status as an outsider among his colleagues in the Berlin faculty see *DB-E* 160–61.

[19.] In the words of his former student Hans Hinrich Flöter, "Bonhoeffer's announcement [of his lecture course] was, as I have said, a fascinating provocation" (letter of May 27, 1987, to Reinhart Staats). See the "Editor's Introduction" above, page 3 and editorial note 7.

[20.] "Das Wesen der Kirche" ("The essence of the church") (*DBW* 11:252) [*GS* 5:235].

these lectures as he may have done already in planning for them. In his view, with due regard for the theories about the different sources behind this biblical primeval history,[21] what mattered was the exegesis of the text "as it presents itself to the church of Christ today."[22] During that winter semester, then, Bonhoeffer accepted that the Bible is the book of the church in the sense of John 5:39: "Search the scriptures . . . it is they that testify on my behalf." The church is founded upon the witness that is borne to Christ on the basis of the new.[23]

II

Looking Back at the "First Time"

Before the winter semester of 1932–33 began, Bonhoeffer must have experienced what he later referred to in the words: "I came to the Bible for the first time."[24] In 1936, the same year in which he wrote these words that looked back in this way, he explained to his brother-in-law, Rüdiger Schleicher:

143

> One cannot simply *read* the Bible like other books. One must really be pre-
> pared to put questions to it. . . . The reason for this is that in the Bible God
> speaks to us. And one cannot just proceed to think about God under one's
> own steam; instead one must ask God questions. Naturally one can read the
> Bible like any other book and so study it from the point of view of textual
> criticism, etc. There is absolutely nothing to be said against this. Only this
> way of going about things does not unlock the essence of the Bible but only
> what lies on its surface. Think of how we come to understand something
> said to us by a person we love not by dissecting it into bits but by simply
> accepting it as the kind of word it is, so that for days it echoes within us sim-
> ply as the word of that particular person whom we love; the more we, like
> Mary, "ponder it in the heart,"[25] the more the person who has said it to us

[21.] Cf. above, page 71 and editorial note 2. Julius Wellhausen (1844–1918) had persuaded almost all scholars that the priestly document (P) was the latest of the sources used in the Old Testament.

[22.] See above, page 83. By relativizing the distinction between the sources in this way Bonhoeffer took the first step on the road that only much later would win respect, also among the specialist exegetes of the Old Testament, above all in the work of Brevard S. Childs, as "canonical criticism."

[23.] See above, page 22.

[24.] Letter later written by Bonhoeffer from the underground seminary at Finkenwalde to Elisabeth Zinn dated January 27, 1936 (*DBW* 14:112–13) [*GS* 6:367].

[25.] Luke 2:19. NRSV has "pondered . . . in her heart."

becomes accessible to us in that word. That is just how we should treat the word of the Bible. . . . Every other place outside the Bible has become too uncertain for me; I am afraid that I will encounter only a divine double [einen göttlichen Doppelgänger] of my own self in it. Is it possible, then, for you to comprehend that I would rather make a sacrificium intellectus[26] by confessing that I do not yet understand this or that passage in Scripture, with the certainty that it too will one day reveal itself as God's own word. I would rather do that than on the basis of my own opinion declare: this is what is divine in it and that is what is human!? (I make the sacrificium intellectus in just these matters and only in these matters, that is, with the true God in view! Who after all would not make a sacrificium intellectus anywhere in this respect?) I also want to say to you now by way of an entirely personal note, that since I learned to read the Bible in this way — which is by no means such a long time ago — it has become more wonderful to me every day. . . . In a few days it will be Easter . . . Resurrection. That is certainly not an idea that is in itself reasonable, an eternal truth. I take it to be what the Bible also takes it to be, of course: resurrection from real death (not from sleep) to real life, from being far away from God [der Gottesferne] and from godlessness [der Gottlosigkeit] to new life with Christ in God. God has spoken — and we know this through the Bible — See, I am making all things new.[27] God made that come true at Easter.[28]

Bonhoeffer used the Easter text in Eph. 5:14, "Sleeper, awake! Rise from the dead. . . ," as the basis for a baptismal address in October 1932.[29] Much of this address recurs in the course of the lectures on Genesis during the winter semester. At the beginning of the course Bonhoeffer viewed creation and resurrection together, and he ended the course with a Christmas hymn: "Once more God opens the gate to fair Paradise today." Easter and Christmas in one — and the word of the Bible "for the first time" stands revealed.

"Pick up, read"

In the seventh book of his *Confessions* Augustine tells us of his intensive preoccupation with problems related to creation, for instance with

---

[26.] By this expression Bonhoeffer means the abandonment of any claim to be able to understand something by means of the intellect. He explains in the words that follow.

[27.] Revelation 21:5.

[28.] Letter to Rüdiger Schleicher dated April 8, 1936 (*DBW* 14:144–48) [*GS* 3:26–31].

[29.] *DBW* 11:463–66 (*GS* 4:150–53).

the question of the origin of evil. In the eighth book he describes how he heard a singsong voice like that of a child saying, "*Tolle, lege; tolle, lege*" ("Pick it up, read it . . ."), understood these words as referring to the Bible, and experienced this as a turning point in his life.[30] The last three books of the *Confessions* are an exposition of the beginning of the Bible as far as Genesis 2:3. Luther in his lectures on Genesis, on which Bonhoeffer drew for "Schöpfung und Sünde" ("Creation and sin"), constantly refers to Augustine. In his series of seminars on "Dogmatische Übungen [Theologische Psychologie]" ("Dogmatic Exercises [Theological psychology]") in 1932–33 Bonhoeffer explicitly mentioned Augustine's *Confessions*. In the seminar that met on December 7, 1932, Hilde Pfeiffer copied down the words: "*Self-knowledge in Augustine. . . .* For Augustine the Christian the split [dividing human beings into will and flesh] has vanished; he sees himself as a creature who is one and undivided."[31]

145

Exercitium

Listening to the word of God involved "*exercitium*,"[32] declared Bonhoeffer, in his oral introduction to the lecture series on "Schöpfung und Sünde" ("Creation and sin").[33] This word occurs again in the final session of the seminar he led in the winter of 1932–33.[34] Discourses on *exercitia*, for example on "the pious practices suitable to a good monk," appear in Thomas à Kempis's book *Imitatio Christi*, which was compiled sometime before 1427 on the basis of the writing of the mystics who were known at the time.[35]

Ignatius of Loyola [1491–1556], the founder of the Jesuit order, thought very highly of this book.[36] In his own *Spiritual Exercises* he gave an account of experiences that were related to spiritual readings. Catalo-

---

[30.] Augustine, *Confessions*, 137–40 [7/3,5], 175–76 [8/12].

[31.] *NL-B* 2.3 (11–12); cf. "Probleme einer theologischen Anthropologie" (Problems of a theological anthropology) (*GS* 5:341, 347).

[32.] "Exercise, practice."

[33.] *EK* (1).

[34.] *HP* (40) (*NL-B* 2.3).

[35.] *The Imitation of Christ*, 40–42 [1/19]. On Bonhoeffer's copy, see *NL* 238, 173.

[36.] For the references to Thomas à Kempis and Ignatius of Loyola, the editors are indebted to Christoph Zimmermann-Wolf.

nia, the district around Barcelona, was the scene of the events in 1522–23 that were decisive for Ignatius. Bonhoeffer could have developed an interest in Ignatius during his time as a curate in Barcelona in 1928–29, and his interest in *exercitia* was renewed before the winter semester of 1932–33.[37]

146

Bonhoeffer later chose this term, designating a literary genre associated above all with the name of Ignatius, in a letter he wrote to his student friend Erwin Sutz in 1934: "I am busy with a work that I would like to call exercises,"[38] on the Sermon on the Mount. It was this work that developed into the book *[The Cost of] Discipleship* that was published in 1937.

III

In this section of the Afterword we will look at basic points in the contents of *Creation and Fall*, in the order in which they appear in the book.

The One God

Bonhoeffer now knew that the one to whom the Bible witnesses is no divine double [Doppelgänger] of the earthly I.[39] In the last sentence of his introduction to the book, which, as he first drafted it, read, "God is God," he inserted the emphatic words, "the one."

The whole of Holy Scripture, the Old as well as the New Testament, bears witness to the one God. Only within this faith did Bonhoeffer wish to pursue scientific, or scholarly, theology. That meant setting himself also against his honored teacher, Adolf von Harnack.

Harnack in 1921 had published a book about Marcion, a heretic who flourished about the middle of the second century. Marcion taught that there were two gods: the good God of the New Testament, who chose to

---

[37.] The remains of Bonhoeffer's library includes a copy of Loyola's *Geistliche Übungen* published in 1932 (English edition: *The Spiritual Exercises of St. Ignatius of Loyola*). Bonhoeffer possessed three other works on the Jesuit order, including Karl Holl's 'psychological study', *Die geistlichen Übungen des Ignatius von Loyola* (The spiritual exercises of Ignatius of Loyola).

[38.] Letter dated April 28, 1934 (*DBW* 13:127) [*GS* 1:41].

[39.] Bonhoeffer chose and used the term *Doppelgänger* for a statement about the I or ego in 1926 (*DBW* 9:377) and again in *Act and Being* (*AB* [*DBWE* 2]:99). By the time he used the expression again in the letter dated April 8, 1936 (*DBW* 14:147) [*GS* 3:29], his use of it was no longer controlled by interest in the I.

be revealed in Jesus, and the Jewish Creator of the world. The first could have had nothing to do with the second. "*The rejection of the Old Testament in the second century*," wrote Harnack,

> *was a mistake which the great church rightly avoided; to maintain it in the six-teenth century was a fate from which the Reformation was not yet able to escape; but still to preserve it in Protestantism as a canonical document since the nineteenth century is the consequence of a religious and ecclesiastical crippling.* . . . Yet the greatest number of objections that 'the people' ['das Volk'] raise against Christianity and against the truthfulness of the church arise out of the recognition that the church still accords to the Old Testament. To clear the table here and to give the truth the place of honor in confession and instruction — that is the great deed that is being demanded today, already almost too late, of Protestantism. . . . For it is not possible to perceive from the Old Testament what is Christian.[40]

147

The elimination of the Old Testament or 'Jewish' element for the sake of 'the people', as Harnack advocated in this passage, and the artificial removal of Jesus from Judaism, became the central demands of National Socialist, and so of 'German Christian', church politics, once Hitler was named Reich Chancellor on January 30, 1933. This demand began to be made, therefore, while Bonhoeffer was lecturing on "Schöpfung und Sünde" ("Creation and sin"). From 1933 until the end of his life Bon-hoeffer fought against this heresy.

Bonhoeffer wrote the introduction to *Creation and Fall* after he had made an in-depth study of Hans Schmidt's *Die Erzählung von Paradies und Sündenfall* (The story of paradise and the fall). This book was writ-ten in the tradition of the history-of-religions school, and in it Schmidt came to the conclusion that Genesis 2:4–3:14 had originally been about a god other than the God of whom Moses and the Israelite prophets spoke. To Bonhoeffer such statements about a text in the Bible, or more exactly about the sources lying behind it, seemed to be an attempt to evade the word of the one God whose name in Genesis is Yahweh.

Beginning out of Nothing

Talk about the 'beginning' is eschatology — i.e., talk about the 'last things' or the end. Bonhoeffer pointed out this paradox in his oral intro-duction to the lecture course and emphasized it in the introduction that

---

[40.] Adolf von Harnack, *Marcion*, 134, 137, 138; italics in the original.

148

he wrote for the printed version.[41] Wilhelm Vischer had put it this way in 1927: "Belief in creation and belief in eschatology are very closely connected in the Bible." In his exposition of Genesis 1:1 Bonhoeffer could express his own agreement with this.[42] He himself related creation and resurrection to each other. Creation out of nothing was for him the death of death that the church knows about from the resurrection of the dead Jesus Christ.[43]

In the lecture course in 1931–32, "Die Geschichte der systematischen Theologie des 20. Jahrhunderts" ("The history of systematic theology in the twentieth century"), Bonhoeffer had connected God's act of bringing forth out of nothing — *ex nihilo* — with Karl Barth's understanding of predestination:

> God remains Lord. God's word brings into being utterly *ex nihilo*, in a predestination and rejection which we cannot rationalize; it is an eternal beginning, not a continuation in which one thing necessarily results from another. . . . This idea of God [in Barth] seems to be the product of philosophical speculation. But it only seems so. . . . God and God alone must declare that God is the absolute beginning.[44]

Hegel's Philosophy of Religion

Bonhoeffer found speculation about creation *ex nihilo* in Hegel. The name Hegel occurs in the book *Creation and Fall* in only one place, in the question about the beginning. According to Hegel there is no place for the beginning in philosophy, for everything in philosophy must be proved, or recognized as necessary. The philosophy of religion never-

---

[41.] On the "beginning" see also Bonhoeffer's meditation on the New Year, written on January 7, 1934 (*DBW* 13:344–46) [*GS* 4:171f.]; his meditation on Psalm 119, written in 1939–40 (*Meditating on the Word*, 101 [*GS* 4:506]); Bonhoeffer's last message from 1945, recounted in *DB-E* 830; and *DBW* 16:468.

[42.] Wilhelm Vischer, "Das Alte Testament als Gottes Wort." On this exposition as what Eberhard Bethge has called an "eschatological interpretation of Creation" (*DB-E*, 163) see Martin Kuske, *The Old Testament as the Book of Christ*, 35–41.

[43.] This combination of creation and Easter was still in 1983 a vivid memory for Ferenc Lehel. See *Internationales Bonhoeffer Forum*, 8:13.

[44.] 1931–32 lectures on "Die Geschichte der systematischen Theologie des 20. Jahrhunderts" ("The history of systematic theology in the twentieth century") (*DBW* 11:198–99) [*GS* 5:218f.].

theless finds it easy to deal with its beginning, for as the last discipline in philosophy it begins at the point where the others come to their conclusion.[45]

None of those who attended the lectures and whose notes are available as part of Bonhoeffer's literary remains copied down the name of Hegel at this point, not even the philosophically trained Hungarian, Ferenc Lehel. Perhaps Bonhoeffer inserted the sentence into his manuscript only after the end of the semester. During the following semester, in the torrid summer of 1933, the first semester under the National Socialist regime, he conducted his seminar on Hegel's philosophy of religion. But Bonhoeffer must already in the winter of 1932–33 have had in his possession the three volumes of Hegel's *Lectures on the Philosophy of Religion* that formed part of the collected works edited by Georg Lasson. There are traces of his having used two of these volumes[46] for the lectures on "Schöpfung und Sünde" ("Creation and sin").

In the *Philosophy of Religion,* Part 1, *The Concept of Religion,*[47] colored and lead pencil markings show that Bonhoeffer worked at least twice through four pages that deal with the idea of God as Creator of the world "out of nothing." In the seminar on Hegel, as Ferenc Lehel's notes show, he analyzed this passage in the book in detail.[48]

In the *Philosophy of Religion,* Part 3, *The Consummate Religion,* Lasson gave the third chapter the heading, "Creation, Humankind and Sin."[49] Under that there is a subsection on "Good and Evil" and a section on

149

[45.] This is how Hegel argues in the volume *The Concept of Religion* with which — after the Introduction — the *Lectures on the Philosophy of Religion* itself begins (257ff., 365ff.). This page and its context in Bonhoeffer's copy of the Lasson edition are heavily marked in indelible pencil. Likewise Bonhoeffer used an indelible pencil in working through a passage which explains "the business of speculation." Speculation encompasses, according to Hegel, "in the form of thought . . . the other, or the difference within itself" (Lasson 1:34); see *Internationales Bonhoeffer Forum,* 8:49, 61, 126–27.

[46.] The second of the three volumes of Bonhoeffer's copy of Lasson's edition of the *Lectures on the Philosophy of Religion, Determinate Religion,* is unmarked; it gives the impression of not having been opened.

[47.] Hegel, *Lectures on the Philosophy of Religion,* Part 1, *The Concept of Religion,* 366ff. (Lasson, 1:146–48). Lasson's text here has no exact parallel in the English edition.

[48.] Cf. *Internationales Bonhoeffer Forum,* 8:81–82.

[49.] Lasson, 3:85–129; see Hodgson, ed., *The Christian Religion,* 109–68.

"The Representation of the Fall." Bonhoeffer's copy is frequently and sometimes heavily marked here.[50] In the 1933 Hegel seminar these pages were skipped. It seems that Bonhoeffer worked through them only for the lectures on "Schöpfung und Sünde" ("Creation and sin"). On the basis of Hegel one could actually say that it was the *fall* that created humankind. Hegel's philosophy posited "dividedness" [Entzweiung] as necessary in its system and as indispensable for humankind's being-human. Bonhoeffer's reaction was to mark not only Hegel's exposition of the fall but also other places in the *Lectures on the Philosophy of Religion* that speak of "absolute dividedness" with question marks and wavy lines expressing reservation.[51]

Bonhoeffer held to the maxim he had set down in his dissertation, *The Communion of the Saints,* in reaction to what idealist philosophy, and in particular Hegel's philosophy of the spirit, had asserted about the spirit: "It is our task . . . to keep the insight without joining in the error."[52] In his exegesis of Genesis 2:7 Bonhoeffer prefers anthropomorphism in thinking about God to an abstract idea of God, and his words come close to Hegel's at this point.[53] He points in particular to God's becoming human, as Hegel also did in favor of anthropomorphism. Important as the concept of God's becoming human was to Bonhoeffer, and remained all through his life, it was just as clear to him where he had to differ with Hegel. The students who attended Bonhoeffer's lectures on Christology in the summer of 1933 copied down these words: "The incarnation of God may not be thought of as derived from an idea of God, in which something of humanity already belongs to the idea of God — as in Hegel. . . . A speculative basis for the doctrine of the incarnation in an idea of God would change the free relationship between Creator and creature into a logical necessity."[54] Bonhoeffer now knew — in agreement with Barth — that it is the *freedom* of God, as the "wholly Other," to which creation owes its coming into being out of nothing, its rising up from the dead.

[50.] See *Internationales Bonhoeffer Forum,* 8:130–31.

[51.] Cf. *Internationales Bonhoeffer Forum,* 8:43, on Hegel, *Lectures on the Philosophy of Religion* (Lasson 1:23).

[52.] *CS* 49 (*DBW* 1:46).

[53.] *Lectures on the Philosophy of Religion* (Lasson, 161).

[54.] *CC* 105–6 (*GS* 3:234).

Cosmos

The Bible witnesses to the one God as Lord of the whole cosmos. In accordance with the cosmic magnitude of the creation event, Bonhoeffer did not limit his exposition of Genesis 1:4ff. to the areas of scholarship of the arts or humanities but also referred to mathematics, natural science, and technology.   151

From 1931 to 1933 Bonhoeffer was a student chaplain at the Charlottenburg Technical College. He found no interest in theology there. His period of service in this post, as Bethge explains, "preceded the upheaval in which the arts faculties [Geisteswissenschaftler] were forced out of the Church under totalitarian pressure and the scientists [Naturwissenschaftler] acquired a new relationship with it."[55]

Dietrich Bonhoeffer's oldest brother, Karl Friedrich, was a physicist who was well acquainted with the fundamental crisis of physics in the 1920s.[56] From him Dietrich must have gained some understanding of the upheaval in the concept of science that had been brought about in the natural sciences "by relativity and quantum theories."[57] Dietrich's older sister Christine had studied biology, until she married Hans von Dohnanyi at the beginning of 1925. Bonhoeffer stated during his lecture course in 1931–32 that "against certain conclusions of natural science" theology had produced "only rearguard actions" and indeed what were frankly irresponsible, unsound apologetics.[58] This applied particularly to the way in which theology had dealt with Darwin's demonstration that humankind was descended from the animals. Bonhoeffer was not interested at all in the rejection of scientific knowledge. The reconstruction of the empirical world by the exact sciences and the reality that this scientific construct represents, in which heavenly bodies and atoms as well as living creatures are to be found, he saw embraced by the one who is most real of all. All that mattered to him was to witness to the revelation of this one God.

[55.] *DB-E* 166 (*DB-G* 70–71).

[56.] *DB-E* 29.

[57.] "Die Geschichte der systematischen Theologie des 20. Jahrhunderts" ("The history of systematic theology in the twentieth century"), *DBW* 11:146 (*GS* 5:186). Cf. above, page 50, concerning the "rapid changes in our own knowledge of nature."

[58.] *DBW* 11:146 (*GS* 5:186).

Freedom

In 1945 Karl Barth published volume 3/1 of his *Church Dogmatics* on
the doctrine of creation; he had been working on this since the summer

152   of 1942. In his treatment in this work of the topic of the *imago Dei*, the
image of God according to Genesis 1:26-27, he states: "*Dietrich Bonhoeffer*
offers us important help in this respect."[59] According to Bonhoeffer it
is freedom in a specific sense, namely, freedom for the other, that constitutes the way in which the image on earth is like God in heaven. This
understanding of it as *analogia relationis,* as a likeness of relationship,
Barth thought, finally cast light on what v. 27 states "in a way that cannot
be overlooked": "Male and female created he them." Humankind is created in the image of God as man and woman and so placed in relationship, to be free for the other. Barth found this exposition convincing,
also as a correction of anthropological speculation about any analogy
between human being and divine being, any *analogia entis.*[60]

"It was a great liberation," wrote Bonhoeffer in 1936 about the change
he had experienced.[61] He knew freedom as a relationship in which one
could abandon oneself without reserve. Plato had expressed this state of
affairs in his image of the puppet pulled in opposite directions by
unyielding strings: it escapes the effects of being pulled like this only
when it keeps its hold on a single string, a golden cord, and yields to it.[62]
Bonhoeffer emphasized in *Creation and Fall* that freedom from the rest
of the created world, and so rule over it, could result only from "being
free for" it, like God.[63] In his *Ethics* he then expressed the matter as follows: "It is this bond of life to human beings and to God that constitutes
the freedom of our own life."[64]

Hanfried Müller has observed that what is generally regarded as freedom of choice was for Bonhoeffer the opposite of freedom. "Being free
between," freedom understood as being suspended between possible

153   choices, falls away when one makes a decision. In his *Ethics* Bonhoeffer
takes up what he had written in *Creation and Fall* in stating that human
beings who bear the image of God "no longer [stand in the position of]

[59.] Karl Barth, *Church Dogmatics,* 3/1:194.
[60.] Ibid., 195–96.
[61.] January 27, 1936 (*DBW* 14:113) [*GS* 6:368].
[62.] Plato, *Laws* 644–45 (*Collected Dialogues,* 1244).
[63.] See above, pages 65–67.
[64.] *E* 224 (*DBW* 6:256). [trans. altered]

those who choose between good and evil" but instead, because they know Christ, recognize and acknowledge "God's election as applying to themselves."[65]

Life

The "creative word of God" calls into life; that is what Bonhoeffer in October 1932 expounded Eph. 5:14 as meaning.

> To be awake means to live before God alone, because God alone is immortal. That is why the text goes on, "Rise from the dead" — that is, live. What is meant by this word that comprehends everything is utterly unutterable. . . . But the word "live" can after all not be a command; instead it is the creative word of God itself. It means . . . you no longer belong to the dead, you belong to eternity.[66]

In this baptismal address, as in his exposition of Genesis 2:7 in *Creation and Fall* in the winter of 1932–33, Bonhoeffer linked this verse in Ephesians to Michelangelo's painting of the creation of Adam, in which God touches the human being who sleeps upon the new earth, who in the ground, as a piece of earth, was dead. That touch calls humankind into (resurrection) life. This life is one in which human beings, "enlightened by Christ," are "wholly in the world, deeply rooted in the earth."[67]

Bonhoeffer did not want to speak of life before God in the same way as Hegel did when the latter described people in their practice of religion as being "lifted up by their spiritual eyes above the hard reality of this world."[68] Bonhoeffer agreed much more with Nietzsche's criticism

---

[65.] Hanfried Müller, *Internationales Bonhoeffer Forum*, 7:159; cf. 155, 163. Müller refers to *E* 33 (*DBW* 6:319) [trans. altered]. When Bonhoeffer wrote the manuscript included in his *Ethics* on "The Love of God and the Decay of the World" (*E* 17–54 [*DBW* 6:301–41]), he knew already about Barth's doctrine of election, or predestination, in the *Church Dogmatics* 2/2.

[66.] Baptismal address, October 1932 (*DBW* 11:465 [*GS* 4:152]) [trans. DSB] Bonhoeffer had quoted the verse from Ephesians already in *Act and Being*, when he repudiated "Heidegger's analysis of 'being towards death' as the 'ownmost potentiality for being' that makes possible 'the whole of Dasein'," *AB* (*DBWE* 2):148, note 15.

[67.] Baptismal address, October 1932 (*DBW* 11:465) [*GS* 4:153]. [trans. DSB]

[68.] Hegel, *Lectures on the Philosophy of Religion* (Lasson 1:3); cf. *Internationales Bonhoeffer Forum*, 8:27.

154 of "afterworldly people" [den "Hinterweltlern"].[69] In opposition to such "afterworldly people" Nietzsche's Zarathustra taught one "no longer to bury one's head in the sand of heavenly things, but to bear it freely, an earthly head, which creates a meaning for the earth."[70] In "Zarathustra's Prologue" there stand the words: "I beseech you, my brothers, *remain faithful to the earth,* and do not believe those who speak to you of otherworldly hopes!"[71] While he was a curate in Barcelona, Bonhoeffer illustrated this exhortation with the myth of the giant Antaeus.[72] In the lecture he gave for the Barcelona congregation on February 8, 1929, "Grundfragen einer christlichen Ethik" ("Basic questions for a Christian ethic"), he stated:

> The profound old saga tells of the giant Antaeus [the son of Gaia, the earth that imparts strength], who was stronger than any man on earth; no one could overcome him until once in a fight someone [Hercules] lifted him from the ground; then the giant lost all the strength which had flowed into him through his contact with the earth. The man who would leave the earth, who would depart from the present distress, loses the power which still holds him by eternal, mysterious forces. The earth remains our mother, just as God remains our Father, and our mother will only lay in the Father's arms him who remains true to her. This is the Christian's song of earth and her distress.[73]

In his exposition of Genesis 2:7 in *Creation and Fall*, Bonhoeffer, who had come to be himself deeply "faithful to the earth," could go along with the plea for an honest yes to life on earth, to the body, to strength, and to health that Nietzsche had made in the section "On the Afterworldly" in *Zarathustra*.

[69.] ["Afterworldly" is analogous to "otherworldly." "Afterworldly" is the word Walter Kaufmann uses to translate *Hinterweltler* in the section, "On the Afterworldly," in *Thus Spoke Zarathustra* (*The Portable Nietzsche*, 142-45). *Hinterweltler* is a neologism that Nietzsche coined because it sounds like *Hinterwäldler*, "backwoods people," i.e., uncouth, ignorant people.] [DSB] The first sentence of Bonhoeffer's lecture "Thy Kingdom Come," from November 19, 1932, uses this expression, *Hinterweltler*, from Nietzsche (*Preface to Bonhoeffer*, 28 [*GS* 3:270]).

[70.] *Thus Spoke Zarathustra*, in *The Portable Nietzsche*, 144.

[71.] Ibid., 125.

[72.] For the first time in a sermon on September 23, 1928 (*DBW* 10:516 [*GS* 5:467]).

[73.] *NRS* 47 (*DBW* 10:344-45 [GS 5:179-80]).

The Limit at the Center

The image that Bonhoeffer portrays on the basis of the creation narrative in Genesis 2:8-17 is one that is strangely cryptic and difficult to picture: the limit of created life is in the center. What he is thinking of is not the central point on a straight line but rather the center of a circle or, better, a point in space from which every direction radiates out. No outward limit is in view, but only one point, namely, the center of everything.[74] In a work that was closely related to his *Monadology* Leibniz used this analogy: God is "as center everywhere, but his circumference is nowhere, since everything is immediately present to him without any distance from this center."[75]

In *Creation and Fall* the "middle" or "center" ["Mitte"] is a metaphor with a double meaning. *After* the fall humankind finds itself in a middle point that is, as it were, one point amidst others in a circle thought of as an empty ring lacking a center. As Bonhoeffer stated in *Act and Being*, the human spirit curving in upon itself constitutes a ring like that.[76] Humankind at this "middle point" knows no center outside itself. The reality, however, is that in the center of the fallen world there stands the cross of the "mediator" ["Mittler"], Jesus Christ, the source of life.[77]

Good and Evil

In his lecture in Barcelona on Christian ethics, "Grundfragen einer christlichen Ethik" ("What is a Christian Ethic?"), Bonhoeffer expressed appreciation for Nietzsche's "discovery of what is beyond good and evil"

[74.] On the connection between center and limit, cf. Ernst Feil, *The Theology of Dietrich Bonhoeffer*, 72-74.

[75.] Gottfried Wilhelm Leibniz, "The Principles of Nature and of Grace, Based on Reason" (13:530 [cf. Überweg 3:336]), was written, like the *Monadology*, in 1714.

[76.] *AB* (*DBWE* 2):41, 46, 58, 80, 89, 137, following Luther's *Lectures on Romans*, 291. Theology, Bonhoeffer explained in his inaugural lecture, "Man [*sic*] in Contemporary Philosophy and Theology," on July 31, 1930 (*NRS* 60 [*DBW* 10:369 (*GS* 3:174)]), sees the philosophical answer to the question about human nature — in the language of Luther's *Lectures on Romans* — as "the thought of the *cor curvum in se* (heart turned in upon itself)."

[77.] On "Jesus Christ: Mediator [*Mittler*] and Center [*Mitte*]" in *CC* (59-65), see Ernst Feil, *The Theology of Dietrich Bonhoeffer*, 74-76.

155

as important for understanding the story of the fall.[78] What this discovery meant became clear to him in a new way in his lectures on "Schöpfung und Sünde" ("Creation and sin"). His exposition of Genesis 2:8-17
156 shows how deeply he had meditated on Nietzsche's notion of what is "beyond good and evil." Nietzsche had set out his thinking about this not only in the work that was published in 1886 with the title *Beyond Good and Evil* but also already in 1883–84 in *Thus Spoke Zarathustra*. The historical Zarathustra (Zoroaster) established a monotheistic religion in ancient Iran about six hundred years before Christ. This took the form of an extreme dualism. According to it the universe had fallen apart into two hostile worlds that proceeded forth from two hostile primeval beings, the "good spirit" and the "bad spirit." Ahura Mazda, the highest and only God, allowed Zarathustra's message of salvation to help human beings choose the good and so take the side of good order. The *Avesta,* the basic text of the followers of Zarathustra, includes hymns, or sermons in verse, by the historical Zarathustra himself. But Nietzsche composed the songs and teachings of his Zarathustra in opposition to the historical Zarathustra's teaching. Nietzsche related "good and evil" in *Thus Spoke Zarathustra* to the concept of creation:

> At one time Zarathustra too cast his delusion beyond man, like all the afterworldly. The work of a suffering [leidenden] and tortured god, the world then seemed to me. . . . Good and evil and joy [Lust] and pain [Leid] and I and you — colored smoke this seemed to me before creative eyes. The creator wanted to look away from himself; so he created the world.
>
> Drunken joy [Lust] it is for the sufferer to look away from his suffering and to lose himself. Drunken joy and loss of self the world once seemed to me. . . .
>
> Alas, my brothers, this god whom I created was man-made and madness, like all gods! Man he was, and only a poor specimen of man and ego: out of my own ashes and fire this ghost came to me, and, verily, it did not come to me from beyond.[79]

[78.] *NRS* 41 (*DBW* 10:327) [*GS* 5:161], dated February 8, 1929 [misdated January 25, 1929, in *NRS*]. The late Jörg Rades of the University of St. Andrew's, Scotland, provided the editors with important suggestions, especially by way of a preliminary essay on "Nietzsche and Bonhoeffer" that he wrote in December 1986 in working toward his tragically unfinished dissertation on "The Intellectual Background of Dietrich Bonhoeffer."

[79.] *Thus Spoke Zarathustra* in *The Portable Nietzsche,* 142–43.

The fourth and last part of *Zarathustra* takes up again the "other dancing song" at the end of the third part, a song that contains the lines, "But all joy [*Lust*] wants eternity."[80] In the section "The Drunken Song," which Zarathustra sings at the end, Nietzsche speaks of another drunkenness than "afterworldly" drunkenness, and when he speaks of "God" here he does not mean the "afterwordly ghost." "God's woe is deeper, you strange world! . . . For joy, even if woe is deep, *joy is deeper yet than agony* [*Herzeleid*]."[81] Bonhoeffer in his exposition on the section on Genesis to which he gave the heading "The Center of the Earth" sets out his view of the split in the unity of good and evil. He had derived this view from what Nietzsche's *Zarathustra* finally points out: the depths of joy or pleasure as revealing a thirst for eternity, a yearning for the unity of goodness that is in God.

157

Bonhoeffer's treatment of good and evil, as not limited to their spiritual and moral aspects, *seems* to go back to Hans Schmidt, whose translation of *tob* and *ra* as "pleasurable" and "painful" Bonhoeffer takes up. Bonhoeffer clearly regarded this pair of ideas as important. This is shown by the exception he makes when he introduces them: he expressly names the author with whom he is in dialogue at this point. Karl Budde is of the opinion that Hans Schmidt chose this way of putting it "doubtlessly with the intent of echoing Clara's 'joyful and painful' in Goethe's *Egmont*, which closes with the words, 'only the soul that loves is happy'."[82] Hans Hellbardt, in his otherwise very positive review of Bonhoeffer's *Creation and Fall*, expressed strong misgivings about this adoption of Hans Schmidt's terms, "pleasurable" and "painful," stating that it "would really have been better if it had not taken place." He attributes Bonhoeffer's idea of good and evil to this fusion of different concepts. "I need to ask: can one speak of 'good' and 'evil' in *such* a way as Bonhoeffer does at the bottom of p. 47 and above all at the bottom of p. 48?"[83] It was, however, not in the first place in Hans Schmidt's translation but in Nietzsche's *Beyond Good and Evil* that Bonhoeffer had found this way of putting things that had come to be so important to him.

[80.] Ibid., 339.
[81.] Ibid., 434.
[82.] Karl Budde, *Die biblische Paradiesesgeschichte*, 23 note 2.
[83.] Hans Hellbardt, "Schöpfung und Fall," 112. Cf. above, pages 88–90.

Being Dead

It is by the grace of the Creator that humankind – before the fall – is allowed to live without knowing about good and evil. As soon as humankind on its own knows about good and evil, it has fallen from life. Instead of living as a creature that stands before the Creator and belongs to eternity,[84] humankind knows itself as an autonomous creator of life that is doomed to be transient. Humankind after the fall no longer possesses life as a gift; instead it *has to* live, and that means – so Bonhoeffer maintained – that it is dead.

In his reflections on the primeval state in his doctoral dissertation, Bonhoeffer had thought of human existence before the fall merely in terms confined to the "spiritual area" [Geistigkeit] and of the fall as an *"ethical failure."*[85] Now, however, he understood creation and the fall not as limited to what is spiritual and ethical but in much more comprehensive terms. He saw that human creativity had also fallen subject to death. In doing so, without going out of his way to be topical, he struck at National Socialist ideology. In the winter of 1932–33, when the German people were deeply depressed, the Hitler movement mobilized the masses with the idea that they could take "German destiny" into their own hands. Behind this idea lay the myth of the exceptionally creative ability of the Aryan human being as a messianic figure glowing with light, a myth that worked all the more effectively by way of contrast, as everything that was undermining, poisonous, and evil was projected onto 'the Jews' and pilloried as the lust of 'Pan-Judah' ['Alljudas'] for intellectual, political, and economic domination. In National Socialist ideology the creative (Aryan) human being was no spiritual being 'superior to nature' but a bodily entity, the bearer of an inherited genetic makeup. In order to protect this being from being impaired, a "Law for the Prevention of Genetically Diseased Progeny" was enacted already on June 15, 1933, soon after Hitler seized power.

Bonhoeffer called that which was wholly cut off from its origin in the good, in the depth of pleasure, "sick." In doing so he was in dialogue with the thinking of Nietzsche. For Nietzsche was at an early stage aware

---

[84.] See the baptismal address of October 1932 (*DBW* 11:465) [*GS* 4:152].

[85.] [The German word *Geistigkeit* can mean either "mental or intellectual activity" or "spirituality, the spiritual area" in the sense of what concerns or involves the spirit only (and not the body).] [DSB] Cf. *CS* 39, 42 (*DBW* 1:221, 224).

158

of what health at this depth meant — and of his own sickness; Nietzsche's mental illness finally overcame him in 1889.

Where one would have expected Bonhoeffer to use the concept 'sin', he spoke instead of "being dead." Consciousness of sin in this all-embracing sense "means, in modern speech, that the I or ego itself, and not certain irrational passions [Affekte] attached to it, is the origin of evil."[86] Bonhoeffer could acknowledge the reality of death in the world of the I without reservation, because he trusted in the miracle of the resurrection.

Possibility versus Reality

Bonhoeffer connected the serpent's question in Genesis 3:1, "Did God really say. . . ?", with the twin concepts of possibility and reality.[87] Karl Holl had used this Aristotelian distinction between δύναμις and ἐνέργεια to explain Luther's expression *pecca fortiter*, "sin boldly." He maintained that it had to do with "the apprehension of reality" instead of battling "only with possibility."[88] Bonhoeffer recognized that the category of "possibility" has no right to be used in theology, in talk about the "most real one."[89] He held onto this recognition throughout his life, even as late as when he wrote the poetic lines in 1944, in prison: "Not by lingering over dreams of the possible, but courageously grasping reality at hand, / Not through ideas soaring in flight, but only through action, / is there ever freedom to be."[90]

[86.] Carl Friedrich von Weizsäcker, "Levels of Christian Theology," in his *Der Garten des Menschlichen*, 485, cf. 479. Von Weizsäcker wrote this essay "so to say as a supplement to the lecture on Bonhoeffer" he had given earlier, on the seventieth anniversary of Bonhoeffer's birth, under the title "Thoughts of a Non-Theologian on Dietrich Bonhoeffer's Theological Development."

[87.] See above, page 103ff. On these concepts, possibility a reality (or actuality), see Ernst Feil, *The Theology of Dietrich Bonhoeffer*, 29–32.

[88.] Karl Holl, *The Reconstruction of Morality*, 95. Bonhoeffer in *Act and Being* took over Holl's quotation of Luther's *pecca fortiter*; see *AB* (*DBWE* 2): 123, which quotes *LW* 48:282. He also quoted it in 1937 in *[The Cost of] Discipleship*, but then in order to warn that when *"pecca fortiter* acquires the character of an ethical principle," this "turns Luther's formula into its very opposite" (*CD* 44 [*DBW* 4:39]).

[89.] See Ernst Feil, "God the *Concretissimum*," in *The Theology of Dietrich Bonhoeffer*, 37–39.

[90.] From "Stations on the Road to Freedom," July 21, 1944 (*LPP* 371). This translation is by Geffrey B. Kelly from *A Testament to Freedom*, 516.

During the lecture course of 1932–33 that was later to be published as *Creation and Fall*, Bonhoeffer characterized the evasion of the reality of a commandment by quoting the statement in Luke 9:61, "let me
160   first . . . ," that is, the condition set by the man who thought he could offer to be Jesus' disciple. Later, in the spring of 1934, Bonhoeffer used this same way of putting things in his appeal to ecumenical bodies – in view of the ideology of the 'German Christians' that had accommodated itself to the National Socialist regime – not to shirk a "one-sided" decision in favor of the Confessing Church: "In the Gospel it is said 'Let me first go . . . ' [Luke 9:59]. Oh, how often we hide behind these words! But precisely at this point what needs to be stated is, Now or never."[91]

The serpent's cunning, pious question – "Did God really say. . . ?" – suggests that humankind is able to evaluate or sit in judgment on God's commandment. Bonhoeffer warned the ecumenical conference at Fanø in the summer of 1934 against this "hypocritical [scheinheilige] question of the serpent," when he summoned it simply to obey the command of Christ to work for peace: "This question is the mortal enemy of obedience, and therefore the mortal enemy of all real peace."[92]

Sicut Deus

Humankind as created in the image of God lived in the freedom of being bound to obey the Creator. Humankind after the fall is, by its own choosing, "like God," *sicut deus* (Gen. 3:5), and so torn away from God.

So truly is fallen humankind *sicut deus* that it can no longer be appealed to on the basis of its creatureliness. It can neither recognize nor acknowledge its utter dependence on a Creator outside itself. Inasmuch as humankind can still be addressed despite that, this does not have its basis in a residual creatureliness; its basis is in God's own speaking. In addressing humankind, God puts humankind-*sicut-deus* to death and creates the creature. Bonhoeffer saw this event in a christological, and consequently in ecclesiological, context; the word of the Creator to the creature is a word "in Jesus Christ, in the cross, in the church."[93] By

---

[91.] Letter of April 7, 1934, to Henri Louis Henriod in Geneva (*DBW* 13:119–21) [*GS* 6:350]. [Trans. DSB] A section of this letter is translated in *DB-E* 294; the crucial biblical text is, however, mistranslated!

[92.] Bonhoeffer's speech at Fanø, August 28, 1934 (*NRS* 289 [*DBW* 13:298–99 (*GS* 1:216)]).

[93.] See above, page 116.

taking seriously humankind's being *sicut deus* Bonhoeffer rejects every 161
natural theology.

In discussing the way in which Hans Schmidt understood Genesis
3:20, Bonhoeffer stressed that even human beings in a world far away
from God are moved by such a thing as gratitude — gratitude that
humankind may be *sicut deus*, gratitude to the Creator from whom
humankind has fallen away.[94] Bonhoeffer's later letters from prison
point to this tremendous paradox. We must recognize that we have to
live without God. "And this is just what we do recognize — before God!
. . . Before God and with God we live without God."[95]

Sexuality

In connection with the community of man and woman as creatures of
God (Gen. 2:24), Bonhoeffer used the German term *Geschlechtlichkeit* for
sexuality. The relationship after the fall, the "perversion of the relation
of one human being to another,"[96] he characterized with a different
term for sexuality, *Sexualität*.

What Bonhoeffer said in his exposition of Genesis 3:7 in 1932–33
strikingly contradicted his earlier utterances about the role of sexuality
in the doctrine of original sin. He persisted with this new understanding, as the lecture notes of a theological candidate at the Finkenwalde
Seminary in 1936–37 show: "According to Gen. 3 sexual impurity has a
special proximity to original sin; there is in fact, as the Catholic doctrine
of original sin expresses it, a particularly close relation between
porneia[97] and original sin."[98]

What caused this change of opinion was not the history-of-religions
discoveries of Hans Schmidt, who characterizes the "view of sexual life"
in the "stories of the 'tree of knowledge' and 'of the tree of life'" in the
following way: "Far removed from all steamy eroticism it sees in sensual
love a holy, a divine, ability."[99] In contrast to Schmidt, Bonhoeffer 162
rejected any sanctioning — "hallowing" — of the so-called "natural"

[94.] See above, page 138.

[95.] Letter of July 16, 1944 (*LPP* 360).

[96.] See above, page 125.

[97.] "Fornication, sexual immorality."

[98.] Notes by Erich Klapproth from 1936–37 (*DBW* 14:735 [*NL-B* 9,6]). Cf.
CD 254 (*DBW* 4:280).

[99.] Schmidt, 40.

aspect of sexuality; in this regard, too, he saw clearly the godlessness of natural theology. But now he knew that the word of God that comes to the world calls human beings along with their bodily nature and all their senses out of death into life.

IV

Reviewers of the book *Creation and Fall* expressed appreciation for Bonhoeffer's "authentic" and "profound" exposition of scripture.[100] They commented that it was "of great topical relevance precisely in view of the question that is much discussed today concerning the 'orders of creation'."[101] "Anyone who is inclined to take cheap shots at the Old Testament today should first take hold of this book and let it introduce him or her to the profoundly serious character of this part of our Bible."[102]

To be sure, hardly anyone seems to have noticed how the book called customary "ethical" speech into question on the basis of a biblical anthropology. Bonhoeffer's later compositions for his *Ethics* took as their point of departure this approach, at some remove from morality, of which Bonhoeffer became convinced in the autumn of 1932. In the manuscript from 1942 on "The Love of God and the Decay [Zerfall] of the World" that is included in the *Ethics*, Bonhoeffer takes up insights from his exposition of Genesis in 1932–33. It begins: "The knowledge of good and evil seems to be the aim of all ethical reflection. The first task of Christian ethics is to invalidate this knowledge" and so to constitute "a critique of all ethics."[103] The final manuscript included in the *Ethics*, on which Bonhoeffer was working when he was arrested on April 5, 1943, defines the new understanding of ethics: ethics and ethicists seek "to help one *to learn to live alongside others [mitleben zu lernen]*."[104]

163

[100.] E.g., H. Hellbardt, "Schöpfung und Fall," 111; cf. the review in the newspaper *Kreuzzeitung*, concerning which Paula Bonhoeffer reported to her son Dietrich in her letter dated January 17, 1934 (*DB-E* 163 [*DBW* 13:79]).

[101.] *Kirchlicher Anzeiger für Württemberg*, November 1934; this was reprinted in a publishing advertisement in the German editions of *[The Cost of] Discipleship* in 1937 (first ed.) and 1940 (second ed.).

[102.] *Kreuzzeitung*; reprinted in the first two German editions of *[The Cost of] Discipleship*.

[103.] *E* 17 (*DBW* 6:302).

[104.] *E* 269 (*DBW* 6:372). [Trans. DSB]

On November 18, 1943, Bonhoeffer mentioned that during the months of his arrest up until then he had "read through the Old Testament two and a half times and learnt a great deal."[105] That in 1944 Bonhoeffer came to dedicate his future work to a nonreligious interpretation of theological concepts[106] is also the fruit of his view of the Old Testament as the word of the one God. The Jewish theologian Pinchas Lapide can describe the process of thought by which Bonhoeffer came to speak of religionless Christianity as "primordially Jewish [urjüdisch]."[107] At the same time it results from a christological interpretation of the Old Testament. Bonhoeffer did not gain his theological insights into the Old Testament *etsi Christus non daretur*.[108] At the same time he could say that he wished to read the Song of Songs "as an ordinary love song, and that is probably the best 'Christological' exposition."[109] "Bonhoeffer understood the Old Testament as the book of Christ at all times, to the extent that it never became the word in itself, but always only in relation to Christ."[110] The name Jesus Christ is the name of the very same One who in Genesis is named Yahweh.

On July 21, 1944, the day after the unsuccessful attempt to assassinate Hitler, Bonhoeffer wrote a letter to his friend Eberhard Bethge about learning to live alongside others in a godless world. In this regard he referred to "the profound this-worldliness of Christianity . . . characterized by discipline and the constant knowledge of death and the resurrection."[111] For Bonhoeffer the knowledge of death and of resurrection had become a truth of the utmost certainty already at some moment during 1932.

[105.] *LPP* 129.

[106.] Cf. *DB-E* 757–95.

[107.] Lapide, *Internationales Bonhoeffer Forum*, 2:122, with reference to *LPP* 280, 282.

[108.] "As if Christ were not there." On July 16, 1944, Bonhoeffer translated Hugo Grotius's Latin phrase "etsi deus non daretur" as "even if there were no God" (*LPP* 359).

[109.] June 2, 1944 (*LPP* 315).

[110.] Martin Kuske, *The Old Testament as the Book of Christ*, 145.

[111.] *LPP* 315.

CHRONOLOGY OF
CREATION AND FALL

February 4, 1906
Dietrich Bonhoeffer and his twin sister, Sabine, born in Breslau, Germany

1912
Dietrich's father, Karl Bonhoeffer, called to the Friedrich Wilhelm University, Berlin

1913
Bonhoeffer begins gymnasium studies

1922
Publication of the second edition of Karl Barth's *Der Römerbrief,* Friedrich Brunstäd's *Die Idee der Religion,* and Emil Kautzsch's *Die Heilige Schrift des Alten Testaments I*

1923
Publication of the third edition of Oswald Spengler's *Der Untergang des Abendlandes*

Summer semester 1923
Bonhoeffer begins year of theological study at the University of Tübingen

1926
Publication of Friedrich Gogarten's *Ich glaube an den dreieinigen Gott*

1927
Publication of Erich Przywara's *Religionsphilosophie katholischer Theologie,* Martin Heidegger's *Sein und Zeit,* and Wilhelm Vischer's essay "Das Alte Testament als Gottes Wort" in *Zwischen den Zeiten*

December 17, 1927
Bonhoeffer receives licentiate in theology; *Sanctorum Communio*, his doctoral dissertation, is accepted by Reinhold Seeberg at the University of Berlin

1928
Publication of Erich Przywara's "Drei Richtungen der Phänomenologie," and Eberhard Grisebach's *Gegenwart: Eine kritische Ethik*

February 15, 1928–February 1929
Bonhoeffer serves as curate for German congregation in Barcelona; he first reads Heidegger's *Sein und Zeit*

1929–1930
Bonhoeffer serves as *Voluntärassistent* to Wilhelm Lütgert at Berlin; *Akt und Sein* written during summer semester 1929 and winter semester 1929–30

1930
Publication of Emil Brunner's *Gott und Mensch*

July 12, 1930
Acceptance of *Akt und Sein*, Bonhoeffer's *Habilitationsschrift* or qualifying thesis, at the University of Berlin

July 31, 1930
Bonhoeffer's inaugural lecture at Berlin, "Die Frage nach dem Menschen in der gegenwärtigen Philosophie und Theologie"

September 1930
Publication of *Sanctorum Communio*

September 5, 1930–May 1931
Postgraduate year at Union Theological Seminary, New York

1931
Bonhoeffer's essay "Concerning the Christian Idea of God" (published in *The Journal of Religion* 1932) and his lecture "The Theology of Crisis and Its Attitude toward Philosophy and Science," at Union Theological Seminary, New York; publication of Emanuel Hirsch's *Schöpfung und Sünde*, and Hans Schmidt's *Die Erzählung von Paradies und Sündenfall*

July 1931
Bonhoeffer meets Karl Barth for the first time in Bonn

August 1, 1931
Bonhoeffer begins his post as lecturer on the theological faculty of the University of Berlin

September 1931
Publication of *Akt und Sein*

October 1931
Bonhoeffer appointed chaplain at the Technical College in Charlottenburg

November 11, 1931
Bonhoeffer's ordination at St. Matthias Church, Berlin

1932
Publication of Emil Brunner's *Das Gebot und die Ordnungen*

Winter semester 1932–33
Bonhoeffer's Berlin lectures "Schöpfung und Sünde," "Jüngste Theologie," "Dogmatische Übungen," and his seminar on "Probleme einer theologischen Anthropologie"

January 30, 1933
Adolf Hitler becomes Chancellor of Germany

Summer 1933
Bonhoeffer's final lecture course at Berlin on "Christologie" and his final seminar on "Hegel"

September 1933
Preliminary work with Pastor Martin Niemöller to organize the Pastors' Emergency League

October 17, 1933
Beginning of Bonhoeffer's pastorate at the German Evangelical Church, Sydenham, and the Reformed Church of St. Paul in London

Autumn 1933
Publication of *Schöpfung und Fall. Theologische Auslegung von Genesis 1–3* by Chr. Kaiser Verlag, Munich. The beginning of the relationship between Chr. Kaiser Verlag and Bonhoeffer's published works

1937
Publication of the second edition of *Schöpfung und Fall*

1955
Publication of the third edition of *Schöpfung und Fall*

1958

Publication of the fourth edition of *Schöpfung und Fall*

1959

Publication of *Creation and Fall* by SCM Press, London, and Macmillan, New York. The translation was made by John C. Fletcher and revised by the staff of SCM

1966

A new English edition, which included Bonhoeffer's Bible study on "Temptation," published by SCM and Macmillan

1968

Publication of the fifth edition of *Schöpfung und Fall* together with "Versuchung"

1989

Publication of the new critical edition of *Schöpfung und Fall*, edited by Martin Rüter and Ilse Tödt, as volume 3 of the *Dietrich Bonhoeffer Werke*

BIBLIOGRAPHY

1. Literature Used by Bonhoeffer

Note: *Creation and Fall* as originally published contained no footnotes. The German editors of the *Dietrich Bonhoeffer Werke* edition of *Schöpfung und Fall* addressed this by citing in their editorial notes those pertinent works in the portion of Bonhoeffer's personal library that survived the war and that they have strong reason to think he consulted in preparing the lectures published as *Creation and Fall*. These sources are cited in the editorial notes of the present volume; all sources cited on this basis are noted below as among those cataloged in the *Nachlaß Dietrich Bonhoeffer*. This section of the Bibliography, "Literature Used by Bonhoeffer," must therefore be understood—in this volume alone of the *Dietrich Bonhoeffer Works*—as an editorial reconstruction of the sources used by the author.

Barth, Karl. *Der Römerbrief.* 2d ed. of the new, rev. version of 1922. Munich, 1923. English translation: *The Epistle to the Romans.* Translated from the 6th German ed. by Edwyn C. Hoskyns. London: Oxford University Press, 1933, 1960.

Bartmann, Bernhard. *Lehrbuch der Dogmatik* (Textbook of dogmatics). 2 vols. Freiburg im Breisgau, 1923. *NL* 6 B 3.

Die Bekenntnisschriften der evangelisch-lutherischen Kirche. Edited and published in the anniversary year of the Augsburg Confession, 1930, vol. 2. Göttingen, 1930. *NL* 2 C 3. English translation: *The Book of Concord: The Confessions of the Evangelical Lutheran Church.* Edited and translated by Theodore G. Tappert, in collaboration with Jaroslav Pelikan, Robert H. Fisher, and Arthur C. Piepkorn. Philadelphia: Fortress Press, 1959.

Die Bibel oder die ganze Heilige Schrift des Alten und Neuen Testaments nach der deutschen Übersetzung D. Martin Luthers (The Bible or all of the Holy Scriptures of the Old and New Testaments in the German translation of Dr. Martin Luther). Supervised by the Commission of the Deutschen Evangelischen Kirchenkonferenz. Mitteloktav-Ausgabe: Stuttgart, 1911. *NL* 1 A 6.

Brunner, Emil. *Gott und Mensch. Vier Untersuchungen über das personhafte Sein.* Tübingen, 1930. *NL* 4.7. English translation: *God and Man: Four Essays on the Nature of Personality.* Translated and with an introduction by David Cairns. London: SCM Press, 1936.

Brunstäd, Friedrich. *Die Idee der Religion: Prinzipien der Religionsphilosophie* (The idea of religion: Principles of the philosophy of religion). Halle, 1922.

Dillmann, August. *Die Genesis* (Genesis). Leipzig, 1886. *NL* 1 C 5.

Gogarten, Friedrich. *Ich glaube an den dreieinigen Gott: Eine Untersuchung über Glauben und Geschichte* (I believe in the triune God: An investigation into faith and history). Jena, 1926. *NL* 3 B 29.

———. *Politische Ethik* (Political ethics). Jena, 1932. *NL* 4.14.

Grisebach, Eberhard. *Gegenwart: Eine kritische Ethik* (The present: A critical ethic). Halle, 1928.

Gunkel, Hermann. *Genesis.* Göttingen, 1910. English translation of the introduction: *The Legends of Genesis: The Biblical Saga and History.* Translated by W. H. Carruth. Introduction by William F. Albright. New York: Schocken Books, 1964.

———, ed. *Die Urgeschichte und die Patriarchen: Das erste Buch Mosis* (Primeval history and the patriarchs: The first book of Moses). In *Die Schriften des Alten Testaments: In Auswahl neu übersetzt und für die Gegenwart erklärt* (The books of the Old Testament: A selection newly translated and explained for today) 1: *Die Sagen des Alten Testaments* (The Legends of the Old Testament). Göttingen, 1920.

Harnack, Adolf von. *Lehrbuch der Dogmengeschichte.* Vol. 3. *Die Entwickelung des Kirchlichen Dogmas.* Tübingen, 1910. English translation: *History of Dogma,* vols. 4–5. Vol. 4 translated by E. B. Speiers; vol. 5 translated by Neil Buchanan, both from the 3d German ed. New York: Russell & Russell, 1958.

———. *Marcion: Das Evangelium vom fremden Gott.* Leipzig, 1921. English translation: *Marcion: The Gospel of the Alien God.* Translated by John E. Steely and Lyle D. Bierma. Durham, N.C.: Labyrinth Press, 1990.

Hase, Carl August von. *Hutterus redivivus oder Dogmatik der evangelisch-lutherischen Kirche* (*Hutterus redivivus* or dogmatics of the evangelical-Lutheran Church). Leipzig, 1883. *NL* 3 B 33.

Hegel, Georg Wilhelm Friedrich. *Vorlesungen über die Philosophie der Religion*, edited by Georg Lasson. Vol. 1, Leipzig, 1925; Vol. 3, Leipzig, 1929. *NL* 7 A 26. English translation: *Lectures on the Philosophy of Religion*. 3 volumes. Edited by Peter C. Hodgson. Translated by R. F. Brown, P. C. Hodgson, and J. M. Stewart, with the assistance of J. P. Fitzer and H. S. Harris. Berkeley: University of California Press, 1984–1987. Volume three of the *Philosophie der Religion* was previously published as *The Christian Religion*. Edited and translated by Peter C. Hodgson. Based on the edition by Georg Lasson. Missoula, MT: Scholars Press, 1979.[1]

Herder, Johann Gottfried. *Älteste Urkunde des Menschengeschlechts*. 2d ed. Riga: Johann Friedrich Hartknoch, 1787.

Holl, Karl. "Der Neubau der Sittlichkeit." In *Gesammelte Aufsätze zur Kirchengeschichte*. Vol. 1, *Luther*, 155–287. Tübingen, 1923. English translation: *The Reconstruction of Morality*. Translated by Fred W. Meuser and Walter R. Wietzke. Edited by James Luther Adams and Walter F. Bense. Minneapolis: Augsburg, 1979.

——. *Die geistlichen Übungen des Ignatius von Loyola* (The spiritual exercises of St. Ignatius of Loyola). Tübingen, 1927.

[1.] Bonhoeffer's quotations from the Lasson edition of the *Vorlesungen über die Philosophie der Religion* pose a peculiar problem in English translation. Lasson's edition was an editorial reconstruction combining the various preceding versions of Hegel's text; because of this, it has been largely abandoned as a reliable source in contemporary editions of Hegel. Thus, there are no contemporary English translations of volumes one and two of the *Philosophie der Religion* that follow Lasson's edition closely. English-language citations to these two volumes, therefore, refer the reader when possible to Peter Hodgson's three-volume edition, *Lectures on the Philosophy of Religion*. However, in many cases there are no exact parallels to citations from Lasson's text in Hodgson's three-volume edition; in these cases only the Lasson edition's pagination has been given in editorial notes. Lasson's edition of volume three of the *Philosophie der Religion*, however, was the basis of Hodgson's earlier edition of volume three, *The Christian Religion*. Despite Hodgson's own subsequent misgivings about the use of Lasson's edition as a textual basis, we have used Hodgson's text when providing English-language parallel-references to volume three of Lasson's edition simply because *The Christian Religion* is the only modern edition of volume three of *Philosophie der Religion* that substantially follows Lasson's text.

Kautzsch, Emil. *Die Heilige Schrift des Alten Testaments* 1: *Mose bis Ezechiel* (The Holy Scripture of the Old Testament 1: Moses to Ezekiel). Tübingen, 1922.

Lilje, Hanns. *Das technische Zeitalter: Versuch einer biblischen Deutung* (The technological era: An attempt at biblical interpretation). Berlin, 1928. *NL* 4.23.

Loyola, Ignatius von. *Geistliche Übungen.* Regensburg, 1932. *NL* 6 B 26. English translation: *The Spiritual Exercises of St. Ignatius of Loyola.* Translated by W. H. Longridge. Rev. ed. Oxford: A. R. Mowbray, 1930.

Luther, Martin. *Werke: Kritische Gesamtausgabe* (Weimarer Ausgabe), vols. 1–58. Weimar, 1883ff. English translation: *Luther's Works.* Vols. 1–30 edited by Jaroslav Pelikan. St. Louis: Concordia, 1958–67. Vols. 31–55 edited by Helmut Lehmann. Philadelphia: Muhlenberg Press and Fortress Press, 1957–67.

———. *Werke: Briefwechsel*, vols. 1–11. English translation: *Letters. Luther's Works*, vols. 48–50. Ed. and trans. Gottfried G. Krodel. See above.

———. *Werke. Tischreden*, vols. 1–5. English translation: *Table Talk. Luther's Works.* Vol. 54. Ed. and trans. Theodore G. Tappert. See above.

———. *Vorlesung über den Römerbrief 1515/1516.* Edited by J. Ficker. Vol. 1 of *Anfänge der reformatorischen Bibelauslegung.* Part 1: "Die Glosse"; Part 2: "Die Scholien." Leipzig, 1925. *NL* 1 D 24. English translation: *Lectures on Romans*, *LW* 25. "Glosses": chaps. 1–2 translated by Walter G. Tillmanns, chaps. 3–16 translated by Jacob A. O. Preus; "Scholia": chaps. 1–2 trans. Walter G. Tillmanns, chaps. 3–15 translated by Jacob A. O. Preus.

———. *Dr. Martin Luthers Auslegung des ersten Buches Mosis I (Chaps. 1–18)* (Dr. Martin Luther's exposition of the first book of Moses, part 1). Edited by Th. Stiasny. Leipzig, 1929. *NL* 1 C 18.

Nietzsche, Friedrich. *Werke.* Part 1:1–8. Leipzig, 1899. *NL* 7 A 61. English translation: *The Complete Works of Friedrich Nietzsche.* Edited by Dr. Oscar Levy. London, 1909.

———. *Jenseits von Gut und Böse. Werke*, 7:1–274. English translation: *Beyond Good and Evil.* Translated, with commentary, by Walter Kaufmann. New York: Random House, 1966.

———. *Also sprach Zarathustra. Ein Buch für alle und keinen.* Leipzig, 1927. *NL* 7 A 58. English translation: *Thus Spoke Zarathustra.* In *The Portable Nietzsche*, 103–439. Translated and edited by Walter Kaufmann. New York: Viking Press, 1968, 103–439.

———. *Götzendämmerung – Der Antichrist – Dionysos – Dithyramben – Ecce homo.* Leipzig, 1928. *NL* 7 A 59. English translation: *Twilight of the Idols and The Antichrist.* In *The Portable Nietzsche,* 463–564, 565–656. Translated and edited by Walter Kaufmann. New York: Viking Press, 1968. *Ecce Homo.* Translated by Walter Kaufmann. New York: Vintage Books, 1969.

Przywara, Erich. *Religionsphilosophie katholischer Theologie* (The philosophy of religion of Catholic theology). Munich and Berlin, 1927. *NL* 7 B 20.

Ritschl, Albrecht. *Unterricht in der christlichen Religion.* 6th ed. Bonn, 1903. *NL* 3 B 59. English translation: *Instruction in the Christian Religion.* In *Three Essays* by Albrecht Ritschl, 219-91. Translated with an introduction by Philip Hefner. Philadelphia: Fortress Press, 1972.

Schmid, Heinrich. *Die Dogmatik der evangelisch-lutherischen Kirche dargestellt und aus den Quellen belegt* (The dogmatics of the evangelical-Lutheran Church set out and demonstrated from its sources). 7th ed. Gütersloh, 1893. *NL* 3 B 65.

Schmidt, Hans. *Die Erzählung von Paradies und Sündenfall* (The story of paradise and the fall). Tübingen, 1931. *NL* 1 C 22.

Seeberg, Reinhold. *Lehrbuch der Dogmengeschichte I: Die Anfänge des Dogmas im nachapostolischen und altkatholischen Zeitalter.* Leipzig, 1922. *NL* 2 C 4.44. English translation: *Textbook of the History of Doctrine.* 2 vols. in one. Translated by Charles E. Hay. Grand Rapids: Baker Book House, 1956.

Spengler, Oswald. *Der Untergang des Abendlandes: Umrisse einer Morphologie der Weltgeschichte. 1: Gestalt und Wirklichkeit.* Munich, 1923. *NL* 7 A 83. English translation: *The Decline of the West,* three vols. in one. Translated by Charles Francis Atkinson. London: Allen and Unwin, 1954.

Thomas à Kempis. *Imitatio Christi. Werke,* vol. 2. Edited by M. J. Pohl. Freiburg, 1904. *NL* 11.8. English translation: *The Imitation of Christ.* Translated by Ronald Knox and Michael Oakley. New York: Sheed and Ward, 1959.

Titius, Arthur. *Natur und Gott* (Nature and God). Göttingen, 1926.

Vischer, Wilhelm. "Das Alte Testament als Gottes Wort" (The Old Testament as the word of God). *Zwischen den Zeiten* 5 (1927): 380-95.

———. "Der Gott Abrahams und der Gott Isaaks und der Gott Jakobs" (The God of Abraham and the God of Isaac and the God of Jacob). *Zwischen den Zeiten* 9 (1931): 282-97.

Zinn, Elisabeth. *Die Theologie des Friedrich Christoph Oetinger* (The theology of Friedrich Christoph Oetinger). Gütersloh, 1932. *NL* 2 C 4.55.

2. Literature Consulted by the Editors

Augustine, Bishop of Hippo. *Des Heiligen Kirchenvaters Aurelius Augustinus Bekenntnisse.* Kempten and Munich, 1914. English translation: *Confessions* and *Enchiridion.* Library of Christian Classics, vol. 7. Translated by Albert C. Outler. Philadelphia: Westminister, 1955.

Barth, Karl. *Die Auferstehung der Toten.* Munich, 1924. English translation: *The Resurrection of the Dead.* Translated by H. J. Stenning. London: Houghton and Stoughton, 1933.

––––––. *Erklärung des Philipperbriefes.* Munich, 1924. English translation: *The Epistle to the Philippians.* Translated by J. W. Leitch. London: SCM, 1962.

––––––. *Die Kirchliche Dogmatik.* 4 vols. Munich and Zurich, 1932–67. English translation: *Church Dogmatics.* 4 vols. Edited by G. W. Bromiley and T. F. Torrance. Translated by G. T. Thomson. Edinburgh: T. & T. Clarke, 1956–77.

––––––. "Schicksal und Idee in der Theologie." *Zwischen den Zeiten* 7 (1929): 309–48. Also published in *Theologische Fragen und Antworten,* 54–92. Vol. 3 of his *Gesammelte Vorträge.* Zollikon: Evangelischer Verlag AG, 1957. English translation: "Fate and Idea in Theology." In *The Way of Theology in Karl Barth: Essays and Comments,* 25–61. Edited by H. Martin Rumscheidt. Allison Park, Pa.: Pickwick Publications, 1986.

Bethge, Eberhard. "The Challenge of Dietrich Bonhoeffer's Life and Theology." In Ronald Gregor Smith, ed., *World Come of Age,* 22–88. Philadelphia: Fortress Press, 1967. Originally published in *The Chicago Theological Seminary Register* 51, no. 2 (February 1961): 1–38.

––––––. *Dietrich Bonhoeffer: Theologe – Christ – Zeitgenosse. Eine Biographie.* Munich, 1968. English translation: *Dietrich Bonhoeffer: Man of Vision. Man of Courage.* Abridged from the 3d German ed. Translated by Eric Mosbacher, Peter and Betty Ross, Frank Clarke, and William Glen-Doepel, under the editorship of E. T. Robertson. New York: Harper and Row, 1970.

Bonhoeffer, Dietrich. "Christologie." *GS* 3:166–242. English translation: *Christ the Center.* A new translation by Edwin H. Robertson. London: Collins; San Francisco: Harper & Row, 1978. [U.K. Title: *Christology.*]

——. *The Cost of Discipleship.* Translated by Reginald H. Fuller, revised by Irmgard Booth. New York: Macmillan, 1963.

——. *Dietrich Bonhoeffer Werke.* 16 vols. Edited by Eberhard Bethge et al. Munich, 1986–. English translation: *Dietrich Bonhoeffer Works.* 16 vols. Edited by Wayne Whitson Floyd, Jr. Minneapolis: Fortress Press, 1996–.

1: *Sanctorum Communio: Eine dogmatische Untersuchung zur Soziologie der Kirche* (*Sanctorum Communio:* A theological inquiry into the sociology of the church). Edited by J. von Soosten. Munich: Chr. Kaiser Verlag, 1986.

2: *Akt und Sein: Transzendentalphilosophie und Ontologie in der systematischen Theologie.* Edited by Hans-Richard Reuter. Munich: Chr. Kaiser Verlag, 1988. English translation: *Act and Being: Transcendental Philosophy and Ontology in Systematic Theology.* Edited by Wayne Whitson Floyd, Jr. Translated by H. Martin Rumscheidt. Minneapolis: Fortress Press, 1996.

3. *Schöpfung und Fall.* Edited by Martin Rüter and Ilse Tödt. Munich: Chr. Kaiser Verlag, 1989.

1933 edition = *Schöpfung und Fall. Theologische Auslegung von Genesis 1–3.* Munich: Chr. Kaiser Verlag, 1933.

EK = The lecture notes of Erich Klapproth from the lecture series "Schöpfung und Sünde," which was published as *Schöpfung und Fall, NL-B 2.*

FL = The lecture notes of Ferenc Lehel from the lecture series "Schöpfung und Sünde," which was published as *Schöpfung und Fall, NL-B 2.*

HP = The lecture notes of Hilde Pfeiffer from the lecture series "Schöpfung und Sünde," which was published as *Schöpfung und Fall, NL-B 2.*

NL-A = A photocopy of the manuscript of the introduction and preface to *Schöpfung und Fall* that Dietrich Bonhoeffer wrote for the publication of the lectures in the winter semester of 1932–33, *NL-A 31.3.*

UK = The lecture notes of Udo Köhler from the lecture series, "Schöpfung und Sünde," which was published as *Schöpfung und Fall, NL-B 2.*

4: *Nachfolge.* Edited by Martin Kuske and Ilse Tödt. Munich: Chr. Kaiser Verlag, 1989.

5: *Gemeinsames Leben. Das Gebetbuch der Bibel.* Edited by G. L. Müller and A. Schönherr. Munich, 1987. English translation: *Life Together.* Edited by Geffrey B. Kelly. Translated by Daniel W. Bloesch. *The Prayerbook of the Bible.* Edited by Geffrey B. Kelly. Translated by James Burtness. Minneapolis: Fortress Press, 1996.

6: *Ethik.* Edited by Ilse Tödt, Heinz Eduard Tödt, Ernst Feil, and Clifford Green. Munich: Chr. Kaiser Verlag, 1992.

9: *Jugend und Studium 1918-1927.* Edited by H. Pfeifer, with Clifford Green and C.-J. Kaltenborn. Munich: Chr. Kaiser Verlag, 1986.

———. *Ethics.* Translated by Neville Horton Smith. New York: Macmillan, 1965.

———. *Gesammelte Schriften.* (Collected works). 6 vols. Edited by Eberhard Bethge. Munich, 1958-74.

———. "Man [*sic*] in Contemporary Philosophy and Theology," *NRS* 50-67 (*GS* 3:62-84).

———. *Meditating on the Word.* Translated and edited by David McI. Gracie. Cambridge, Mass.: Cowley Publications, 1986.

———. *No Rusty Swords: Letters, Lectures and Notes. 1928-1936. From the Collected Works of Dietrich Bonhoeffer,* vol. 1. Edited and introduced by Edwin H. Robertson. Translated by Edwin H. Robertson and John Bowden. London: Collins; New York: Harper and Row, 1965.

———. *Sanctorum Communio.* Munich: Chr. Kaiser Verlag, 1960. English translation: *The Communion of Saints.* Translated by Ronald Gregor Smith et al. London: Collins, 1963; New York: Harper and Row, 1964. [U.K. title: *Sanctorum Communio: A Dogmatic Inquiry into the Sociology of the Church.*]

———. *Schöpfung und Fall. Versuchung.* Munich, 1968. English translation: *Creation and Fall. Temptation.* Translated by John C. Fletcher and Kathleen Downham. New York: Macmillan, 1966.

———. *A Testament to Freedom: The Essential Writings of Dietrich Bonhoeffer.* Edited by Geffrey B. Kelly and F. Burton Nelson. San Francisco, 1990.

———. "Thy Kingdom Come: The Prayer of the Church for God's Kingdom on Earth" [sermon]. Translated by John Godsey. In *Preface to Bonhoeffer: The Man and Two of His Shorter Writings,* 28-47. Philadelphia: Fortress, 1965.

———. "The Theology of Crisis and Its Attitude toward Philosophy and Science." In *NRS* 361-72 (*GS* 3:110-26). [Written by Bonhoeffer in English.]

——. *Widerstand und Ergebung: Briefe und Aufzeichnungen aus der Haft.* New edition edited by Eberhard Bethge. Munich, 1985. English translation: *Letters and Papers from Prison.* 4th ed. Translated by Reginald H. Fuller, revised by Frank Clarke et al. Additional material translated by John Bowden for the enlarged edition. London: SCM, 1971; New York: Macmillan, 1972.

——. *Worldly Preaching.* Translated by Clyde E. Fant. New York: Crossroad, 1990.

Brown, F., S. R. Driver, and C. A. Briggs. *The New Brown-Driver-Briggs-Gesenius Hebrew and English Lexicon.* Peabody, Mass.: Hendricksen, 1979.

Brunner, Emil. *Der Mittler: Zur Besinnung über den Christusglauben.* Tübingen, 1927. *NL* 3 B 15. English translation: *The Mediator.* Translated by Olive Wyon. New York: Macmillan Press, 1934.

——. *Das Gebot und die Ordnungen: Entwurf einer protestantisch-theologischen Ethik.* Tübingen, 1932. English translation: *The Divine Imperative.* Translated by Olive Wyon. Philadelphia: Westminster Press, 1947.

Büchmann, Georg. *Geflügelte Worte: Der Zitatenschatz des deutschen Volkes gesammelt und erläutert* (Familiar quotations: A dictionary of quotations of the German people collected and explained). Frankfurt, 1986.

Budde, Karl. *Die biblische Paradiesesgeschichte* (The biblical narrative of paradise). Giessen, 1932.

Childs, Brevard S. *Biblical Theology in Crisis.* Philadelphia: Westminster Press, 1970.

——. *Old Testament Theology in a Canonical Context.* Minneapolis: Fortress Press, 1989.

——. *Introduction to the Old Testament as Scripture.* Philadelphia: Fortress Press; London: SCM Press, 1979.

Darwin, Charles. *The Descent of Man, and Selection in Relation to Sex.* With an introduction by John Tyler Bonner and Robert M. May. Princeton, N.J.: Princeton University Press, 1981.

——. *The Origin of Species by Means of Natural Selection; The Descent of Man and Selection in Relation to Sex.* 2d ed. Chicago: Encyclopedia Britannica, 1990.

De Gruchy, John W., ed. *Dietrich Bonhoeffer: Witness to Jesus Christ.* London: Collins, 1988.

Denzinger, Henricus, and Adolfus Schönmetzer, eds. *Enchiridion Symbolorum definitionum et declarationum de Rebus fidei et morum.* Freiburg, 1976. English translation: *The Sources of Catholic Dogma.* Translated by Roy J. Defarrari. St Louis: Herder, 1957.

Dietrich, Albrecht. *Mutter Erde: Ein Versuch über Volksreligion* (Mother earth: an inquiry regarding folk-religion). Leipzig, 1925.

Dumas, André. *Dietrich Bonhoeffer: Theologian of Reality.* Translated by Robert McAfee Brown. New York: Macmillan, 1971.

Evangelisches Gesangbuch für Brandenburg und Pommern (Protestant hymnbook for Brandenburg and Pommerania). Edited by the provincial councils of Brandenburg and Pommerania. Berlin/Frankfurt an der Oder, 1931.

Evangelisches Gesangbuch erarbeitet im Auftrag der Evangelischen Kirche in Deutschland, seit 1992 (Protestant hymnbook compiled under commission by the Evangelical Church in Germany, since 1992). Hanover: Lutherisches Verlagshaus, 1994.

Farrar, Frederic W. *History of Interpretation.* Grand Rapids: Baker Book House, 1961.

Glenthøj, Jørgen. *Dokumente zur Bonhoeffer-Forschung 1928–1945* (Documents for Bonhoeffer Research, 1928–1945). Munich, 1969.

Godsey, John. *The Theology of Dietrich Bonhoeffer.* London: SCM, 1960.

Goethe, Johann Wolfgang von. *Plays: Egmont, Iphigenia, Torquato.* Edited by Frank Glessner Ryder. New York: Continuum Publishing Group, 1993.

———. *Faust,* part 1 and sections from part 2. The original German and a new translation and introduction by Walter Kaufmann. Garden City, N.Y.: Doubleday, 1961.

Heidegger, Martin. *Sein und Zeit.* Halle, 1927. English translation: *Being and Time.* Translated by John Macquarrie and Edwin Robinson. London: SCM Press, 1962.

———. *Was ist Metaphysik?* Bonn, 1929. English translation: "What Is Metaphysics?" In *Martin Heidegger: Basic Writings,* 95–112. Rev. and expanded ed. edited by David Farrell Krell. New York: Harper Collins, 1977, 1993.

———. *Vom Wesen des Grundes.* Halle an der Saale, 1929. English translation: *The Essence of Reasons.* Translated by Terrence Malick. Evanston, Ill.: Northwestern University Press, 1969.

Hirsch, Emanuel. *Schöpfung und Sünde in der natürlich-geschichtlichen Wirklichkeit des einzelnen Menschen* (Creation and sin in the natural historical reality of the individual human being). Tübingen, 1931. *NL* 3 B 40.

Internationales Bonhoeffer Forum. (International Bonhoeffer forum). Vols. 1–10. Munich, 1976–1996.

1: Pfeifer, Hans, ed. *Genf '76: Ein Bonhoeffer-Symposion* (Genf '76: A Bonhoeffer symposium). *Internationales Bonhoeffer Forum* 1. Munich: Chr. Kaiser, 1976.

2: Feil, Ernst, ed. *Verspieltes Erbe?: Dietrich Bonhoeffer und der deutsche Nachkriegsprotestantismus* (A Lost heritage?: Dietrich Bonhoeffer and German postwar protestantism). Munich: Chr. Kaiser, 1979.

6: Gremmels, Christian, ed. *Bonhoeffer und Luther: Zur Sozialgestalt des Luthertums in der Moderne* (Bonhoeffer and Luther: The social form of Lutheranism in modernity). Munich: Chr. Kaiser, 1983.

7: Gremmels, Christian and Ilse Tödt, eds. *Die Präsenz des verdrängten Gottes: Glaube, Religionslosigkeit und Weltverantwortung nach Dietrich Bonhoeffer* (The presence of the God who has been driven out: Faith, religionlessness, and worldly responsibility according to Dietrich Bonhoeffer). Supplement: Heinz Eduard Tödt, *Der Bonhoeffer-Dohanyi-Kreis im Widerstand gegen das Hitlerregime* (Zwischenbilanz eines Forschungsprojekts) (The Bonhoeffer-Dohanyi circle in the resistance against the Hitler regime [Status report on a research project]). Munich: Chr. Kaiser, 1987.

8: Tödt, Ilse, ed. *Dietrich Bonhoeffers Hegel-Seminar 1933: Nach den Aufzeichnungen von Ferenc Lehel* (Dietrich Bonhoeffer's Hegel seminar 1933: According to the notes of Ferenc Lehel). Munich: Chr. Kaiser, 1988.

Jahrbuch für Biblische Theologie 3: Zum Problem des biblischen Kanons (Concerning the problem of the biblical canon). Neukirchen-Vluyn, 1988.

Jonas, Hans. *Gnosis und spätantiker Geist*. 1st ed. Göttingen, 1964. English translation: *The Gnostic Religion: The Message of the Alien God and the Beginnings of Christianity*. 2d rev. ed. Boston: Beacon Press, 1963.

Kant, Immanuel. *Werke in zehn Bänden*. Edited by W. Weischedel. Darmstadt, 1968. English translation: *The Cambridge Edition of the Works of Immanuel Kant*. Cambridge University Press, 1992–.

———. *Groundwork of the Metaphysic of Morals*. Translated and analyzed by H. J. Paton. New York: Harper and Row, 1964.

——. *Critique of Pure Reason.* Translated by Norman Kemp Smith. New York: St. Martin's Press, 1965.

——. *Critique of Practical Reason.* Translated by Lewis White Beck. Indianapolis: Bobbs-Merrill, 1977.

Kirchlicher Anzeiger für Württemberg (Zeitschrift des evangelischen pfarrvereins) 43, no. 11 (1934):43. "[A review of] Dietrich Bonhoeffer, *Schöpfung und Fall,*" edited by Dr. Sannwald.

Kreuzzeitung (Neue Preussische Zeitung) 86, nos. 11, 13 (January 1934): 14. "[A review of] Dietrich Bonhoeffer, *Schöpfung und Fall,*" edited by Dr. Lic. Uhl of Budapest.

Lapide, Pinchas. "Bonhoeffer und das Judentum" (Bonhoeffer and Judaism). In *Internationales Bonhoeffer Forum* 2. Munich, 1979.

Leibniz, Gottfried Wilhelm von. *Essais de Théodicée sur la bonté de Dieu, la liberté de l'homme et l'origine du mal; Principes de la nature et de la grace; Monadologie.* In *Die Philosophischen Schriften von G. W. Leibniz,* vol. 6. Edited by C. J. Gerhardt. Berlin, 1885.

English translation: *Theodicy: Essays on the Goodness of God, the Freedom of Man and the Origin of Evil.* Translated by E. M. Huggard. London: Routledge & Kegan Paul Ltd., 1951.

English translation: *The Principles of Nature and of Grace, Based on Reason.* In *Leibniz: Selections,* 522–33. Edited by Philip P. Wiener. New York: Charles Scribner's Sons, 1951.

English translation: *Discourse on Metaphysics, Correspondence with Arnauld, Monadology.* Translated by George R. Montgomery. Chicago : Open Court, 1968.

Nachlaß Dietrich Bonhoeffer: Ein Verzeichnis. Archiv – Sammlung – Bibliothek (Dietrich Bonhoeffer's literary estate: a bibliographical catalog). Edited by Dietrich Meyer and Eberhard Bethge. Munich, 1987.

Neuner, Josef, and J. Dupuis, eds. *The Christian Faith in the Doctrinal Documents of the Catholic Church.* London: Collins, 1982.

Oetinger, Friedrich Christoph. *Sämtliche Werke* (Collected works). Stuttgart, 1827–52.

Phillips, John A. *The Form of Christ in the World.* London: Collins, 1967.

Plato. *The Collected Dialogues of Plato.* Edited by Edith Hamilton and Huntington Cairns. Princeton, N.J.: Princeton University Press, 1963.

Smend, Rudolf. "Nachkritische Schriftauslegung." In *Parrhesia: Karl Barth zum achtzigsten Geburtstag am 10 Mai 1966.* ("Postcritical biblical exegesis," in Parrhesia: Karl Barth's eightieth birthday, 10 May 1966.) Zurich, 1966.

Sproul, Barbara. *Primal Myths: Creating the World*. San Francisco: Harper-SanFrancisco, 1979.

Staats, Reinhart. "Das patristische Erbe in der Theologie Dietrich Bonhoeffers" (The patristic inheritance in the theology of Dietrich Bonhoeffer). *Berliner Theologische Zeitschrift* 5 (1988): 178–201.

Stace, W. T. *The Philosophy of Hegel: A Systematic Exposition*. New York: Dover, 1955.

Trible, Phyllis. "Eve and Adam: Genesis 2–3 Reread." In *Womanspirit Rising: A Feminist Reader in Religion*. Edited by Carol P. Christ and Judith Plaskow. New York: Harper and Row, 1979.

Tucker, Gene M. "The Creation and the Fall: A Reconsideration." *Lexington Theological Quarterly* 13 (October 1978): 113–24.

Turretin, Francis. *The Doctrine of Scripture*. Grand Rapids: Baker Book House, 1981.

Überweg, Friedrich. *Friedrich Überwegs Grundriss der Geschichte der Philosophie* (Friedrich Überweg's outline of the history of philosophy).
1: *Die Philosophie der Altertums* (The philosophy of antiquity). Edited by Karl Prächter. Tübingen, 1926.
3: *Die Philosophie der Neuzeit bis zum Ende des XVIII. Jahrhunderts* (The philosophy of modern times to the end of the 18th century). Edited by Max Frischelsen-Köhler and Willy Moog. Tübingen, 1924.

Weizsäcker, Carl Friedrich von. "Gedanken eines Nichttheologen zur theologischen Entwicklung Dietrich Bonhoeffers." In *Internationales Bonhoeffer Forum* 1. Munich, 1976. Also published in Friedrich von Weizsäcker, *Der Garten des Menschlichen: Beiträge zur geschichtlichen Anthropologie* (The garden of the human: Contributions to a historical anthropology), 454–78. Munich and Vienna, 1977. English translation: "Thoughts of a Non-Theologian on Dietrich Bonhoeffer's Theological Development." *The Ecumenical Review* 28, no. 2 (April 1976): 156–73.

Wellhausen, Julius. *Prolegomena zur Geschichte Israels*. Berlin, 1895. *NL* 1 C 29. English translation: *Prolegomena to the History of Israel*. Edinburgh, 1885.

Zimmermann, Wolf-Dieter, ed. *Begegnungen mit Dietrich Bonhoeffer*. Munich, 1964. English translation: *I Knew Dietrich Bonhoeffer: Reminiscences by His Friends*. Edited by Wolf-Dieter Zimmermann and Ronald Gregor Smith. Translated by Käthe Gregor Smith. New York: Harper and Row, 1966.

3. Other Literature Related to *Creation and Fall*

Alternähr, Albert. *Dietrich Bonhoeffer – Lehrer des Gebets. Grundlagen für eine Theologie des Gebets bei Dietrich Bonhoeffer* (Dietrich Bonhoeffer — teacher of prayer: Fundamentals for a theology of prayer according to Dietrich Bonhoeffer). Würzburg, 1976.

Bax, Douglas S. *A Different Gospel: A Critique of the Theology Behind Apartheid.* Johannesburg: Presbyterian Church of Southern Africa, 1979.

Burtness, James. "Als ob es Gott nicht gäbe. Bonhoeffer, Barth und das lutherische finitum capax infiniti," in *Internationales Bonhoeffer Forum* 6. Munich: 1983. English translation: "As Though God Were Not Given: Barth, Bonhoeffer and the *Finitum Capax Infiniti.*" *Dialog* (Minnesota) 19 (Fall 1980): 249–55.

Butler, William Warren. *A Comparison of the Ethics of Emil Brunner and Dietrich Bonhoeffer with Special Attention to the Orders of Creation and the Mandates.* Ph.D. dissertation, Emory University, 1970.

Class, Gottfried. *Der verzweifelte Zugriff auf das Leben. Dietrich Bonhoeffers Sündenverständnis in "Schöpfung und Fall"* (The desperate grasp at life: Dietrich Bonhoeffer's understanding of sin in Creation and Fall). Vol. 15 of Neukirchener Beiträge zur Systematischen Theologie. Neukirchen-Vluyn: Neukirchener Verlag, 1994.

De Gruchy, John W. *Bonhoeffer and South Africa: Theology in Dialogue.* Grand Rapids: Eerdmans, 1984.

Ericksen, Robert P. *Theologians under Hitler: Gerhard Kittel, Paul Althaus and Emanuel Hirsch.* New Haven: Yale University Press, 1985.

Feil, Ernst. *Die Theologie Dietrich Bonhoeffers. Hermeneutik, Christologie, Weltverständnis.* English translation: *The Theology of Dietrich Bonhoeffer.* Translated by H. Martin Rumscheidt. Philadelphia: Fortress Press, 1985.

Floyd, Wayne W., Jr. "Christ, Concreteness and Creation in the Early Bonhoeffer." *Union Seminary Quarterly Review* 39 (1984): 101–14.

———. "The Search for an Ethical Sacrament: From Bonhoeffer to Critical Social Theory." *Modern Theology* 7, no. 2 (January 1991): 175–93.

Green, Clifford. *The Sociality of Christ and Humanity: Dietrich Bonhoeffer's Early Theology, 1927–1933.* Missoula, Mont.: Scholars Press, 1972.

Hellbardt, Hans. "Schöpfung und Fall" (Creation and fall) [book review]. *Theologische Blätter* 13 (1934): 110–12.

Krause, Gerhard. "Bonhoeffer, Dietrich (1906–1945)." *Theologische Realenzyklopädie* 7 (1981):55–66.

Kuske, Martin. *Das Alte Testament als Buch von Christus: Dietrich Bonhoeffers Wertung und Auslegung des Alten Testaments.* Berlin, 1970. English translation: *The Old Testament as the Book of Christ: An Appraisal of Bonhoeffer's Interpretation.* Translated by S. T. Kimbrough. Philadelphia: Westminster Press, 1976.

Mayer, Rainer. *Christuswirklichkeit: Grundlagen, Entwicklung und Konsequenzen der Theologie Dietrich Bonhoeffers* (The reality of Christ: Foundations, development, and consequences of Dietrich Bonhoeffer's theology). Stuttgart, 1980.

Moser, Peter. *Gewissenspraxis und Gewissentheorie bei Dietrich Bonhoeffer* (The praxis and theory of conscience according to Dietrich Bonhoeffer). Theology dissertation, Heidelberg, 1983.

Müller, Gerhard Ludwig. *Bonhoeffers Theologie der Sakramente* (Bonhoeffer's theology of the sacraments). Frankfurt, 1979.

Müller, Hanfried. "Stationen auf dem Wege zur Freiheit" ("Stations on the way to freedom"). In *Die Präsenz des verdrängten Gottes: Glaube, Religionslosigkeit und Weltverantwortung nach Dietrich Bonhoeffer* (The presence of the hidden God: Faith, religionlessness and responsibility for the world according to Dietrich Bonhoeffer). Munich, 1987, 145–65.

Peters, Tiemo Rainer. *Die Präsenz des Politischen in der Theologie Dietrich Bonhoeffers: Eine historische Untersuchung in systematischer Absicht* (The presence of the political in the theology of Dietrich Bonhoeffer: A historical investigation with a systematic aim). Munich, 1976.

Schollmeyer, Matthias. "Die Bedeutung von 'Grenze' und 'Begrenzung' für die Methodologie und Grundstruktur der Theologie Dietrich Bonhoeffers" (The significance of 'limits' and 'limitation' for the methodology and structure of the theology of Dietrich Bonhoeffer). In *Die Aktualität der Theologie Dietrich Bonhoeffers* (The actuality of the theology of Dietrich Bonhoeffer). Edited by N. Müller. Halle an der Saale, 1985.

Sweeney, Arthur Norman. *A Critique of Dietrich Bonhoeffer's Thesis on Temptation.* B.D. thesis, Andover Newton Theological School, 1955.

Wendel, Ernst Georg. *Studien zur Homiletik Dietrich Bonhoeffers: Predigt – Hermeneutik – Sprache* (Studies on Dietrich Bonhoeffer's homiletics: Preaching, hermeneutics, language). Tübingen, 1985.

Woelfel, James W. *Bonhoeffer's Theology: Classical and Revolutionary.* Nashville: Abingdon Press, 1970.

Wüstenberg, Ralf K. *Glauben als Leben: Dietrich Bonhoeffer und die nichtreligiöse Interpretation biblischer Begriffe* (To live as to believe: Dietrich Bonhoeffer on religionless Christianity). *Kontexte*, vol. 18. Peter Lang: Frankfurt, 1996.

INDEX OF
BIBLICAL REFERENCES

Index of Names

INDEX OF SUBJECTS

Editors and Translator

Wayne Whitson Floyd, Jr. (M.Div., Ph.D., Emory University) is visiting professor and director of the Dietrich Bonhoeffer Center at the Lutheran Theological Seminary at Philadelphia. He is the author of *Theology and the Dialectics of Otherness: On Reading Bonhoeffer and Adorno* (University Press of America, 1988); he co-authored the *Bonhoeffer Bibliography: Primary Sources and Secondary Literature in English* (American Theological Library Association, 1992); and he co-edited *Theology and the Practice of Responsibility: Essays on Dietrich Bonhoeffer* (Trinity Press International, 1995).

John W. de Gruchy (B.D., Rhodes University, D.Th., University of South Africa, D.Soc.Sc., University of Cape Town) is the Robert Selby Taylor Professor of Christian Studies at the University of Cape Town and Director of the Research Institute on Christianity in South Africa. A member of the Editorial Board of the *Dietrich Bonhoeffer Works* English Edition, he is also the author of several books on Dietrich Bonhoeffer, including *Bonhoeffer and South Africa*, and is the editor of *Bonhoeffer for a New Day*.

Douglas S. Bax (B.D., Rhodes University) is the minister of the Rondebosch United Church (Congregational/Presbyterian) in Cape Town and a former Moderator of the Presbyterian Church of Southern Africa. He did postgraduate studies at Princeton Theological Seminary and the Georg August University in Göttingen and is the author of *A Different Gospel: A Critique of the Theology Behind Apartheid.*